Eisenhower

PROFILES IN POWER

General Editor: Keith Robbins

Eisenhower

Peter G. Boyle

PEARSON

Longman

Harlow, England • London • New York • Boston • San Francisco • Toronto
Sydney • Tokyo • Singapore • Hong Kong • Seoul • Taipei • New Delhi
Cape Town • Madrid • Mexico City • Amsterdam • Munich • Paris • Milan

PEARSON EDUCATION LIMITED

Edinburgh Gate
Harlow CM20 2JE
United Kingdom
Tel: +44 (0)1279 623623
Fax: +44 (0)1279 431059
Website: www.pearsoned.co.uk

First edition published in Great Britain in 2005

© Pearson Education Limited 2005

The right of Peter G. Boyle to be identified as author
of this work has been asserted by him in accordance
with the Copyright, Designs and Patents Act 1988.

ISBN 0 582 28720 0

British Library Cataloguing in Publication Data
A CIP catalogue record for this book can be obtained from the British Library

Library of Congress Cataloging in Publication Data
Boyle, Peter G.
    Eisenhower / Peter G. Boyle.
        p. cm. — (Profiles in power)
    Includes bibliographical references and index.
    ISBN 0–582–28720–0
    1. Eisenhower, Dwight D. (Dwight David), 1890–1969. 2. United States—Politics and
    government—1953–1961. 3. United States—Foreign relations—1953–1961. 4.
    Presidents—United States—Biography. I. Title. II. Profiles in power (London, England)
    E836.B696 2005
    973.921′092—dc22
    [B]

                                                                                    2004048606

10 9 8 7 6 5 4 3 2 1
08 07 06 05 04

Set by 35 in 9.5/12pt Celeste
Printed and bound in Malaysia

The Publisher's policy is to use paper manufactured from sustainable forests.

Contents

Preface

This book rests upon study of various aspects of Eisenhower's career on the part of the author over many years, in particular Eisenhower's correspondence with Winston Churchill, 1953–55, his correspondence with Anthony Eden, 1955–57, the Suez crisis, the Hungarian Revolution and Eisenhower's relations with the Soviet Union. Expression of gratitude for assistance with regard to this book must first, therefore, be to all to whom I have been indebted for assistance in these earlier studies, whom I shall not attempt to specify in detail.

With regard to this book, I wish to express my gratitude to the British Academy for a research grant in 2003. I am grateful to the University of Nottingham for a sabbatical leave for a semester in 2003. I express my appreciation for assistance to the librarians and archivists at the Dwight D. Eisenhower Library in Abilene, Kansas, especially David Haight. I am grateful for assistance to the staff of the Public Record Office, National Archives, Kew, Surrey.

I am very grateful to Christine Worthington for typing the manuscript. I am very appreciative of the assistance of my editor at Pearson, Heather McCallum, and of the General Editor of the Profiles in Power series, Keith Robbins.

My greatest debt is to the authors and editors of the very extensive historiography on Eisenhower and to innumerable colleagues and students with whom I have discussed ideas on Eisenhower over many years.

All of this assistance has not only helped to improve the quality of my understanding of the subject but has saved me from many particular errors. For errors that remain I accept responsibility.

Nottingham
April 2004

Abbreviations

AEC	Atomic Energy Commission
AWF	Ann Whitman File
CAT	Civil Air Transport
CIA	Central Intelligence Agency
D.	Democrat
DDEL	Dwight D. Eisenhower Library, Abilene, Kansas
FBI	Federal Bureau of Investigation
FRUS	Foreign Relations of the United States
ICBM	Intercontinental Ballistic Missile
IRBM	Intermediate Range Ballistic Missile
JCS	Joint Chiefs of Staff
NA	National Archives, Kew, Surrey
NSC	National Security Council
OF	Official File
OSS	Office of the Staff Secretary
PP	Public Papers of the Presidents
PRO	Public Record Office
R.	Republican
SACEUR	Supreme Allied Commander, Europe
WHCF	White House Central File
WHO	White House Office

Introduction

When George Washington died in 1799, he was acclaimed in an address in Congress by his fellow Virginian, Henry Lee, as 'first in war, first in peace and first in the hearts of his countrymen'.[1] During the presidency of Dwight D. Eisenhower in the 1950s, many Americans would have regarded Eisenhower as a close second. A hero of the Second World War, he presided over a decade of peace and prosperity, while he provided a symbol of stability in a time of anxiety.

Many sophisticated commentators in the 1950s, however, along with the earliest historians of Eisenhower writing in the 1960s, judged Eisenhower's presidency in a very different light.[2] He was viewed as weak and politically inexperienced, dominated by powerful subordinates and presiding over an era of postponement and illusion. Yet, by the end of the 1960s a revisionist interpretation of Eisenhower was advanced, which was accepted by most historians of Eisenhower writing in the 1970s and 1980s.[3] Revisionists dismissed the portrayal of Eisenhower as a Ulysses S. Grant type of figure – a military hero out of his depth in the political arena – and suggested that Eisenhower was shrewd and surprisingly cunning in his political methods as well as intelligent and conscientious in his conduct of affairs.

By the 1990s, post-revisionists began to argue that the pendulum had swung too far in the direction of an overly favourable view of Eisenhower as president. Among the qualifications and reservations that post-revisionists made to the revisionist view, the most significant was the point that revisionist accounts had placed too much emphasis upon style and method rather than upon substantial achievement. Chester Pach and Elmo Richardson, in the leading post-revisionist study of Eisenhower, argued that 'revisionists mistook Eisenhower's cognisance of politics for brilliance and his avoidance of war as promotion of peace'. Pach and Richardson accepted 'the basic revisionist argument that Eisenhower was a thoughtful and skilful leader', but they concluded that 'the Eisenhower presidency was more complex and not as successful as many revisionists have maintained'.[4]

The present study adopts a methodology and organisation that places emphasis on substance, policy and achievement. Following a chapter on Eisenhower's early life and military career, his presidency is divided into two-year periods, with a chapter on domestic affairs and a chapter on foreign affairs for each of the two-year periods. While this can have a disadvantage on some matters of being a little stilted and can interrupt the continuity of discussion of issues that run beyond a two-year period, it has the advantage of allowing a discussion in reasonable depth of the major issues and providing a more precise measurement of Eisenhower's achievements. Each period is divided by elections at the end of the period – Congressional elections every second year and presidential elections every four years. This approach is designed to fulfil the overall purpose of this study, as part of the Profiles in Power series, of attempting to evaluate the impact of a statesman on his times. Eisenhower is a useful example for such a study, since his military career as well as his political career mark him as clearly one of the major historical figures of the twentieth century, while the issues of his time, with the Cold War at its height and serious social, economic and racial tensions at home, made his conduct of affairs of great historical significance.

There are, moreover, several reasons why a re-evaluation of Eisenhower as a political leader seems particularly appropriate at this time. First, Eisenhower's papers are very full, well-organised and nearly completely open. Among his very able assistants, Eisenhower was very well-served by his long-serving secretary, Ann Whitman, who kept his papers very carefully filed for administrative purposes during his presidency.[5] These papers, the so-called Ann Whitman File in the Dwight D. Eisenhower presidential library in Abilene, Kansas, constitute the bulk of his papers for the purposes of historical research. Eisenhower was also very well-served by assistants who kept full accounts of meetings and conversations, especially Andrew Goodpaster, his Staff Secretary, his son, John S. D. Eisenhower, who served for a few years as Goodpaster's assistant, L. Arthur Minnich, an assistant Staff Secretary who took the minutes of Cabinet meetings and of meetings with Congressional leaders and who kept, in addition to formal minutes, a notebook containing frank comments by Eisenhower and others attending those meetings, and S. Everett Gleason, a distinguished historian who wrote the minutes of the meetings of the National Security Council. These minutes and memoranda of conversations are not only quite lengthy but include indications of the president's emotional reactions as well as his statements of views on issues. The bulk of Eisenhower's papers have been open since the 1970s, but in recent years a great deal of formerly classified material, especially on the later 1950s and on matters such as intelligence operations, has been opened.

The opening of all of this material has produced a plethora of excellent monographs and articles on a wide variety of issues of the Eisenhower era. This flood of newly-published work necessitates a constant re-evaluation of Eisenhower in a synthesis that benefits from these specialist studies. There has, moreover, been a very extensive literature on the American presidency by historians and political scientists. This literature has raised a wide variety of issues and questions with regard to the institution of the presidency in its varied capacities, from the president as head of state and symbol of the nation's ideals and aspirations to the president as party leader and political operator. This very extensive literature on the American presidency has made possible a deeper and more sophisticated understanding of any one particular president, such as Eisenhower.[6]

Finally, the perspective of the intervening years since the end of Eisenhower's presidency is of great relevance in an evaluation of his time in office. The historian of any statesman at any time is bound to take a relativist view to a greater or lesser extent and to evaluate that statesman's achievements in the light of succeeding events up to the historian's own time. Yet, it might be suggested that this matter is of special relevance with regard to Eisenhower. Eisenhower's presidency was marked by relative placidity, which led contemporary critics and early historians to make the criticism of a lack of excitement. The events in succeeding decades in America have been marked by rather too much excitement, with crises ranging from the Vietnam war, race riots and terrorism to economic fluctuations and massive budget deficits. An evaluation of Eisenhower at the beginning of the twenty-first century benefits from comparison between Eisenhower and his successors in their handling of the critical issues of the second half of the twentieth century.

Following the detailed discussion of the issues of Eisenhower's presidency in the chapters covering each two-year period, the Conclusion provides a broad evaluation of Eisenhower as a statesman in the context of his time. The Conclusion sums up the main theme developed throughout the book, which is the presentation of a broadly very favourable evaluation of Eisenhower's substantial accomplishments, with reservations with regard to his political skills. The interpretation of Eisenhower that is offered goes beyond post-revisionism. It is suggested that post-revisionists have been too grudging and carping in their assessment of Eisenhower's accomplishments. It is argued that, especially in the light of comparisons with his successors, Eisenhower's conduct of the presidency was, aside from some blemishes, extremely effective and that his achievements in office mark Eisenhower as clearly one of America's greatest presidents. On the other hand, reservations are made to the revisionist view that Eisenhower was very skilful politically. It is argued that, while in many ways Eisenhower was indeed politically shrewd and cunning, in other respects he displayed serious weaknesses as a politician, such as in his role as party leader, his ineffectiveness in grooming a successor and his inability to capitalise on his accomplishments for party political advantage.

Military Man to President

Dwight D. Eisenhower was born in Denison, Texas, on October 14, 1890. A year later his family moved to Abilene, Kansas, where Eisenhower grew up and where he lived until he went to West Point Military Academy in 1911. Eisenhower came from humble, German-American origins. His father's family had emigrated from the Rhineland to Pennsylvania in the eighteenth century. His grandfather moved west to Kansas in 1878. His father, David, married Ida Storer, who was of a similar humble German-American background, and they had six sons. David ran a general merchant store in a small hamlet named Hope in Kansas, but his business partner and a lawyer engaged in dishonest dealings, which led to the failure of the business. David took his wife and their first son to Denison, Texas, where he worked for the Missouri–Texas–Kansas railroad. While the family were in Denison two more sons were born, Edgar in 1899 and Dwight David in 1890.

In 1891 the family returned to Kansas and settled in Abilene. Abilene had won a brief moment of fame as a cowboy town in the early 1870s. As the railhead of the Kansas and Pacific Railroad it stood at the northern end of the Chisholm Trail, over which longhorns were driven up from Texas. In 1871 Wild Bill Hickok served as marshal, when shootouts were common. The railhead soon moved further west, however, to such towns as Dodge City, and Abilene descended into the rural, small-town, provincial atmosphere, which it maintained thereafter. David found employment in Abilene as a mechanic in the Belle Spring Creamery, where he worked for the rest of his life. The family lived in a modest home south of the railroad tracks on the outskirts of Abilene. Three more sons were born, while David's father also made his home with the family from the time of his wife's death in 1890 until he died in 1906. There was some land around the house for crops, vegetables and animals, which allowed the family to be almost self-sufficient, and which, together with David's pay for twelve-hour shifts six days per week at the creamery, enabled the family to live modestly. They were a hard-working, God-fearing, German-American family, though with the boisterous atmosphere inevitable in a family of six boys. It was, as Tom Wicker puts it, a 'Tom Sawyer-like upbringing'.[1] The family belonged to the Brethren of Christ, a sect of the Mennonites who were popularly known as the River Brethren, because they held baptisms in rivers. Members of the sect, including David and Ida, were pacifists. Eisenhower's forebears had similarly been pacifists, although one ancestor, Frederick Eisenhower, fought in George Washington's army at the Battle of Long Island in 1776 and Eisenhower's grandfather's brother, Samuel, fought in the Civil War in the Union Army's Ninth Cavalry.[2]

At school, Ike, as he began to be called, was reasonably intelligent, but not particularly academically oriented and more interested in football. His passion for football was one reason why at the age of fourteen he vigorously opposed amputation of a leg, which was advocated by doctors when he suffered from a serious infection. Eisenhower pleaded with his parents, who supported his wish to risk death rather than to undergo amputation, which would, of course, have drastically altered his future career. Fortunately, he recovered from the infection without the need for the proposed drastic remedy.

When Eisenhower graduated from Abilene High School, the yearbook predicted his future as a professor of History at Yale. He had always had quite an interest in history, but his prospects of studying in college, let alone teaching in college, were restricted, not only by modest academic attainment but by financial impediments. He graduated from high school in the same class as his brother Edgar, and it was financially impossible for both of them to go on to college. Edgar went to the University of Michigan, while Ike went to work in the Belle Springs Creamery, partly to help Edgar with his expenses and also to save up sufficient funds so that he could likewise go to university in a year or two.

After a year working at the creamery, the suggestion was put to him by his friend Everett ('Swede') Hazlett that he should apply to a military academy, since this would enable him to obtain a college education free of charge. Eisenhower followed up the suggestion and after passing the required tests and obtaining the recommendation of a Congressman was accepted for West Point Military Academy. Eisenhower was extremely grateful for the suggestion to Swede, with whom he later engaged in an extremely interesting correspondence.[3] Swede's career progressed modestly, while Eisenhower, with pacifist parents and attracted to a military academy as a means to obtain a free education, went to the very top.

At West Point, 1911–15, Eisenhower was an average student. He was ranked 61st in a graduating class of 164. Most of his courses were in science and technology. In his one combined English and History course, he was tenth in his class and displayed a natural ability in writing. His roommate, P. A. Hodgson, who became a lifelong friend, noted in a letter home that Eisenhower had 'naturally a very direct and pleasing style of writing'.[4] He continued to be a very keen football player and became varsity team half back in his second year at West Point. Unfortunately, however, he then suffered a serious knee injury, which ended his playing career. Thereafter, his passion for football found an outlet in coaching.

After graduation from West Point in 1915 Eisenhower was posted to Fort Sam Houston in Texas. There he met Mary Geneva ('Mamie') Doud, the daughter of a wealthy meat-packer from Denver, Colorado, whose family wintered in San Antonio, Texas. They were married in July 1916, and in 1917 a son, Doud Dwight ('Icky') was born. Eisenhower became involved in training recruits, especially in tank warfare, a matter in which he took a special interest. He was engaged in this duty from 1916 to 1918 at postings at Fort Oglethorpe, Georgia, Fort Leavenworth, Kansas, and Camp Colt near Gettysburg, Pennsylvania, an area where he felt very much at home as the land in which his ancestors had lived and to which he would eventually retire. Eisenhower's abilities in training in tank warfare became all the more important after the United States entered the First World War in April, 1917. It made him more useful, however, at a base in the United States involved in training than in active service overseas. Eisenhower was keen to be sent overseas and eventually persuaded his commander to allow him to go to France with the next contingent of troops he trained. He received orders to embark from Fort Dix, New Jersey, on November 18, 1918. The Armistice on November 11, 1918, led to the cancellations of these orders. Eisenhower, therefore, did not engage in active duty in the First World War, a fact that he felt would impede his future military career.

In 1919 Eisenhower became an instructor at the Infantry Tank School at Camp Meade, Maryland. He participated in a cross-country convoy, which impressed upon him the inadequacy of the national highway system. In 1920 he suffered a serious blow in his personal life when Icky died. Ike and Mamie had hired a maid, who had recently been ill with scarlet fever and had not fully recovered, so that Icky caught the disease and died. The Eisenhowers blamed themselves for the tragedy, and Eisenhower felt the loss for the rest of his life. 'This was the greatest disappointment and disaster in my life', he wrote, 'the one I have never been able to forget completely.'[5] In 1922, however, another son was born, John, who was their only other child.

At Camp Meade, Eisenhower worked with George Patten, who shared his enthusiasm with regard to the use of tanks and the general issue of swifter mobility in warfare. Their ideas caught the attention of General Fox Conner, who had been Chief of Staff to General John Pershing during the First World War. Conner was very impressed by Eisenhower and when Conner was given command of the 20th Infantry Brigade in the Panama Canal Zone in 1922 he appointed Eisenhower as his executive officer. Conner acted as a mentor to Eisenhower and had a great influence on his career, encouraging him to read widely in military strategy, military history and more generally in history and philosophy. Conner was sure that there would be another world war and that Eisenhower was of the generation who should prepare themselves to lead American forces in such a war. After Eisenhower's return to the United States to postings in 1924–25 at Camp Meade, Maryland, and Fort Bemis, Georgia, Conner helped him to be admitted to the Infantry Command and General Staff School at Fort Leavenworth, Kansas, which Eisenhower attended in 1925–26 and from which he graduated first in a class of 275. This was a clear indication of how Eisenhower, after his undistinguished record at West Point, applied himself with great diligence in the interwar years to the development of his considerable innate talents in military leadership and acquired a remarkably wide range of experience in an impressive career. As Matthew Holland observes, when George Marshall summoned Eisenhower to Washington in 1941 after Pearl Harbor to be his right-hand man, it was not out of the blue but 'a culmination of twenty years of brilliant effort in challenging and difficult duties'.[6]

In 1927 Eisenhower went on to the Army War College in Washington, DC, where he again graduated first in his class. This was followed in 1928–29 by his first assignment in Europe, writing a Battle Monuments Commission guide to the battlefields in which American soldiers had fought in the First World War. This involved touring the First World War battlefields, which gave him a greater sense of the strategy and the tragedy of the war. The Battle Monuments Commission booklet was published in Pershing's name but was in fact written by Eisenhower. Eisenhower was then posted in 1929 to Washington, DC, to serve as staff officer to the Assistant Secretary of War. This gave him experience in such matters as budgets, Congressional liaison and Federal government administration. In 1932 he was appointed as an assistant to Army Chief of Staff Douglas MacArthur. One of his tasks, which Eisenhower found very distasteful, was to stand at MacArthur's side in clearing out of Washington the veterans who had set up a camp on waste ground while they petitioned Congress for full payment of their First World War bonus. Eisenhower continued as MacArthur's assistant in Washington until 1935, which brought him into contact with the New Deal and increased his innate dislike of Federal bureaucracy and consolidated his conservative political philosophy.

In 1935 MacArthur became military adviser to the President of the Philippines, which was an American colony. Eisenhower went to the Philippines as MacArthur's assistant. Since the Philippines was being prepared for self-government, Eisenhower's task was to build up a Philippine army that could protect the country's independence. The basic lack of success of the task was demonstrated when the Japanese overran the Philippines in 1941, but the challenges and frustrations of working with MacArthur and President Manuel Quezon had added considerably to Eisenhower's range of experience.

Following the outbreak of the Second World War in September, 1939, Eisenhower returned to the United States. He had various postings in 1940–41, including Chief of Staff of the Third Army, which won against the Second Army in an elaborate war games battle organised in 1941 by Army Chief of Staff George Marshall. Following Pearl Harbor in December, 1941, Marshall brought Eisenhower to Washington and appointed him head of the War Plans Division in the War Office in February, 1942. When the decision was taken in early 1942 that American forces should be sent to North Africa, Marshall's choice as commander was Eisenhower, over a large number of more senior American officers.

In June, 1942, Eisenhower arrived in London to prepare for operation TORCH, the landings in North Africa. In the organisation of the landings and in the successful prosecution of the North African campaign from November, 1942, to May, 1943, Eisenhower demonstrated the main characteristics of his military leadership. He had sound technical knowledge of strategic and practical details. He had an unpretentious manner, which made him popular with colleagues and troops. At the same time, he had a quiet authority which led him not to shrink from difficult decisions, such as the replacement of ineffective subordinates. Above all, Eisenhower's skill lay in his ability to bring people to work together, including prima donnas and prickly personalities, and to facilitate cooperative working relations between allies. His experience in Washington had improved his skills as a political military leader. His years with MacArthur had improved his ability to work with people with an outsize ego. His need to cooperate with the British brought out his diplomatic skills.

The differences of views between the Americans and the British in the North African campaign were, in fact, very considerable. As Mark Stoler has demonstrated, the degree of suspicion of the British within the American Joint Chiefs of Staff went very deep.[7] Nationalistic rivalry went well beyond friendly banter. Eisenhower's son, John, records that in November, 1943, even after the British and Americans had worked together in the Combined Chiefs of Staff for over a year, 'the Combined Chiefs of Staff could still meet below the Pyramids of Egypt in an atmosphere so acrimonious that one witness was not ruling out a fist fight, even hoping for it'.[8] Eisenhower made every effort to eliminate nationalistic differences and to emphasise Allied cooperation. He smoothed out disagreements with General Alan Brooke, Chief of the Imperial General Staff, and the abrasive General Bernard Montgomery, commander of the Eighth Army in the Western desert. His relations were very good with his British deputies, General Harold Alexander, Admiral Andrew Cunningham and Air Marshal Arthur Tedder. Above all, he formed a very close relationship with Prime Minister Winston Churchill. They disagreed strongly on many issues, but the personal rapport between the two was strong. As John Eisenhower puts it, 'There was something about the chemistry of the two men that gave them a mutual affinity from the start.'[9] Eisenhower later wrote that 'History testifies to the ineptitude of coalitions in waging war . . . Differences there were . . . but these faded into insignificance alongside the miracle of achievement represented in the shoulder-to-shoulder march of the Allies to complete victory in the West.'[10]

In the North African campaign Eisenhower faced not only formidable military problems in organising amphibious landings and in engaging German troops but also extremely difficult diplomatic issues with the French authorities in Algeria and French Morocco, which involved him in compromises of principle. French North Africa was part of Vichy France, which was committed to side with Nazi Germany against the Allies, though the majority of the population were pro-Ally. As a result of complicated negotiations and behind-the-scenes dealings, Eisenhower supported the accession to power in Algeria in November, 1942, of Admiral Jean Darlan, who ruled in an authoritarian manner and persecuted Jews, but who was willing to order the French in North Africa not to resist the Allied invasion. As a result, the Allied landings met little resistance from the French, but there was widespread criticism in Britain and in the United States of the moral compromise of working with Darlan. Darlan's assassination on December 24, 1942, somewhat fortuitously solved the problem, and Eisenhower felt that pragmatically the correct course had been followed. With British progress in Egypt and Libya, following victory at El Alamein in November, 1942, the British and American forces met up in Tunisia in May, 1943, with German and Italian troops driven out of North Africa.

After the North African campaign, Eisenhower had command of the campaigns in Sicily and Italy. With their success, the decision was taken to launch the most important campaign, OVERLORD, the cross-Channel invasion into northern France, in 1944. It had been assumed that Marshall would be given command of this campaign, but Roosevelt decided that he needed to keep Marshall in Washington. When Roosevelt consulted with Churchill at the conference in Cairo in November, 1943, with respect to command of OVERLORD, Churchill told him that the British 'had the warmest regard for General Eisenhower and would trust our fortunes to his direction with hearty good will'.[11] Eisenhower was given the appointment as commander of the Allied invasion of Europe. He came to London in January, 1944, to prepare for the cross-Channel invasion. Churchill remained apprehensive over a cross-Channel invasion and continued to suggest alternative approaches, such as an attack through the Balkans. As Churchill not infrequently told Eisenhower, his nightmare was the repulsion of a cross-Channel invasion, leaving thousands of British and American dead bodies in the English Channel. Eisenhower was very respectful of Churchill's concerns and appreciated the enormous dangers and difficulties involved in a landing in France. But Eisenhower demonstrated inner self-confidence as well as impressive organisational and leadership skills. Allied forces not only successfully landed on D-Day but avoided becoming bogged down in France and instead advanced quite rapidly to liberate Western Europe.

Eisenhower continued to be the popular commander who felt that it was important for morale for him to make frequent visits to ordinary soldiers, while as Supreme Commander he took the difficult final decisions on overall strategy. His deputy, Montgomery, not infrequently exasperated him, while Churchill was awkward on such matters as advancing to take Berlin before the Soviets, despite earlier agreements. As John Eisenhower wrote, Eisenhower 'was the one high leader whose position as Supreme Commander carried no national label. When issues became deadlocked along national lines, therefore, the deciding vote tended to fall to him.'[12] Eisenhower, however, won the confidence and respect of those under his command and was regarded as fair-minded as well as effective. After the German surrender at Rheims on May 7, 1945, Churchill wrote to Harry Truman, who had succeeded Roosevelt as president, expressing his 'admiration of the firm, far-sighted and illuminating character and qualities of General of the Army Eisenhower' and adding that

'In him we had a man who set the unity of the Allied armies above all nationalistic thoughts.'[13]

Eisenhower returned to the United States as a war hero. He gave an address to a Joint Session of Congress. A ticker tape parade was held for him in New York and he went on a triumphant tour by train across the country, including a visit to his home town of Abilene. His immense prestige and popularity, together with his photogenic smile, inevitably increased speculation that his next step would be the presidency of the United States. This idea had been mooted since 1943, but Eisenhower dismissed talk of such matters, asserting that he was fully occupied with the war. He wrote to his friend Swede Hazlett that 'Once this war is over, I hope never again to hear the word "politics".'[14] At the end of the war, Eisenhower denied that he had political ambitions. At Potsdam in July, 1945, Truman, who was a great admirer of Eisenhower until they fell out in the election campaign in 1952, said to him, rather extraordinarily, 'General, there is nothing that you may want that I won't help you get. That specifically includes the presidency in 1948.'[15] Eisenhower replied that he had no intention of seeking the presidency in 1948. It was never-theless widely rumoured at the end of the war that Eisenhower would be a future president. He firmly denied such ambitions, but his denials were interpreted as coyness and were not taken as final.

If Eisenhower had political ambitions, there was a potential impedi-ment with respect to his personal life. According to Truman, at the end of the war Eisenhower wrote to Marshall that he intended to seek a divorce in order to marry Kay Summersby, whom he had met in London in 1942 and who had been his driver and personal assistant throughout the war. By the social standards of the time divorce was unacceptable for a presidential candidate, while, even more so, much of the gloss would have been knocked off Eisenhower's image if he had divorced his wife who had waited for him at home and married a younger woman whom he had met overseas and who was not an American. Truman said in an interview in 1973 that 'Right after the war was over, he wrote a letter to General Marshall saying that . . . he wanted to come back to the United States and divorce Mrs Eisenhower, so that he could marry this English woman.' In response, according to Truman, 'Marshall wrote him back a letter, the like of which I never did see. He said that if . . . Eisenhower even came close to doing such a thing, he'd not only bust him out of the Army, he'd see to it that he never for the rest of his life would he ever be able to draw a peaceful breath.' Truman then rather astonishingly related that 'One of the last things I did as President, I got those letters from the file in the Pentagon and I destroyed them.'[16]

Rumours had circulated throughout the war with regard to Eisenhower's relationship with Kay Summersby. Affairs between American military and political figures and British women were a common wartime occurrence. C. D. Jackson, Eisenhower's assistant for psychological warfare, had an affair with Beatrice Eden, the wife of Foreign Secretary Anthony Eden. Averell Harriman, Roosevelt's special envoy for Lend-Lease, had an affair with Pamela Churchill, the wife of Winston Churchill's son, Randolph. The evidence, though not completely conclusive, would tend to suggest that Eisenhower's relationship with Kay Summersby was of a more innocent nature. Kay was the daughter of an Irish landowner and an English mother, who had been brought up in County Cork but came to England in 1924 at the age of sixteen when her parents separated. She moved in the London society of balls, debutantes and parties. She married and divorced a young publisher, Gordon Summersby, and worked as a model. With the outbreak of war, she joined the Motor Transport Corps and, when in 1942 the American embassy asked for drivers for Americans in London, was assigned as a driver to Eisenhower. Eisenhower was attracted to the 33-year-old Kay's Anglo-Irish good looks and charming vivacity, and he saw her frequently in the course of her duties as his driver, which included taking drives in the countryside for relaxation from time to time and driving Eisenhower at weekends to Chequers, the Prime Minister's country estate in Buckinghamshire. Eisenhower then made Kay his personal assistant and, although she was a British citizen, arranged for her to be commissioned in the American Women's Army Corps. She went with Eisenhower as he relocated throughout the war, to Algiers, for example, in 1942, and she was in the group photograph at Rheims on May 7, 1945, when the German surrender was accepted.

Gossip spread throughout the war about Eisenhower's relationship with Kay, especially after an article in *Life* magazine, which featured Eisenhower's personal staff, with a photograph which included 'Kay Summersby, a pretty Irish girl who drives for General Eisenhower'.[17] This caused concern to Eisenhower's wife, Mamie.[18] Eisenhower, in his letters to Mamie, which he wrote regularly almost every day throughout the war, gave strong re-assurances of his love and fidelity. 'You are all that any man could ask as a partner and a sweetheart,' he wrote. 'If anyone is banal or foolish enough to lift an eyebrow to an old duffer such as I am in connection with WAACS, Red Cross workers, nurses and drivers, you will know that I've no emotional involvement and will have none.'[19] At the end of her life, Kay published a book on her relationship with Eisenhower, which she claimed was for the most part not physically intimate but was emotionally very close and which made the possibility of divorce and re-marriage a definite possibility, even though Kay did not know of the alleged letter to Marshall.[20]

The veracity of the accounts by Truman and by Kay Summersby are open to question. Although rumours of Eisenhower's letter to Marshall circulated in political circles, no copy has ever been discovered, while Truman's report of his action in destroying such documents seems somewhat incredible. John Eisenhower denies that such a letter existed and dismisses Truman's account as 'spiteful falsehood'.[21] Stephen Ambrose suggests that the story was related 'at a time when Truman was approaching senility'.[22] With regard to Kay Summersby's version of events, John Eisenhower writes that 'her imagination played a stupendous role' and that 'there is no evidence that divorce ever seriously crossed Dad's mind'.[23] Whatever the nature of Eisenhower's relationship with Kay Summersby during the war, on his return to America after the war, Kay essentially disappeared from his life and he re-established his marital home with Mamie. His son John was married in 1947, producing a grandson, David (after whom Eisenhower named Camp David), and three granddaughters. By the time Eisenhower entered the political arena, any possible skeletons in his personal life had been firmly locked in the closet and he had the strong credentials of a family man with a popular wife, Mamie, and young grandchildren.

In June, 1945, Eisenhower returned to Germany to become head of the American occupation zone. He established good relations with his Soviet counterpart, Marshal Georgi Zhukov, who had been in command of Soviet forces in the Second World War. In early August, 1945, Eisenhower went to Moscow. He attended a football match at Moscow Dynamo stadium, where he and Zhukov were introduced to the crowd and received a rapturous reception.[24] He met Stalin, who said to Averell Harriman, American ambassador to the Soviet Union, that 'General Eisenhower is a very great man, not only because of his military accomplishments but because of his human, friendly, kind and frank nature.'[25] Eisenhower was optimistic about the prospects for postwar US–Soviet cooperation. He felt, however, that American use of the atomic bomb against Japan had a worsening effect on US–Soviet relations. Eisenhower had been opposed to the use of the atomic bomb, since he felt that Japan was on the point of collapse and that use of the atomic bomb was unnecessary. He thought that use of the bomb would taint the reputation of the Allies, while it would have an intimidating effect on the Soviet Union. Eisenhower was in Moscow when the atomic bomb was dropped on Hiroshima. He said, with regard to its impact on relations with the Soviet Union, that 'Before the atom bomb was used, I would have said yes,

I was sure we would have peace with Russia. Now, I don't know. I had hoped the bomb wouldn't figure in this war . . . People are frightened and disturbed all over. Everyone feels insecure again.'[26] Nevertheless, in 1945–47 he retained the hope that good relations with the Soviet Union could be attainable, especially on account of Soviet exhaustion. 'Russia has not the slightest thing to gain by a struggle with the United States,' he said in testimony before the House of Representatives Military Affairs committee in November, 1945. 'There is no one thing, I believe, that guides the policy of Russia more today than to keep friendship with the United States.'[27] He said to Truman in June, 1946, that he did not believe that 'the Reds want a war. What can they gain by armed conflict? They've gained about all they can assimilate.'[28] By 1947, however, he had swung to a strongly anti-Soviet position, which he maintained thereafter. 'Russia is definitely out to communise the world,' he wrote in his diary in September, 1947. 'We face a battle to extinction between the two systems.'[29]

In November, 1945, Eisenhower returned to the United States to succeed Marshall as Army Chief of Staff. He had the disheartening experience of presiding over demobilisation, which took place, in his view, at too rapid a pace and was guided by political considerations rather than by military concerns. His duties as Chief of Staff involved him in extensive travel to give speeches to various organisations, where he met influential figures, many of whom encouraged him to run for president. In 1947 Truman rather extraordinarily said to him that if Eisenhower accepted the Democratic presidential nomination, Truman would take the vice-presidential nomination.[30] Eisenhower did not accept this offer, as he also rejected the advances of many leading Democrats who, realising Truman's low rating in the opinion polls, wished to dump Truman and to replace him by Eisenhower. Eisenhower did not declare his party political preference, but a clear sign of his political position was given by his growing association with successful business magnates, with whom he played golf and bridge and went hunting and fishing. His 'gang', as he called them, which included such business leaders as Robert Woodruff, chairman of Coca-Cola, and Ellis Slater, president of Frankfurt Distilleries, encouraged him to seek the Republican nomination in 1948. He firmly refused, however, to allow his name to be entered for the Republican nomination in the New Hampshire primary and removed himself from the race in 1948.

In February, 1948, Eisenhower retired from the army to engage in writing and to become president of Columbia University in New York in June, 1948. In the spring of 1948 he wrote an account of his wartime experiences, *Crusade in Europe*, which became an enormous best-seller and brought him for the first time in his life a reasonable amount of money, especially since, as a special dispensation, he was allowed to treat the income as a capital gain, on which he paid much less tax. He used the income from the book, along with assistance from some friends, to buy a farm near Gettysburg in Pennsylvania. In the late 1940s, however, he lived in Morningside Heights in New York as president of Columbia University.

Churchill wrote to Eisenhower with regard to his decision not to run in 1948 that 'My feeling is that you were right not to intervene on this occasion. Because if you had stood as a Democrat, it would have looked like going to the rescue of a party which has so long held office and is now in difficulties. On the other hand if you had stood as a Republican it would have been hard on the party whose president you served. However, luckily there is plenty of time.'[31] In fact, Eisenhower did not have plenty of time. He later recorded that he had voted for the Republican candidate, Thomas Dewey, in 1948 – the first vote that Eisenhower had cast in an election.[32] If Dewey had won in 1948, as was widely expected, and had been re-elected in 1952, Eisenhower would have been sixty-six in 1956, with the Second World War receding into history. By narrow political calculations, 1948 would have seemed to have been the time for Eisenhower to seek the presidency, whereas delay carried with it a very real chance that the opportunity would not arise again.

After Truman's re-election in 1948, however, the pressure was unrelenting on Eisenhower to run as the Republican candidate for president. The surprising Republican defeat in the presidential election of 1948, together with Republican defeat in the Congressional elections in 1948 after their victory in the Congressional elections in 1946, led many Republicans to look to Eisenhower the war hero as the only possible Republican saviour. As Eisenhower wrote in his memoirs, the drive for him to run for president in 1952 began 'almost within hours of Truman's defeat of Dewey'.[33]

At Truman's request, Eisenhower spent one day per week in 1949 as a consultant to the Secretary of Defense and as acting chairman of the Joint Chiefs of Staff, following the re-organisation of the Department of Defense. Most of his time, however, he spent as president of Columbia and in 1950 he was able to devote all of his time to that role. He encountered frustrations at Columbia, where he felt that he was too remote from faculty and students and too much involved with fund-raising and administration, while many intellectuals sneered that the soldier whose favourite reading was Westerns lacked the qualifications desirable for the presidency of an elite Ivy League university. Nevertheless, he found some aspects satisfying, such as the American Assembly, which consisted of seminars attended by leading figures in business, politics, finance, labour and higher education at the upstate New York home of Averell Harriman. His period at Columbia was his only time of employment outside military service before he became president. As Travis Jacobs observes, 'Columbia, thus, played a significant role in the General's education as a civilian.'[34]

In 1950 Truman asked Eisenhower to return to active duty as Supreme Allied Commander in Europe, following the formation of NATO. Taking up his post in February, 1951, Eisenhower enjoyed the experience of living in Paris and working with some of his old military and political colleagues in an enterprise to which he was fully committed. He had become increasingly concerned over the neo-isolationism of Congressional conservatives, especially Senator Robert Taft, who had criticised the Marshall Plan as a 'vast give-away program' and who was emerging as the leading contender for the Republican nomination for president in 1952.[35] With the ongoing pressure on Eisenhower to run for president and his reluctance to do so, but with his fear that Taft would win the nomination while committed to a neo-isolationist standpoint, Eisenhower decided to meet Taft in December, 1950, before he left for Europe. Eisenhower brought to the meeting a statement that he intended to issue if Taft agreed to the principles of collective security. The statement read that 'Having been recalled to military duty, I want to announce that my name will not be used by anyone as candidate for President – and if they do I will repudiate such efforts.'[36] At the meeting, Taft, however, was equivocal about America's commitment to NATO, so Eisenhower tore up the statement.

Pressure therefore continued to build on Eisenhower in 1951 to run for president. In the summer of 1951, some of his business friends set up a Citizens for Eisenhower organisation, and Ike Clubs sprang up all over America. On September 4, 1951, Henry Cabot Lodge, senator from Massachusetts, visited Eisenhower in Paris as a spokesman for a number of East Coast Republicans who wished Eisenhower to be the Republican candidate for president and who wished to enter his name in the presidential primaries. Eisenhower replied to Lodge that he would think about the matter. Eisenhower had strong reservations, especially over seeking the presidential nomination while in uniform, which, as H. W. Brands puts it, might 'smack of Caesarism, at least of MacArthurism'.[37] His brother, Milton, wrote that Eisenhower 'earnestly believed that it would be wrong to take advantage of the wave of popularity and affection that resulted from military victory, won by the toil and blood of men under his command'.[38] On January 6, 1952, Lodge decided to force the issue and announced that he was entering Eisenhower's name in the New Hampshire primary. Eisenhower announced for the first time his party preference as a Republican and did not repudiate Lodge's action.[39] Eisenhower would have preferred to have won the nomination by acclamation, but he agreed in February, 1952, to enter the contest against Taft and other contenders for the Republican nomination. In the New Hampshire primary on March 11, 1952, Eisenhower won 50 per cent of the vote, compared to 38 per cent for Taft. On March 18, he won 108,692 write-in votes in the Minnesota primary, compared to 129,076 for Harold Stassen, the Governor of Minnesota, who assured Eisenhower that he would support him. On April 12, 1952, Eisenhower announced that he would resign as NATO commander in June and return to America to campaign for the Republican nomination for president. On June 1, 1952, he returned to the United States to begin his campaign.

Eisenhower had been ambivalent about running for president since 1945. William Pickett concludes that 'Eisenhower decided he had a duty – which he called "transcendent" – to make the United States a stabilising force in the postwar world. It was this responsibility . . . that sustained him and brought him, finally, to enter the race.'[40] The mixture of motives was in fact probably rather greater. On the one hand, Eisenhower was exhausted at the end of the war and looked forward to a less demanding future. Moreover, his health, as Robert Ferrell has shown, was much worse than historians have generally realised.[41] He gave up smoking in 1949, but a lifetime of smoking several packs of cigarettes per day had taken its toll. He also had a long history of stomach and heart problems. The prospect of taking on the presidency at the age of sixty-two in much less than perfect health was in many ways off-putting. Moreover, the world of professional politics had little appeal to him. On the other hand, his sense of duty made him feel that he should ensure that America played its proper role in world affairs and that at home responsible fiscal and social policies were pursued. He was not immune, however, to the flattering allure that he was the indispensable man who had a rendezvous with destiny. If, like MacArthur, he had been consumed with ambition to be president, he would have run in 1948. If, like Sherman, he had no desire whatever to be president, he would not have run in 1952. His position was somewhat between the two, resulting in his rather vacillating record until he finally decided to run.

Once in the race, his nomination was far from a foregone conclusion. Taft's supporters had control of the party machinery in a large number of states, so that a majority of the delegates to the Republican convention in July, 1952, favoured Taft. A key issue lay with the credentials of the delegations from several Southern states. Since these states were solidly Democratic, their delegations, which supported Taft, had been dubiously selected and lacked authority. Alternative delegations, consisting of mainly former Democrats who supported Eisenhower, claimed to be more representative, but the Committee on Rules at the convention decided that the Taft delegates should be seated. Eisenhower's supporters then introduced a Fair Play amendment that the Eisenhower delegates should be seated. The close vote in favour of the Fair Play amendment was crucial to Eisenhower's narrow victory over Taft for the Republican nomination.[42]

As his running mate Eisenhower chose Richard Nixon, a senator from California. Nixon balanced the ticket very well. He was young, aged thirty-nine, compared to Eisenhower's maturity. He was from the west, whereas Eisenhower was associated with the plains states and the east. He was right-of-centre, having won a reputation as a red-baiter, while Eisenhower was regarded as a moderate centrist. He had helped to swing the California delegation to support the Fair Play amendment. There were many good political reasons, therefore, for Nixon's selection.

On the campaign trail, Eisenhower demonstrated a natural gift as a campaigner. He used the techniques of old and new politics to equal effect. He conducted a traditional whistle-stop campaign, with short speeches from the rear of a train, with distribution of 'I like Ike' badges and lots of hoopla. At the same time, he used the new medium of television to excellent effect, especially spot commercials on popular programmes. He had a folksy image which, along with his attractive smile and engaging manner, made him a much more appealing candidate than his Democratic opponent, Adlai Stevenson, Governor of Illinois.

Two slight crises upset Eisenhower's campaign, over Nixon and over Joseph McCarthy. On September 18, 1952, a story broke that Nixon had illegal funding, provided by wealthy supporters in California, which Nixon used for personal as well as for political purposes. Nixon denied that the fund was for personal use and stated that it was a legitimate political fund, such as Stevenson also had. The story created such controversy, however, that many of Eisenhower's advisers wished Nixon to be dropped from the ticket, lest Eisenhower's image be tarnished. Eisenhower did not support the move to drop Nixon but neither did he give Nixon his full support. He agreed with the suggestion that Nixon should make a speech on television explaining the matter but he did not make a commitment that, if strong public support resulted, Nixon should remain on the ticket. Nixon was furious that Eisenhower was not more decisive. In a telephone conversation Nixon said to Eisenhower that 'there comes a time in matters like this when you've either got to shit or get off the pot'.[43] Eisenhower was taken back by Nixon's intemperate outspokenness. Nixon's television speech, which included the sentimental story of a dog named Checkers, was a great success. A few days later, with wide support for Nixon in the Republican party, Eisenhower assured Nixon of his support. The incident, however, made Eisenhower even less inclined than previously to include Nixon in his inner circle of advisers.

The McCarthy incident arose in early October, 1952. Eisenhower loathed McCarthy, especially McCarthy's charges of Communist leanings on the part of George Marshall on the very spurious grounds that Marshall had negotiated with Chinese Communists in 1946. Eisenhower planned to make a personal tribute to Marshall when he came to campaign in Wisconsin, McCarthy's home state. His speechwriter, Emmet John Hughes, drafted a paragraph praising Marshall as 'a man and as a soldier ... dedicated with singular selflessness and the profoundest patriotism to the service of America' and repudiating charges of disloyalty against Marshall as 'a sobering lesson in the way freedom must *not* defend itself'.[44] On the campaign train from Illinois to Wisconsin, however, Governor Walter Kohler of Wisconsin argued that a public repudiation of McCarthy in his home state could cost the Republicans Wisconsin, a state that the Democrats had won in 1948. Although newspaper reporters had been told of Eisenhower's passage defending Marshall, he agreed to eliminate it from his speech in Milwaukee on October 3.[45] Reports of the episode made Eisenhower appear to be an unprincipled political coward. Even Eisenhower's sympathetic biographer Stephen Ambrose suggests 'that he was ashamed of himself, there can be little doubt'.[46]

Despite these episodes, Eisenhower remained far ahead in the polls of his Democratic opponent. On October 24, 1952, Eisenhower then played a trump card by saying that between the election and the inauguration, 'I shall go to Korea'.[47] The statement was ambiguous, since he did not spell out proposals to bring about an end to the Korean War. He implied, however, that his election could lead to peace in Korea after two and a half years of war and frustration.

On election day, November 4, 1952, Eisenhower won 55 per cent of the popular vote to 44 per cent for Stevenson. In the electoral college he won by 442–89, even winning four Southern states and Stevenson's home state of Illinois. His victory gave him access to the greatest source of power on earth, the presidency of the United States. How he utilised this power will be examined in an analysis of his policies over the next eight years.

Chapter 1

Creating Domestic Stability, 1953–54

On assuming the presidency, Eisenhower's overall goal was to provide leadership that would instil confidence and stability in the American people. The United States was still in a state of slow recovery from the traumas of the Great Depression and the Second World War. Moreover, the last months of the Truman presidency and the hysteria of the Red Scare had poisoned the political atmosphere in America and heightened the underlying sense of anxiety and fear. Eisenhower's leadership in the first two years in office played a major part in restoring greater equilibrium within America. On the other hand, anxieties over the economy persisted, with a recession in 1953–54, which was a major contributory factor in Eisenhower's lack of success politically in failing to establish the Republican party as the dominant majority party. Moreover, race emerged as an issue of primary importance that was both potentially explosive and divisive. Eisenhower had the advantage of a strong mandate of a new president elected by a sweeping margin of victory and with a Republican majority in both houses of Congress, but the majority was paper thin, with 48 Republicans, 47 Democrats and one independent in the Senate, and 221 Republicans, 210 Democrats and one independent in the House of Representatives.

In the 1952 campaign Republicans had criticised the 'mess in Washington', and while this was partly an electioneering slogan, Eisenhower was very critical of Truman with regard to administrative disorderliness, a lack of presidential dignity and decorum, and the excessive influence of interest groups. Eisenhower had enjoyed a good relationship with Truman in the last months of the Second World War and during his time as Army Chief of Staff, 1947–48, and as SACEUR, 1951–52. The relationship soured, however, when Eisenhower became a candidate for president on the Republican ticket. The episode in the election campaign when Eisenhower backed down from public condemnation of McCarthy's charges against Marshall was the catalyst that led Truman to begin to express severe criticism and contempt for Eisenhower. Following Eisenhower's victory in the 1952 election, Truman was in no way gracious in defeat. Eisenhower had only one perfunctory meeting with Truman between the election in November, 1952, and the Inauguration on January 20, 1953. On Inauguration Day, Truman did not follow tradition by inviting the incoming president into the White House before the Inauguration ceremony, and when the president and president-elect were driven by limousine from the White House to Capitol Hill for the Inauguration, Truman maintained a stony silence. Eisenhower felt that in the latter part of his presidency Truman lacked the bearing and command that an effective president should exude and that he demeaned the office of president by acts of pettiness and intemperate rhetoric. Eisenhower sought to win respect through an orderly style of government that would win confidence as well as create goodwill.

Eisenhower's system of government was developed from the military staff system. This left him open to the criticism that he delegated too much and that he did not appreciate the difference between a military system and a political system. In fact, Eisenhower's administrative system was quite efficient, and he maintained control over the major decisions and the main lines of policy. Although he had spent virtually his entire career in the army, he showed no inclination to act in a military manner as president. His long experience in civilian and military matters had reinforced within him an innate respect for constitutional procedures. But Eisenhower had been very critical of Franklin Roosevelt's somewhat chaotic approach to administrative matters, and he criticised Truman along the same lines.

Eisenhower chose Sherman Adams, Governor of New Hampshire, as Special Assistant for Domestic Affairs, effectively White House Chief of Staff. Adam's meticulous conscientiousness and rather gruff and abrasive manner enabled Eisenhower to delegate routine matters effectively and to be protected from unnecessary intrusions on his time. At the same time, Adams, like some other Eisenhower appointees, such as Nixon and John Foster Dulles, acted as a lightning rod to attract criticism and allow Eisenhower to appear to be the genial, unifying head of state rather than the demanding executive who was responsible for some of the difficult decisions that Adams ensured were implemented. For Congressional relations, Eisenhower chose a very different type of figure, Wilton ('Jerry') Persons, an old friend, who had had long experience as a War Department Congressional liaison officer. As Press Secretary, Eisenhower chose Jim Hagerty, who had long experience in presidential politics as Press Secretary for Tom Dewey. As speech-writer, Eisenhower appointed Emmet

John Hughes, a well-known journalist with *Life* and *Time* magazines, while Eisenhower used the actor Robert Montgomery as an adviser on the delivery of speeches. On economic affairs, he chose Joseph Dodge, a banker with wide experience in international affairs, as Director of the Budget, but he also consulted extensively with Arthur Burns, chairman of the Council of Economic Advisers. A very important informal adviser was Eisenhower's youngest brother, Milton, who had a four-day per week contract as president of Pennsylvania State University, so that he could spend the other days as adviser to the president. In 1956 Milton moved to the presidency of Johns Hopkins University in Baltimore, Maryland, to be closer at hand to the White House. 'Every Friday, Saturday and often Sunday I was in the oval office or the family rooms of the White House,' Milton wrote, 'save when assignments took me abroad.'[1] Eisenhower described Milton as 'my most intimate general advisor'.[2] Eisenhower also took advice to some extent – though the association was primarily social – from his 'gang', namely, his friends with whom he played golf and bridge and went hunting and fishing. They were virtually all wealthy, successful businessmen, such as Pete Jones, head of the Cities Services Oil Company, George Allen, Bill Robinson, Ellis Slater and Cliff Roberts.

Eisenhower held press conferences and meetings with the Cabinet and with Congressional leaders on a very regular basis. Meetings with Republican Congressional leaders were held on Mondays, with Joint Congressional leaders on Tuesdays, press conferences on Wednesdays and Cabinet meetings on Fridays. Eisenhower was criticised for the appointment of Cabinet officers who for the most part lacked political experience, such as George Humphrey, Secretary of the Treasury, and Charles Wilson, Secretary of Defense, both of whom were businessmen from a narrow social and economic background. While such criticisms have validity, Eisenhower strove to a much greater extent than most presidents to develop collegiality in the Cabinet and to use the Cabinet as a team of advisers on all issues of government policy and not only on their department's affairs. Aside from formal meetings with Congressional leaders and with the Cabinet, Eisenhower made extensive use of informal contacts through 'stag' dinners at the White House, invitations to weekends at Camp David or to the Eisenhower farm at Gettysburg.

Eisenhower's fairly orderly, well-organised system was, however, obscured by the processes of what Fred Greenstein has called 'the hidden-hand presidency'. As Greenstein has observed, Eisenhower was 'a politician with apolitical protective coloration'.[3] Eisenhower had considerable innate political skills, which he had developed during his military career. Among these skills was a surprising degree of calculated cunning, which, paradoxically, made him appear, quite incorrectly, to be an amateurish political innocent. In fact, Eisenhower was 'a far more complex and devious man than most people realized', as it was expressed by Richard Nixon – a man who was well-qualified to speak with authority on the arts of guile.[4] This was illustrated, for example, on occasion in his press conferences. Eisenhower held regular weekly press conferences, which made him appear to be more open than most presidents, and his apparently open and friendly manner, together with his infectious smile and his air of authority, won him support from the public. Sophisticated commentators derided answers which he occasionally gave which were garbled and ungrammatical and mocked him in their newspaper reports, failing to realise that Eisenhower was deliberately employing a folksy style and convoluted prose to evade awkward questions and to appeal to the general public, who responded favourably to an apparently 'non-political' approach. Similarly, Eisenhower was not overly concerned that the sophisticated commentators suggested that he spent more time on the golf links than in the Oval Office, while Sherman Adams ran the country. Eisenhower was aware that the public, as Gallup polls consistently indicated, preferred a more human president rather than a narrow politician, and Eisenhower was able to shield himself behind such figures as Adams while conducting affairs more effectively in the background. With regard to Congress, Eisenhower perhaps did not match President Lyndon Johnson in the extent of the detail which he knew of the wishes and vulnerabilities of every Congressman, but his intelligence on these matters was very extensive and professionally organised, while in formal and informal meetings with Congressmen, whether at a regular Legislative Leaders meeting or at a barbecue at his farm, Eisenhower demonstrated the skills of manipulation and persuasion that LBJ made famous with 'the Johnson treatment'.

Eisenhower's political methods were, of course, not an end in themselves but a means to achieve particular policy goals as well as his overall goal of providing the leadership to allay the anxieties of the American people and restore the self-confidence that could enable the underlying strength of the country to come more fully into play. This was also demonstrated in such matters as religion. Although Eisenhower had been brought up in a deeply religious environment in his boyhood in Abilene, and he maintained a strong religious conviction, he had not regularly practised his religion throughout his army career. He felt, however, that as president he should provide leadership and an example. Moreover, he was well aware of the power of civic religion as a central gelling force within American society. He therefore joined his wife's National

Presbyterian church and attended church regularly throughout his presidency. He also supported the proposal in 1954 for the insertion of the phrase 'In God we trust' on American coins and the phrase 'under God' in the Pledge of Allegiance, which was recited daily by American schoolchildren. Cabinet meetings opened with a minute's silent prayer. Such actions seemed to blur the constitutionally declared separation of the power of church and state and generated a piety that was somewhat superficial and hypocritical. It helped to produce, however, a cohesive force of major significance in a time of uncertainty.

An issue that added greatly to the uncertainty of the times and poisoned American politics and society was the Red Scare. The deep fears and anxieties of America in the Cold War created the irrationality of the Red Scare, which found its most bizarre and grotesque expression in the figure of Senator Joseph McCarthy. In some ways McCarthy seemed an unlikely figure to lead such an anti-Communist crusade. He was a little-known junior senator from Wisconsin, who had encountered serious political difficulties over dubious gifts from lobbyists, excessive drinking and gambling and flagrant disregard for veracity. In other ways, however, McCarthy had the ideal qualifications to embody the anxieties of Americans in the early Cold War years, especially less-educated Americans. He was an Irish-American Catholic, at a time when the Catholic Church was a leading exponent of anti-Communism. Moreover, he had considerable demagogic skills and a gift for attracting the attention of the press, while his slippery style enabled him to change the subject and to move on to another issue when the lack of substance in his charges was demonstrated. McCarthy's wild charges and irresponsible accusations with regard to Communists in government kept him in the front pages of American newspapers. Congressional committees and serious newspaper commentators demonstrated the speciousness of McCarthy's claims, but his accusations won widespread support in the popular and provincial press and hit a responsive chord in the mass of the American public. His political strength grew even greater when figures who challenged him, such as Senator Millard Tydings (D. – Maryland) and Senator Thomas Benton (D. – Connecticut), found that McCarthy campaigned against them in their re-election bids and helped to bring about their electoral defeat.

The Republicans found that McCarthy was a useful tool with which to smear the Truman administration. With their victory in 1952, the Republicans had no further need for McCarthy as an attack dog against the Democrats, but they had helped to create a monster that would not quietly disappear. Eisenhower therefore faced a major problem in deciding on how to deal with McCarthy. Eisenhower loathed McCarthy, especially on account of McCarthy's attack on Marshall, and Eisenhower realised that McCarthy was a worthless charlatan and political opportunist. But Eisenhower also realised the strength of McCarthy's following and the grave dangers involved in engaging in a public confrontation with McCarthy that could seriously smear the new administration at its outset and add to the divisions within the Republican party.

Eisenhower was, of course, concerned over the security risk of Communists in government. But he appreciated the significant difference between sensible security measures to guard against infiltration by subversives and McCarthy's foolish accusations of guilt by association, which linked any kind of liberal political views to Communism and disloyalty. Eisenhower pursued a hard line on internal security. He endorsed the death sentence in 1953 on Julius and Ethel Rosenberg, who had been involved in a spy ring that passed atomic information to the Soviets. He supported the withdrawal of the security clearance from Robert Oppenheimer who, although one of the leading physicists responsible for the development of the atomic bomb, had become critical of further nuclear development and whose wife had Communist associations. Eisenhower extended Truman's loyalty programme to a wide security programme, which involved checks on security risks, such as homosexuals and heavy drinkers, as well as people with left-wing views. The Eisenhower administration was disingenuous in claiming that in 1953–54 there were large numbers of dismissals from government, with the implication that these were loyalty risks, whereas the dismissals were for incompetence or more general security risks. Nevertheless, the matter of how to deal with McCarthy posed a grave dilemma for Eisenhower.

With Republican victory in the 1952 Congressional elections, Republicans organised Congress and chaired Congressional committees. McCarthy was given a place on the Government Operations Committee and chaired its sub-committee on Investigations. This presented McCarthy with a splendid forum from which to attract attention and to inflict damage and embarrassment. He held two investigations in 1953, on the Voice of America and on the United States Information Service, in which he alleged that there were disloyal influences within these agencies. This was illustrated, for example, McCarthy charged, by the placement in USIS libraries in American embassies of liberal, left-wing books. Two young aides of McCarthy, Roy Cohn and G. David Schine, went on a tour of USIS libraries in Europe, which led to the removal from the shelves of liberal authors. In one case a number of books were burned, raising ominous comparison with Nazi book burnings. When Schine was drafted into the army and was refused exemptions from some duties to enable him to continue to serve on McCarthy's committee, McCarthy decided to hold investigations into Communist infiltration into the Department of the Army. This produced the usual chaotic hearings, with harassment of Army officers and a lack of serious substance in any of the charges. Since the Army–McCarthy hearings were broadcast live on television, the public became aware of McCarthy's boorish personality, with his constant rude interruptions calling for a 'Point of Order' in very disorderly proceedings. This encouraged attacks on McCarthy by such figures as the broadcaster Ed Murrow in his 'See It Now' programme and by senators such as Ralph Flanders (D. – Florida). The outcome was a Senate vote in December, 1954, to condemn McCarthy, which marked his demise. He ceased to wield influence or to attract attention, and sank into obscurity. He died of cirrhosis of the liver in 1957.

Eisenhower's critics fiercely condemn him for failure to speak out against McCarthy in 1953–54. Eisenhower did speak out over the book burning incident, saying to students at Dartmouth College Commencement ceremony on June 14, 1953, 'Don't join the book burners . . . Don't be afraid to go in your library and read every book.'[5] Otherwise, however, Eisenhower remained in the background and refused to confront or to challenge McCarthy. Eisenhower's critics argue that, as a newly-elected Republican president with a strong popular mandate and as a war hero with enormous prestige, Eisenhower was uniquely well-placed to expose McCarthy at the outset of his presidency. Instead, it is charged, Eisenhower cowered in the background, while McCarthy wreaked grave damage, severely harming America's international reputation as well as undermining civil liberties at home. Robert Griffith writes that 'The new president was a decent man, but he possessed neither the ability nor the inclination to deal with a potential problem of this complexity.'[6] James Patterson writes that 'His refusal to challenge McCarthy represented a major blot on his presidency.'[7]

Eisenhower's judgement, however, was that public denunciation of McCarthy would be the wrong approach and could seriously backfire. A fair case can be made in defence of Eisenhower's judgement. Senator Millard Tydings, for example, had denounced McCarthy in damning terms in a Senate sub-committee report, stating that 'We are constrained fearlessly and frankly to call the charges and the methods employed to give them ostensible validity, what they truly are: a fraud and a hoax perpetrated on the Senate of the United States and the American people.'[8] McCarthy skilfully deflected this condemnation, stating that the Tydings report was 'a signal to the traitors, Communists and fellow travellers in our government that they need have no fear of exposure from this administration . . . The most loyal stooges of the Kremlin could not have done a better job of giving a clean bill of health to Stalin's Fifth Column in this country.'[9] McCarthy then worked for Tydings' opponent in the Maryland Senate election in November, 1950, smearing Tydings with Communist associations and helping to bring about his defeat. Dean Acheson, Truman's patrician Secretary of State, made frequent haughty denunciations of McCarthy, but McCarthy's scurrilous counterattacks helped to render Acheson politically vulnerable and ineffective by the end of Truman's administration. Eisenhower resolved, therefore, that as he put it, 'I will not – I refuse – to get into the gutter with that guy.'[10] Eisenhower wrote that 'This particular individual wants, above all, publicity. Nothing would please him more than the publicity that would be generated by public repudiation by the President. Whether a Presidential "crack-down" would better, or would actually worsen, the situation, is a moot question.'[11] Eisenhower did not rely entirely on the tactics of ignoring McCarthy. As Fred Greenstein has shown, Eisenhower also employed 'hidden-hand' methods of working behind the scenes to undermine McCarthy, such as denying him access to government files and providing information on McCarthy to Congressional figures who were working against McCarthy.[12] As Jeff Broadwater has shown, however, these tactics were of marginal significance in bringing about McCarthy's downfall.[13] Essentially, Eisenhower defused the McCarthy crisis by providing McCarthy with the rope with which to hang himself. Such an approach was not heroic, but a good case can be made that the method of gradual deflation was the most effective and sensible means of dealing with McCarthy. Patience, prudence and behind-the-scenes manoeuvring were called for rather than a dramatic public confrontation, which was likely to produce a bruising, smearing counterattack from McCarthy that could wreak severe damage on the dignity, prestige and authority of the presidency.

Eisenhower's main aim in domestic affairs was to work for a healthy economy and to keep in check the role of government in social and economic affairs. 'Maintenance of prosperity is one field of government concern that interests me mightily,' he observed to his brother, Milton.[14] Indeed, the ludicrous falsity of the caricature of Eisenhower as a disengaged president who preferred golf to government is demonstrated, perhaps more than by any other matter, by Eisenhower's deep involvement in every aspect of economic policy. Historians and commentators may legitimately agree or disagree with the economic policies that Eisenhower pursued, but, as the studies of Eisenhower's economic management by Iwan Morgan and John Sloan amply illustrate, there can be no dispute over the degree of his absorption in all aspects of economic policy.[15] He was in constant contact with his main advisers, Joseph Dodge, Director of the Bureau of the Budget, Arthur Burns, chairman of the Council of Economic Advisers, and George Humphrey, Secretary of the Treasury. Receiving disparate advice and refusing to subscribe to any one economic theory, he reached his own decisions on the various aspects of economic policy.

Eisenhower's economic policies were derived from his political philosophy. To some extent this consisted of banal statements of pedantic common sense, regurgitating conservative clichés and verities of homespun, small town wisdom. But this was embedded in a wide range of knowledge and experience, so that, as John Sloan puts it, 'Eisenhower had evolved a fairly sophisticated philosophy that was often camouflaged by folksy rhetoric.'[16] Eisenhower adhered to the fundamental conservative viewpoint that incentives, private enterprise and free markets were the bases of American national prosperity and that the traditional virtues of thrift, hard work and self-reliance were the dynamics of wealth creation, whereas the collectivist tendencies of big government would stifle creative enterprise. 'Our development since the early days of the Republic', he said, 'has been based on the fact that we left a great share of our national income to be used by a provident people with a will to venture. Their actions have stimulated the American genius for creative initiative and this multiplied our productivity.'[17] Yet this basic conservative position was qualified and amplified in a variety of ways. Cooperative partnership between government and business and the importance of personal sacrifice and societal discipline were perennial themes in his speeches, which were evocative of cherished ideals deeply rooted in the American tradition. On the key issue of the proper role of government in social and economic affairs, Eisenhower often quoted Abraham Lincoln that 'The legitimate object of government is to do for a community of people whatever they need to have done, but can not do at all, or can not so well do, for themselves, in their separate and individual capacities. In all that the people can individually do as well for themselves, government ought not to interfere.'[18] The application of this principle in practice, he suggested, should be that 'In all those things which deal with people, be liberal, be human. In all those things which deal with people's money or their economy or their form of government, be conservative.'[19] He conceded, however, that 'there can be no distinct line drawn between the economy and individual, and I am ready to say also that such a capsule sort of description of an attitude can be pulled to pieces if you want to'.[20] Moreover, as a Republican president and an heir of Herbert Hoover, he appreciated the need to avoid creating any impression of a negative attitude of an uncaring government. 'To help build a floor over the pit of personal disaster,' he said, 'Government must concern itself with health, security and welfare of the individual citizen.'[21] On the other hand, it was essential to restrain the role of government and to curb the activities of the state. Eisenhower tried to pinpoint the dividing line between proper government intervention for legitimate social reasons and excessive government interference for unjustified reasons. 'Necessity, rather than mere desirability', he said, should be 'the test for our expenditures.'[22]

The application of Eisenhower's philosophy in practice was demonstrated above all in his policy with regard to the budget, especially his determination to try to achieve a balanced budget. In his first State of the Union message Eisenhower declared that 'The first order of business is the elimination of the annual deficit.'[23] He reiterated this point frequently. 'A great deal of my waking moments are given over to that problem', he said in answer to a question on the balanced budget at a news conference, 'And we're going to do it.'[24] Eisenhower placed a high premium on fiscal constraint, which in his view was the key to social stability. James Patterson writes that 'His tenacity in support of prudent financing . . . stamped a definite character on his presidency.'[25]

Eisenhower inherited from Truman a budget for Fiscal 1954 (July 1, 1953–June 30, 1954) of $68.7 billion in revenue, $78.6 billion in expenditure, leaving a deficit of $9.9 billion. Eisenhower regarded this as unacceptable and he took measures to reduce the deficit. He placed economy-minded Republican businessmen in administrative positions, with instructions to reduce bloated bureaucracies. Downward pressure was applied on expenditures across the board, with reductions in the number of Federal employees and a shift of many Federal activities to the states and local government or to private enterprise. At the same time, Eisenhower emphasised the need to take only prudent first steps towards fiscal discipline rather than precipitate measures that could damage the economy. 'Hasty and ill-considered action of any kind', he said, 'could seriously upset . . . the general economic health of the nation. Our goals can be clear, our start towards them can be immediate – but action must be gradual.'[26] Eisenhower believed that budget deficits contributed to inflation, which was destructive of social harmony, leading workers to press for excessive wage claims and penalising thrift and savings, which was the basis for sustained investment and long-term economic growth. Nevertheless, he did not aim at the attainment of a balanced budget immediately. Indeed, he felt a higher short term priority was a significant tax cut of $7 billion in 1954 to stimulate the economy and to raise incentives, with the goal of a balanced budget deferred until later. An even higher priority was the immediate abolition in the spring of 1953 of the price and wage controls of the Truman era.

Eisenhower sought to set an example of frugality and simplicity in the presidency. He dispensed with some of the more luxurious perks of the office, which had existed since Franklin Roosevelt's time. He decided to forego the use of the presidential yacht, the *Williamsburg*. He gave up the presidential quarters at Key West in Florida. He retained the president's place of retreat in Maryland but dropped Roosevelt's name of 'Shangri-La'. 'It has been renamed "Camp David",' Eisenhower wrote. '"Shangri-La" was a little fancy for a Kansas farm boy.'[27]

One area in which Eisenhower wished to save a significant amount of Federal money was agriculture. From his rural Kansas background and with his farm in Pennsylvania, Eisenhower was very interested in matters relating to agriculture. His conservative political philosophy made him appalled by the panoply of subsidies and other such mechanisms that distorted the market in agriculture and involved a great deal of political interference. As Secretary of Agriculture Eisenhower appointed Ezra Taft Benson, who was an elder in the Mormon church in Salt Lake City, Utah, and who had considerable experience in agriculture and a similar wish to Eisenhower's to free the farm economy from government control as far as possible and to reduce Federal government expenditure on subsidies and storage of surpluses. Eisenhower was sufficiently realistic, however, to appreciate that he faced deeply-entrenched vested interests and that the agricultural economy could not be wholly exposed to free-market forces. He felt, however, that he might eventually be able to bring about changes to the system of subsidies and price supports that had developed in the depression and the Second World War but that, in the very different circumstances of the 1950s, only added to the problems of over-production and to government storage costs. Eisenhower had made a campaign promise to maintain the existing system until the current legislation expired in 1954. The Agricultural Act of 1954 attempted some significant changes, which would take effect from 1955 onwards. In the first two years of his administration Eisenhower accepted that he would not achieve significant savings in agriculture.

As Eisenhower realised, therefore, there was only one area in which really significant cuts in government expenditure could be made, namely, defence. Defence amounted to 73 per cent of government expenditure in 1953, and much of the remaining 27 per cent was for fixed expenditures, such as interest on the national debt. The major battle of Eisenhower's campaign for fiscal prudence and a balanced budget was in the field of defence. One of the most surprising and extraordinary features of Eisenhower's presidency was the advocacy of severe reductions in defence expenditure by a Republican former general, in the face of strong opposition from civilian politicians, often Democrats, as well as from other vested interests.

Eisenhower spoke with remarkable eloquence on the theme of the tragic waste of resources in the diversion from civilian to military purposes. 'Every gun that is made,' he said, in the most memorable speech of his presidency, 'every warship launched, every rocket fired, signifies in the final sense, a theft from those who hunger and are not fed, those who are cold and are not clothed . . . This is not a way of life at all, in any true sense. Under the cloud of threatening war, it is humanity hanging from a cross of iron.'[28] He expressed the hope that the day would come when 'the world may turn its energies and resources to serving the needs, rather than the fears, of mankind'.[29] As a realist, however, Eisenhower faced the necessity of investing sufficient resources into America's defence to ensure American security without overstraining the American economy. Eisenhower devoted a great deal of time, thought and political capital to this 'great equation' of how to equate essential military strength with tolerable economic strain. His emphasis was on cutting back on military spending in order to protect the economy. 'Our problem', he said, 'is to achieve adequate military strength within the limits of endurable strain upon our economy. To amass military power without regard to our economic capacity would be to defend ourselves against one kind of disaster by inviting another.'[30] He wrote to Al Guenther, his successor as commander of NATO forces, that 'we are trying to bring the total expenditure of the American government within reasonable limits. This is not because of any belief that we can afford relaxation of the combined effort to combat Soviet communism. On the contrary, it grows out of a belief that our organised, effective resistance must be maintained over a lengthy period of years and that this is possible only with a healthy economy.'[31] Of symbolic as well as practical importance Eisenhower made the Secretary of the Treasury and the Director of the Bureau of the Budget members of the National Security Council. As Saki Dockrill puts it, 'US national security policy was not to be seen as inhabiting a different realm to the nation's domestic concerns . . . Instead, he insisted that economic factors were to become the main elements in the formulation of the nation's security policy.'[32] In a reorganisation of the Department of Defense he stated that 'We must not endanger the very things we seek to defend. We must not create a nation mighty in arms but that is lacking in liberty and bankrupt in resources.'[33]

Eisenhower frequently expressed his fear that, if military expenditure was not kept in check, a 'garrison state' would be created in America, subsuming liberal democracy and bringing in censorship, price controls and government allocation of materials. He warned against the dangers of 'a permanent state of mobilization' in which 'our whole way of life would be destroyed'.[34] Such fears had been expressed by a number of figures in America since 1945, but Eisenhower more than anyone else focused attention on this threat to liberty as well as to economic prosperity from excessive military expenditure.[35] If the United States adopted a defence policy 'to try to play safe in all the possible kinds of warfare', he said, 'we might just as well stop any further talk about preserving a sound economy and proceed to transform ourselves forthwith into a garrison state'.[36]

Eisenhower, however, of course paid due attention to the other side of the 'great equation', namely, the need for adequate levels of expenditure on defence in order to safeguard American security. As he said to the Cabinet, 'National security must not be endangered merely for the sake of balanced budgets.'[37] The reorganization of defence, the 'New Look', allocated greater resources to air power and to the nuclear deterrent, with cuts in conventional forces, especially the army. By 1954, army personnel had been reduced from 1.6 million to 1 million, whereas resources for Atlas missiles had been increased. Eisenhower argued with regard to cuts in military spending that 'these savings result from revisions in programs, from shifts in emphasis, from better balanced procurement, from improved management and operations. Our security is being strengthened, not weakened.'[38] His policy came under attack from critics who derided the New Look as a simplistic search for a 'Bigger Bang for a Buck' and who argued in favour of greater military expenditure. Eisenhower's emphasis was on the economic benefits of his cuts in military spending. 'Our approach to a position of military preparedness', he reported to Congress, 'now makes it possible for the United States to turn more of its attention to a sustained improvement of national living standards.'[39]

The recession of 1953–54 presented Eisenhower with a serious challenge to his economic management. The role of government in general and of the president in particular had evolved since the 1930s to the extent that, as John Sloan writes, 'The Keynesian notion that the economy can be managed by intelligent and compassionate policymakers so as to avoid the ravages of unemployment and inflation helped to spread the belief that uncaring policymakers are responsible when these maladies occur.'[40] As Clinton Rossiter puts it, the president had become the 'manager of prosperity'.[41] Moreover, the Republican party had the albatross of the Great Depression around its neck. Democratic victory in 1948 had been due fundamentally to the lingering belief that the Republicans were the party of slump. Eisenhower was well aware of the need to take action to avert a recession or to stimulate recovery in the event of the occurrence of recession. In February, 1953, he instructed his economic assistant, Gabriel Hauge, to use the highway programme in such a way that 'the timing of construction should be such as to have some effect in levelling out peaks and valleys in our economic life'.[42] When the economy sank into recession in the autumn of 1953, Eisenhower made clear that he was not a do-nothing Republican president. 'The arsenal of weapons at the disposal of government for maintaining economic stability is formidable,' he said. 'We shall not hesitate to use any or all of those weapons as the situation may require.'[43]

Eisenhower's conservative instincts, however, made him inclined to move cautiously in introducing interventionist measures. In the recession of 1953–54 he made use of monetary measures and minor public works rather than tax cuts or more extensive public works, which he feared could add significantly to the budget deficit and cause inflation. Unemployment reached its highest level since the Second World War at 6 per cent in January, 1954, but by June, 1954, the economy had recovered. His Democratic opponents accused him of moving too slowly, rejecting, for example, the Democratic proposal of raising the personal tax exemption from $600 to $800 in 1954 and to $1,000 in 1955. Eisenhower felt vindicated that his approach to the recession of 1953–54 of a clear statement of government responsibility and intention to take whatever action was necessary, combined with relatively mild interventionist policies in practice, had been successful in bringing the economy out of recession. His critics charged that he had been overly cautious and caused unnecessary economic pain.

Apart from the economy, the most important issue in domestic affairs facing Eisenhower was civil rights. Eisenhower's approach on this issue was even more conservative than on other social and economic issues. Eisenhower's upbringing in Abilene had been in a small town with an entirely white population. He had served in a segregated army. He had been posted to several bases in Southern states, such as Georgia and Texas. Many of his closest associates in the army had been Southerners, such as Fox Conner, George Patten and George Marshall. Eisenhower undoubtedly had the racial prejudices that such an upbringing and background produced. Furthermore, his position on constitutional issues reinforced his views on race in inclining him towards non-interference by the courts or the federal government. On the other hand, Eisenhower was aware of the growing pressure to improve the condition of black

Americans, many of whom had served under his command in the Second World War and returned to discrimination and poverty in America. At the same time, blacks in colonial countries were pressing for freedom and independence, while new civil rights leaders and organisations were emerging in America to champion the cause of black Americans. Above all, as an internationalist, Eisenhower realised that America's record on civil rights presented a propaganda gift to the Soviets, which they exploited endlessly. As the Justice Department brief in the case of Brown v. Board of Education in 1954 put it, 'It is in the context of the present world struggle between freedom and tyranny that the problem of racial discrimination must be viewed.'[44] Eisenhower therefore supported moves against racial discrimination, but he felt that, on such a delicate and sensitive issue, a gradualist approach should be taken, with due regard to Southern sensibilities and an avoidance of precipitous action and intrusive, morally self-righteous attitudes.

Eisenhower's first public statement on race relations as president was of a vague, very gradualist nature. He suggested that racial discrimination could be alleviated through the power 'of fact, fully publicized; of persuasion, honestly pressed; and of conscience, justly aroused'.[45] Eisenhower was punctilious in implementation of measures that were required by law. He completed the process of the desegregation of the armed forces, such as the integration of schools on military bases. He ended segregation within the Federal government, with blacks appointed to clerical and sometimes higher administrative positions in the executive branch of the government. His appointments were favourable to civil rights, especially Attorney-General Herbert Brownell and Solicitor-General Simon Sobeloff and liberal and moderate judges appointed to the circuit courts. The most important appointment was Earl Warren, whom Eisenhower appointed Chief Justice of the Supreme Court in September, 1953, following the death of Chief Justice Fred Vinson. Eisenhower did not foresee that Warren would take a very liberal standpoint on a wide range of issues, but Eisenhower did deliberately select Warren as a moderate, who, as an experienced politician as Governor of California, would give weight to the Supreme Court on such decisions as Brown v. Board of Education, which had come before the Court. Of clear symbolic significance was the appointment to the Supreme Court in October, 1954, of John Marshall Harlan, the grandson of the only Justice who had dissented in the case of Plessy v. Ferguson, the Supreme Court decision of 1896 that was overturned in Brown v. Board of Education in 1954. With regard to appointments to the lower courts, Stanley Kutler writes that Eisenhower 'appointed an array of outstanding judges throughout the federal system . . . who steadily advanced the cause of desegregation and civil rights in the late 1950s and in the next decade'.[46]

On May 17, 1954, the Supreme Court ruled in Brown v. Board of Education that 'in the field of public education the doctrine of "separate but equal" has no place. Separate educational facilities are inherently unequal.'[47] In response Eisenhower adopted a position of constitutional correctness, but with clear signs of coolness, which reflected his distaste for social engineering, especially when imposed on local communities from outside. He accepted the constitutional ruling on segregation in schools, but he hoped that the process of implementation would be gradual and as far as possible left to local initiative. 'The Supreme Court has spoken', he said at a news conference, 'and I am sworn to uphold the constitutional processes of this country; and I will obey.'[48] Eisenhower asked the District of Columbia Board of Commissioners to set an example of peaceful school desegregation. In June, 1954, the DC Superintendent of Schools drew up a desegregation plan that was smoothly introduced in the following school year without disturbances. But Eisenhower made no public statement supporting the Court's decision in the Brown case or directly urging states to comply. Such silence was interpreted as encouragement to those who wished resistance or the slowest possible implementation of the Court's ruling. Chester Pach and Elmo Richardson suggest that 'His sympathy clearly lay with southern whites, who he patiently said needed time to adjust, not with southern blacks, whom he impatiently criticised for wanting basic rights too soon.'[49] Eisenhower's greatest fear was of a backlash that could lead to social disturbance and to the closure of public schools in some Southern states, with private schools receiving state aid. 'It's all very well to talk about school integration,' he said to his aide, Emmet John Hughes, 'if you remember that you may also be talking about school disintegration . . . Feelings are deep on this, especially where children are involved . . . We can't demand perfection in moral things . . . And the fellow who tries to tell me that you can do these things by force is plain nuts.'[50] As Michael Mayer puts it, Eisenhower 'was not the obstructionist that some historians have portrayed . . . His quarrel was with the Court's methods, not its intent. He had qualms about the exercise of judicial power represented in the school segregation decision and even more doubts about the extension of federal power. The doubts did not, however, extend to the *principle* of desegregation.'[51] In spite of Mayer's argument, however, the issue of race and desegregation seems the weakest part of Eisenhower's record. It is one issue on which post-revisionists and other critics have clear validity in their unfavourable judgement of Eisenhower's performance.

Eisenhower's policies on civil rights were also influenced to some extent by party political considerations. With a very thin Republican majority in Congress, Eisenhower needed the support of Southern Democrats in Congress. Moreover, having won four Southern states in the presidential election of 1952, Eisenhower hoped to build up further support in the South for the Republican party. He was consequently very aware of the danger of alienating the South over civil rights. His need for good relations with Southern Democratic Congressional leaders, especially Senate Minority Leader Lyndon Johnson and House Minority Leader Sam Rayburn, grew greater after Robert Taft's death in July, 1953. Following their intense rivalry in 1952, Eisenhower had developed a good working relationship with Taft, who became Senate Majority Leader. Although they had an almost explosive disagreement on one occasion over the level of Federal government expenditure, they worked together smoothly. Indeed, Eisenhower noted in his diary that 'I think it is scarcely too much to say that Taft and I are becoming right good friends.'[52] Taft was succeeded by Senator William Knowland (R. – California), with whom Eisenhower did not develop a very good relationship. Knowland, Eisenhower wrote in January, 1954, 'means to be helpful, but he is cumbersome'.[53] By the middle of 1954, Eisenhower dismissed Knowland as 'the biggest disappointment I have found since I have been in politics'.[54] Eisenhower had a strong need for cooperation from Southern Democrats to enable him to pass his programme in Congress. Eisenhower did not adopt a Calvin Coolidge-type of approach as an aloof president. Although his constitutional principles led him to oppose overactive government intervention, he accepted the transition in the public expectancy of the post-Second World War presidency that, as James Pfiffner puts it, 'both the public and Congress now expect that presidents will have a legislative agenda and actively fight for it on Capitol Hill'.[55] At one of his earliest press conferences in 1953 Eisenhower said that 'If the Republican party can show as its record over the next two years a progressive, sane program of accomplishment, one that is in keeping with the constitutional processes of this country, which takes care of the welfare, the interest, of all our people and doesn't give itself away to any section or any group, any class, and that program, that accomplishment, is properly advertised, we will be back with a greatly enhanced majority.'[56] The record of legislative accomplishment in 1953–54 was reasonably substantial, but it was not a cohesive programme of a united, moderate Republican party, as Eisenhower would have wished, but a series of incremental measures, attained with the support of Southern Democrats. Some liberal measures were passed, such as an increase in minimum wage from 75 cents to

$1 per hour, expansion of Social Security to cover ten million additional workers and the establishment of a Department of Health, Education and Welfare, headed by a woman, Oveta Culp Holby. Most measures were more conservative, such as on public utilities, which Eisenhower was prepared to support if they were local, but he was opposed to Federal public power projects, which he felt gave too much economic control to the Federal Government. He supported, however, the St Lawrence Seaway Act, which funded the construction of the St Lawrence Seaway by Canada and the United States, and which Eisenhower felt had been obstructed by the selfish regional interests of New England congressmen. In many of the issues of domestic policy, as well as on the key issues of the budget and overall economic policy, the Republican party was quite divided. Eisenhower failed to achieve a greater degree of party unity. He was dismayed by the stridency of his critics on the right, such as Styles Bridges and Barry Goldwater. The British ambassador, Roger Makins, noted that Eisenhower was 'involved in a struggle for the soul of the Republican party'.[57] He was much more in tune with Southern Democrats who joined the Republican party, such as his protégé, Robert Anderson from Texas, whom he appointed Secretary of the Navy. He wrote of Anderson that he hoped 'that he can be sufficiently publicised as a young, vigorous Republican, so that he comes to the attention of Republican groups in every state of the union'.[58] In his exasperation with the Old Guard right wing Republicans, he wondered if 'I should set quietly about the formation of a new party'. He considered writing to every senator, congressman and governor 'whose general political philosophy is "the middle way"'. But he decided instead to try to educate the Old Guard Republicans.[59] He wrote that 'If we could get every Republican committed as a Moderate Progressive, the Party would grow so rapidly that within a few years it would dominate American politics.'[60]

In the Congressional election campaign in 1954, Eisenhower was initially reluctant to become involved. He had a temperamental disdain for the practice of party politics. He realised that blatant involvement in partisan politics detracted from his role as national unifier. He was aware of the disastrous presidential interventions in Congressional elections by Woodrow Wilson in 1918 and Franklin Roosevelt in 1938. On the other hand, with the parties so finely balanced, he was prepared to enter the field. He travelled extensively and made over two hundred speeches across the country.

Since the party that holds the White House has traditionally lost seats at mid-term Congressional elections, the swing of 2 per cent to the Democrats in 1954 was within the margins of a normal mid-term swing, especially following the recession of 1953–54. Nevertheless, it had been hoped that Eisenhower's personal popularity would have brought benefit to the Republican party and enabled the party to retain its majority in Congress. This did not prove to be the case. The Democrats gained two seats in the Senate and seventeen in the House of Representatives, giving the Democrats a majority in both houses of Congress. The Democrats gained eight governships, including the largest state, New York, where the Democrat Averell Harriman was succeeded after three terms by Tom Dewey. Eisenhower had attained a reasonable record of accomplishment in his first two years in office. But he had not, as he had hoped, won broad national support within the Republican party nor within the country for the programme of the Middle Way of dynamic conservatism, which he wished to become established as the majority political standpoint in the United States. The greater focus of his attention in 1953–54, however, had not been on domestic affairs but on foreign affairs.

Chapter 2

Waging Peace, 1953–54

Issues of foreign policy, to a greater extent than domestic affairs, had led Eisenhower to seek the presidency. His military career had given him considerable experience in foreign affairs, and as president he regarded foreign policy as his most important area of responsibility and his major area of interest. His primary objective was the attainment and preservation of peace. He assumed the presidency with the nation at war in Korea, and his first order of business was to bring the Korean War to an end. The danger was great, however, of the outbreak of another much more terrible war, a nuclear war with the Soviet Union. Eisenhower came to power with the Cold War at its height in the last days of Stalin's rule in the Soviet Union. Eisenhower's military career had given him endless experience of the horrors of war, and he had a clear appreciation of the calamitous devastation that nuclear war would bring. In a very dangerous world situation, then, Eisenhower above all sought peace. There was wide debate, however, over the best means to attain peace, while at the same time safeguarding America's interests and ideals.

Even more than with regard to domestic affairs, Eisenhower had a well-organised system for his conduct of foreign policy.[1] He delegated extensively but maintained control over the major decisions and the overall direction of foreign policy. As part of his overall style as president, however, his control over foreign policy was not always clear to the general public or to foreign leaders and public opinion abroad. This had advantages in allowing him not to be associated with some of the more controversial decisions on foreign policy matters. As part of his 'hidden-hand' approach to the presidency, Eisenhower often deliberately conducted foreign policy in an ambiguous manner. On the other hand, the disadvantage in this approach was that many Americans as well as foreign leaders thought that Eisenhower left control over foreign policy to subordinates, which reduced respect for Eisenhower and weakened his authority in foreign relations.

Eisenhower's most important adviser on foreign policy by far was his Secretary of State, John Foster Dulles. In some respects, Dulles seemed an excellent choice as Secretary of State, but in other ways he was a very controversial figure. Dulles seemed almost to have been preparing all his life for the post of Secretary of State. His grandfather, John W. Foster, was Secretary of State in the last year of Benjamin Harrison's administration, 1888-89, and his uncle, Robert Lansing, was Woodrow Wilson's Secretary of State, 1915-20. Dulles was a brilliant student at Princeton University and he went on to an extremely successful career in law in New York. He maintained an interest in foreign affairs, and was an adviser at the Versailles Conference in 1919 and an active participant in the Council on Foreign Relations. He also wrote many articles for the journal, *Foreign Affairs*, as well as a book, *War, Peace and Change*.[2] In 1948 Dulles became foreign policy adviser to Thomas Dewey. If Dewey had, as expected, won the presidential election in 1948, Dulles would have become his Secretary of State. Instead, Dulles provided bipartisan support for Truman by acting as negotiator of the Japanese Peace Treaty in 1951. In 1952 Dulles acted with skill in drawing up a foreign policy plank for the Republican platform that was acceptable to supporters of both Eisenhower and Taft. Eisenhower had wide general experience in foreign policy, but he needed a Secretary of State with expertise on the technical aspects of diplomacy. Dulles seemed the ideal, obvious choice.

On the other hand, there were facets of Dulles' personality that made him a controversial figure. He was the son of a Presbyterian minister and was heavily involved in the affairs of the Presbyterian Church for most of his life. He came across as a narrow-minded, moralistic, self-righteous preacher rather than as a seasoned, polished diplomat. His stern manner, inability to make eye contact or to engage in small talk made him an offputting figure, while his tendency to speak in moralistic terms and apocalyptic phrases caused consternation. To Eisenhower, however, Dulles was not only a very skilled and experienced professional in the technicalities of diplomacy but also a figure who would win him support in conservative circles within the Republican party. He was also a figure who would act as a lightning rod to deflect from Eisenhower some of the consequences of more difficult foreign policy decisions. At the same time, Eisenhower was one of the few people who had a good personal relationship with Dulles. They became good friends and frequently met for cocktails at the end of the working day.

For the organisation of foreign policy Eisenhower developed the National Security Council, which had been established in 1947 but had not been widely used in Truman's administration. The NSC held very regular meetings, almost every Tuesday, with the president normally in attendance. Eisenhower chose as his National Security Adviser Robert Cutler, who was a low-key figure with ability in administration rather than a high-profile policy adviser. The minutes were taken by S. Everett Gleason, who had served in the Office of the Historian in the State Department and who was a distinguished diplomatic historian. Gleason's historical sense ensured that the decisions at NSC meetings were very fully recorded, and the record brings out that the discussions were lively and extensive, with the president playing a very full part and displaying emotion as well as engaging in discussion. In 1954 Andrew Goodpaster became Staff Secretary, with administrative duties that included taking notes of conversations in which the president engaged. Goodpaster became such a close aide to Eisenhower as to become his alter ego.

Regular meetings of the NSC brought the Director of Central Intelligence more fully into foreign policy discussions. As Director of Central Intelligence Eisenhower appointed Allen Dulles, elder brother of John Foster Dulles. A much more urbane and sophisticated figure than his brother, Allen Dulles had a long association with the murkier, undercover side of foreign policy, dating back to his service in Berne in Switzerland during the First World War, through to his involvement with OSS in the Second World War and service as Deputy Director of the CIA in 1950–52. Allen Dulles provided experience and heavyweight input on the clandestine aspects of foreign policy, in which Eisenhower had longstanding interest and experience from his Second World War days. The combination of the two Dulles brothers, however, added to the sense of their domination over foreign policy and gave the incorrect impression that Eisenhower was little more than a figurehead.

In his campaign for president, Eisenhower had pledged that, if elected, he would 'go to Korea' between the election and his inauguration, which was widely viewed as a coded message of a promise to bring the Korean War to an end swiftly. Public opinion had supported America's original intervention in Korea in June, 1950, when the North Koreans, who were viewed as pawns of the Soviet Union, invaded South Korea. There was even stronger support for American involvement when General Douglas MacArthur made a spectacularly successful amphibious landing at Inchon in South Korea in September, 1950, and very rapidly drove the North Koreans back across the 38th Parallel, the border between North Korea and South Korea. The decision to cross the 38th Parallel and invade North Korea in October, 1950, however, brought about the intervention of Communist China, with the result that, instead of a swift victory, the war bogged down into a stalemate, with mounting casualties and with no end in sight. Peace negotiations had been taking place at Panmunjon on the 38th Parallel since July, 1951, but they had proved frustrating and inconclusive.

After the election in 1952, Eisenhower went to Korea as promised, on December 2–5. Once inaugurated, Eisenhower pursued diplomacy to bring an end to the war through various channels. Towards the Chinese, he took a threatening line. As he recorded in his memoirs, he let the Chinese know that, unless there was progress in the peace negotiations, the United States would 'move decisively, without inhibitions in our use of weapons'.[3] Towards the Soviet Union, after Stalin's death in March, 1953, Eisenhower took a more conciliatory approach, pressing the new Soviet leadership for a gesture of goodwill, such as the use of their good offices to persuade the Chinese and North Koreans to make peace in Korea. Towards India, whose leader Pandit Nehru he found sanctimonious, Eisenhower swallowed his pride and accepted India's lead in arranging a solution for the difficult issue of an exchange of prisoners-of-war, accepting that prisoners should go to India for a 120-day period for questioning before they decided whether to return them to their home country or not. The outcome was that on July 23, 1953, an armistice was signed and the fighting in Korea came to an end.

With the opening of new archives in China and the Soviet Union as well as in the United States and Britain, historians have been able to make more fully-informed assessments of Eisenhower's diplomacy in ending the Korean War. Dulles claimed that 'The principal reason we were able to obtain the armistice was because we were prepared for a much more intensive scale of warfare . . . We had already sent to the theatre means for delivering atomic weapons. This became known to the Chinese through their good intelligence sources, and in fact we were not unwilling that they should find out.'[4] William Stueck has shown, however, that 'The Chinese viewed enemy use of atomic weapons as unlikely, both because of world opinion and of the Soviet Union's retaliatory capacity.'[5] Stueck concludes that 'More influential than Eisenhower's nuclear diplomacy was war weariness and pressure from the post-Stalinist leadership of the Soviet Union.'[6] Nevertheless, for whatever reasons agreement on an armistice was reached, the ending of the Korean War serving as an excellent opening chapter in Eisenhower's record in foreign policy. He inherited a war and in six months there was peace. During the remainder of his presidency, peace was preserved and almost no American soldiers died in conflict.

At the centre of Eisenhower's policy to maintain peace and to protect America's interests was solid commitment to a policy of containment.

This had been confused by the apparent criticisms of containment and support for liberation in the 1952 campaign and by an apparent willingness on the part of the new administration to explore policies that went beyond containment. In practice, however, Eisenhower's policy was firmly based on the principles of containment, which had been established in the late 1940s. George Kennan, the head of the Policy Planning Division in the State Department, had provided the intellectual framework for containment, arguing that in the ideological conflict between Communism and liberal democracy, the deeper spiritual roots of Western liberal democracy and its broader popular support would ultimately prevail over the unnatural, forcefully imposed system of Soviet Communism. Kennan warned against a provocative policy of attempting to overthrow Communism, which could lead to war. Instead, Kennan advocated the containment of Communism, preventing its further expansion, which in the course of time would result in its collapse from within.[7] Eisenhower strongly endorsed a policy of firm and patient containment, which found expression in the late 1940s in the Truman Doctrine, the Marshall Plan and NATO. Eisenhower's appointment as commander of NATO forces in 1950 made him a clear embodiment of the American rejection of isolation and commitment to the long-term containment of Communism.

American impatience, however, made containment a difficult policy to sustain. An intellectual challenge to Kennan's position was mounted by such figures as James Burnham, who argued that containment was a negative, reactive policy that handed the initiative to the other side. 'Its inner law is', as Burnham put it, 'let history do it.'[8] This was a superficially reasonable argument, and it won wide support in the highly-charged political atmosphere of the late 1940s and early 1950s, with accusations that disloyalty and incompetence had been responsible for the loss of China, the Soviet atomic bomb and the stalemate in Korea. This culminated in the plank in the Republican platform on liberation in the 1952 campaign, which denounced the Truman–Acheson policy of containment as 'negative, futile and immoral'.[9] John Foster Dulles advocated a 'policy of boldness', which would proclaim America's intension that 'it wants and expects liberation to occur'.[10] Eisenhower realised that this stance not only helped to unite the Republican party but also won support from East European ethnic minorities who normally voted Democratic, such as Polish-Americans. In the election campaign, however, Eisenhower was very circumspect and always careful that his position was support for liberation by peaceful means. When Dulles made a speech on August 27, 1952, in which he spoke in a less reserved manner about strategies for stirring up resistance in the satellites, Eisenhower reproached Dulles, leading to a clearer statement by Dulles in a speech on October 4, 1952, about commitment to 'a more dynamic foreign policy, which, by peaceful means, will endeavour to bring about the liberation of the enslaved people'.[11]

In office, Eisenhower's policy on containment and liberation was very little different from Truman's. The opening of new material on American policy towards Eastern Europe, from CIA sources as well as State Department sources, has produced a spate of books on liberation.[12] Those new sources have revealed that Truman's policy was not altogether passive but that there was always strong support in the Truman administration for what one historian described as 'the invigorated version of containment'.[13] Eisenhower had been very interested in psychological warfare since the Second World War. In 1953 he appointed his wartime aide, C. D. Jackson, as Special Assistant for Psychological Warfare. Eisenhower was, however, a cautious realist with respect to Eastern Europe. In June, 1953, the revolt in East Germany illustrated very clearly the limits and dangers of an uprising in Eastern Europe. On June 16–21, 1953, protests over working practices in East Berlin led to large-scale demonstrations and calls for reform, but in the face of brutal suppression by Soviet troops and East German police, which left over a hundred dead, the United States was unable to do more than lodge a diplomatic protest and distribute food aid in East Berlin.

An alternative approach to relations with the Soviet Union was by means of direct personal contact in the pursuit of détente, which was the approach suggested to Eisenhower by Winston Churchill. Churchill had gained a reputation as a Cold War hardliner, especially as a result of his Iron Curtain speech in Fulton, Missouri, in March, 1946. But once Western strength had been built up with the formation of NATO and re-armament in the late 1940s, Churchill was eager, when he returned to office as prime minister of Britain in 1951, to make his last dramatic contribution to history with a summit meeting to reduce tensions.[14] Churchill did not win Truman's support for a summit meeting, but, following Eisenhower's election, Churchill met Eisenhower in New York in December, 1952, and pressed his idea of a personal meeting between the leaders of the United States, Britain and the Soviet Union. Eisenhower was cautious on the matter, but Churchill raised the issue frequently in the personal correspondence in which Churchill and Eisenhower engaged while they were simultaneously in office as prime minister of Britain and president of the United States, from January 20, 1953, to April 5, 1955. When Stalin died in March, 1953, and was succeeded by an apparently more moderate successor, Georgi Malenkov, Churchill wrote to Eisenhower to propose a summit meeting with the Soviets. 'I have the feeling', Churchill wrote, 'that we might both of us together or separately be called to account if no attempt were made to turn over a leaf so that a new page would be started with something more coherent on it than a series of casual and dangerous incidents at the many points of contact between the two divisions of the world.'[15] Eisenhower replied, however, that 'I tend to doubt the wisdom of a formal multilateral meeting since this would give our opponent the same kind of opportunity he has so often had to use such a meeting simultaneously to balk every reasonable effort of ourselves and to make of the whole occurrence another propaganda mill for the Soviet.'[16] Churchill persisted with his argument, however, writing in March, 1954, that 'I recur to my earlier proposal of a personal meeting between Three. Men have to live with men, no matter how vast, and in part beyond their comprehension, the business in hand may be. I can even imagine that a few simple words, spoken in the awe which might at once oppress or inspire the speakers might lift this nuclear monster from our world.'[17] Eisenhower maintained his view, however, that, as he replied to Churchill, 'I doubt whether the project on which we are engaged would, at this moment, be advanced by a meeting of heads of government. In fact, I can say that such a meeting might inject complications.'[18] Churchill became exasperated and wrote with passion that 'It will seem astonishing to future generations – such as they may be – that with all that is at stake no attempt was made by personal parley between the Heads of Government to create a union of consenting minds on broad and simple issues ... Fancy that you and Malenkov should never have met, or that he should never have been outside Russia, when all the time in both countries appalling preparations are being made for measureless mutual destruction.'[19] But Eisenhower maintained his position that 'while I would like to be more optimistic, I cannot see that a top-level meeting is anything which I can inscribe on my schedule for any predictable date'.[20]

Eisenhower's critics suggest that his rejection of Churchill's proposal of a summit meeting illustrated a lack of imaginative leadership, which resulted in a loss of a historic opportunity to initiate a new departure in relations with the Soviet Union following Stalin's death. Instead, Eisenhower pursued a cautious policy, arguing that the new Soviet leadership must provide evidence of good faith before he was prepared to engage in a summit meeting. Eisenhower's defenders argue that realistically there was no such historic opportunity for a breakthrough in East–West relations in 1953. Stalin was gone, but his successors, it is suggested, had been his close associates and were committed to the same lines of policy.

As they jockeyed for position in the Kremlin, none of the contenders could have risked a dramatic change of policy towards the West for fear of being overthrown. With State Security chief Lavrenti Beria arrested in June, 1953, and executed in December, 1953, and with a supposedly collectivist leadership in place consisting of Chairman of the Council of Ministers Georgi Malenkov, First Secretary of the Communist Party Nikita Khrushchev, Minister of Defence Nikolai Bulganin and Foreign Minister Vyacheslav Molotov, there was no prospect of a bold change of direction in Soviet policy. At the same time, a summit meeting was liable to raise false hopes in public opinion in Western countries and to create divisions and weaken support for defence spending. It was significant that Eisenhower's cautious step-by-step approach was supported not only by Dulles and the State Department but also by British Foreign Secretary Anthony Eden and the British Foreign Office. It was felt that Churchill was an old man in a hurry, advocating an imprudent and unrealistic approach, because he had reached the age of seventy-eight and his health was failing, so that the step had to be taken immediately or Churchill would have passed from the scene. Moreover, the political situation in the United States ruled out an early meeting between Eisenhower and Soviet leaders. With American suspicions of summit meetings, such as the alleged sell-out at Yalta, with McCarthy at the height of his power and the Republican party divided between the supporters of Eisenhower and Taft, it was inconceivable that Eisenhower could have flown off to meet with Soviet leaders in the first year or two of his presidency. Political considerations, then, dictated what Eisenhower had already concluded on the basis of foreign policy considerations, namely, that there was no prospect of a significant change in relations with the Soviet Union in the immediate future.

Eisenhower's distrust of the Soviet Union deepened with the rejection of his Atoms for Peace proposal. In a speech at the United Nations on December 8, 1953, Eisenhower proposed that each of the nuclear powers should set aside for peaceful purposes an amount of fissionable material from their weapons stockpile in a programme under United Nations auspices. The United States would contribute, Eisenhower proposed, five units for every one unit contributed by the Soviet Union. Eisenhower had become enthusiastic about this idea as a step, he felt, 'to help the fearful atomic dilemma and find a way by which the miraculous invention of man shall not be dedicated to his death but consecrated to his life'.[21] He set great store in this proposal 'to bring some hope and replace fear in the world'.[22] It was, moreover, as Richard Hewlett and Jack Holl suggest, in line with his basic strategy 'to approach world disarmament not in one dramatic proposal, but in small steps in tune with existing realities and simple enough for the public to understand'.[23]

The Soviet Union, however, brusquely rejected the Atoms for Peace proposal. The Soviets claimed that the scheme would be to America's advantage, since the United States had a vastly larger weapons stockpile of fissionable material, so that, even at a five to one American rate to the Soviet contribution to the programme for peaceful purposes, the strategic impact on the Soviet stockpile would be much greater. The Soviets suggested that the American proposal was advanced simply for propaganda purposes. The Soviets made a familiar counterproposal of a universal abolition of all atomic weapons, but without any acceptable system of inspection. The Atoms for Peace proposal led to the establishment of the International Agency for Atomic Energy in Vienna, which had a useful function but did not fulfil Eisenhower's purpose in drawing the Soviet Union into cooperation with the United States in the use of nuclear energy for peaceful purposes. The Soviet rebuff added significantly to Eisenhower's suspicions of Soviet purposes.

With little faith in diplomacy as a means to bring about a peaceful settlement, Eisenhower placed greater reliance on the consolidation of the Western alliance and on strong defence, especially the nuclear deterrent. Eisenhower was eager to maintain the Anglo-American special relationship as one of the pillars of the Western alliance. But whereas Churchill wished to make the Anglo-American relationship exclusive, Eisenhower wished to develop closer relations with all NATO countries, particularly West Germany. Eisenhower supported German rearmament as essential to Western defence and to the rehabilitation of West Germany, and when France rejected the complicated scheme of German rearmament within the European Defence Community, Eisenhower supported West German admission to NATO. Eisenhower gave consistently strong support to the Mutual Assistance Programme for economic and military aid to allies. Despite budget cuts in other areas of defence, military and economic assistance to allies was always high on Eisenhower's agenda, in order to consolidate the Western alliance and to give military substance to the policy of containment. At an NSC meeting in March, 1953, for example, 'The President said we should never forget that in defending Europe with $6 billion of Mutual Security assistance we are getting a very great deal for our money, because we are avoiding the necessity of using our own troops. The money in the program was not merely "giveaway" money. With it we are bringing something concrete in terms of United States security.'[24]

Eisenhower's unequivocal commitment to international involvement on the part of the United States was also made clear by his fierce opposition to neo-isolationist proposals by right-wingers, such as repudiation of the Yalta Agreement or the constitutional amendment sponsored by Senator John Bricker (R. – Ohio), the so-called Bricker Amendment. Since Yalta had taken on connotations of disloyalty and betrayal, right-wingers pressed for the new Republican administration to repudiate the Yalta Agreement. Eisenhower realised that the reality of the Yalta Agreement, rather than the mythology surrounding it, was that Soviet failure to adhere to its terms had been the source of the difficulties rather than the agreement itself. Eisenhower was able, therefore, to demonstrate that repudiation of Yalta was contrary to America's interests, since repudiation would not only be a dangerous precedent in international relations but would be contrary to America's interests, giving up rights that the agreement conferred, such as with regard to Berlin. The Bricker Amendment, however, proved much more difficult to defeat. It was a very complicated proposal, which in essence sought to curb the power of the president in the conduct of foreign policy by requiring Congressional approval of executive agreements and stipulating that treaties required supporting legislation, which must not conflict with legislation of individual states. The details became so confusing and obscure as to make the proposal seem unworkable in practice. Much more important than the details of the Amendment was its symbolism. The Bricker Amendment symbolised the deeply-rooted isolationist, unilateralist tradition in America. For this reason, rather than concern over particular details, Bricker, as Eisenhower noted, 'has gotten almost psychopathic on the subject'.[25] For the same reason, however, Eisenhower was absolutely determined that the Bricker Amendment must be rejected. Attempts at compromise proved impossible. The matter took up a great deal of Eisenhower's time in his first two years in office. The defeat of the Bricker Amendment, though by a narrow margin, was a very important symbolic victory in the clear commitment of America to international involvement.[26]

The more controversial aspect of Eisenhower's defence policy was his greater reliance on the nuclear deterrent. Eisenhower concluded that an attempt by the United States and its allies to develop a sufficient military deterrent with conventional forces would bankrupt the West. His solution was the 'New Look' in defence policy, with much greater reliance on air power and nuclear weapons, which were much less expensive than conventional forces but which raised controversial issues of morality and practicality. The threat of massive retaliation against a minor act of aggression was likely to give serious pause for thought to the other side, but such a threat somewhat lacked credibility, since it seemed unbelievable that an American president would use nuclear forces over a relatively minor issue in the virtually certain knowledge that this would produce a Soviet nuclear counterattack against the United States. Dulles argued in favour of 'brinkmanship', that is, willingness to go to the brink of war in any situation as a means to deter aggression and to maintain peace, but the practicality of such a policy was open to doubt and it tended to scare allies as much as adversaries.

When Eisenhower first learned about the atomic bomb, in a briefing by Secretary of War Henry Stimson at the Potsdam conference in 1945, his reaction had been expression of the hope that 'we would never have to use such a thing'.[27] As president, the possible use of increasingly powerful nuclear weapons was his most important responsibility. He made abundantly clear his view that the use of nuclear weapons would produce catastrophe. In his conduct of nuclear diplomacy, however, it was vital that he did not display an attitude that nuclear weapons were unusable. His foreign policy was dependent upon fear and uncertainty in the minds of America's adversaries that the United States might employ formidable destructive power against them, perhaps even over a relatively minor matter. Eisenhower's conduct of nuclear diplomacy revealed his 'hidden-hand' approach to an even greater extent than in the less vital area of domestic politics. McGeorge Bundy, in his well-balanced study of nuclear diplomacy, refers to Eisenhower's 'enigmatic but self-commanding' approach.[28]

Of crucial importance to Eisenhower with regard to decisions on defence was information from intelligence sources. The creation of the CIA in 1947 had made America's approach to intelligence gathering much more professional than before the Second World War. Eisenhower took a keen interest in the information which was gathered with respect to Soviet military developments, especially in the nuclear field. Yet, as Eisenhower made clear at an NSC meeting, 'The President once again expressed his chagrin that the United States encountered such awful difficulties in trying to discover anything about Soviet capabilities . . . while, thanks to our habit of publicizing everything, it was so much easier for the Soviets to find out what they needed to know about our capabilities.'[29] America's greatest fear since Pearl Harbor in 1941 had been surprise attack, and with the development of Soviet nuclear weapons, America's nightmare was a nuclear Pearl Harbor. In the tightly closed society of the Soviet Union, intelligence from human sources was very limited. The United States, as well as Britain, with whom the United States worked closely on intelligence matters, began to employ more effective mechanical means, especially aerial photography, which became more technically advanced by the 1950s. British and American aircraft took aerial photographs from as close to the Soviet border as possible and made many missions across the Soviet border, though it was rarely possible to penetrate Soviet airspace in any depth. The opening of archives on intelligence sources in recent years has revealed the vast extent of those operations on the Soviet border and intrusions into Soviet airspace, which involved great risks and resulted in the loss of many aircraft and crew, which was not reported at the time.[30] Nevertheless, surveillance from outside the Soviet Union, which included from submarines and radar stations as well as from aircraft, had severe limitations. In 1954, however, technological breakthroughs enabled the CIA Director of Operations, Richard Bissell, to report that it seemed possible to construct an aircraft, the U-2, that could fly at such a height over the Soviet Union that it could not be shot down but could gather vital intelligence on Soviet military capabilities. Eisenhower was well aware of the risks in such U-2 flights, but he supported its construction.[31] In the first years of his presidency, however, decisions on strategic policy and defence spending needed to be made on the basis of limited information with respect to Soviet military strength.

The most acute crises in the first two years of Eisenhower's presidency occurred in the Far East. Following the Chinese Communist victory in the Chinese Civil War in 1948, the United States had refused to recognise the Communist régime as the government of China but had continued to recognise the Nationalist régime of Chiang Kai-shek, which controlled Taiwan, also known as Formosa, which was a very large island a hundred miles off the coast of China. Since the issue of the so-called 'loss of China' was highly emotive in American politics, the Republican party exploited the issue in the election campaign of 1952, inferring that Communist victory was due to the incompetence or even disloyalty of the Truman administration. Eisenhower was sufficiently realistic to appreciate that Communist victory in China had been beyond American power to prevent and that the continuation of American support for Chiang's claim to be the legitimate ruler of China was provocative to the Chinese Communists. Nevertheless, political pressures within the United States led him to make gestures in support of Chiang. The Truman administration had instructed the US Seventh Fleet to patrol the Taiwan Straits to prevent either a Communist invasion of Taiwan or Nationalist raids against Communist China. The Eisenhower administration announced in February, 1953, a new policy to 'unleash' Chiang, with revised instructions that the Seventh Fleet's task was only to prevent a Communist attack on Taiwan and not to interfere with Nationalist forays against the Communists on the mainland. This pleased the right wing in America, such as Senator

William Knowland (R. – California), whose persistent support for Chiang led him to be referred to as the 'senator from Formosa' and whose influence greatly increased when he succeeded Taft as Senate Majority Leader in July, 1953.[32] Eisenhower observed that 'Knowland has no foreign policy except to develop high blood pressure whenever he mentions the words "Red China".'[33] In practice, however, as Admiral Arthur Radford said at an NSC meeting, although Eisenhower 'had publicly changed the orders of the Seventh Fleet in such fashion as to permit the Chinese Nationalists to make raids on the mainland, in point of fact we had privately informed Chiang Kai-shek that he must undertake no such actions without U.S. concurrence'.[34]

Relations with China deteriorated even more sharply in the autumn of 1954 when the Chinese Communists began to shell the islands of Quemoy and Matsu, which, like Taiwan, were controlled by the Nationalists. Quemoy and Matsu were in fact not individual islands but chains of a number of small islands located less than ten miles from the coast of China. Quemoy and Matsu were, therefore, very vulnerable to attack and were within shelling distance from the Chinese coast. Since the islands were so small and there were few civilians on them, there seemed to be a good case for their evacuation, with the main line of defence established to protect Taiwan. Chiang, however, adamantly refused to evacuate Quemoy and Matsu and Eisenhower supported him. Eisenhower felt that, in order to maintain Nationalist morale, the possibility must be retained of a return by the Nationalists to the mainland, whereas, if the stepping stones of Quemoy and Matsu were given up, Nationalist morale would sink and make the Nationalists less willing to defend Taiwan, which would fall to the Communists.

Eisenhower's hardline policy towards the Chinese Communists has come in for heavy criticism. His decision to 'unleash' Chiang has been denounced as irresponsible pandering to right-wing extremists for domestic political reasons. His willingness to support Chiang's stance on Quemoy and Matsu rather than to withdraw to more defensible ground on Taiwan has been widely condemned as militarily foolish as well as diplomatically unwise. The criticism has also been made that these policies drove the Chinese Communists into closer alliance with the Soviet Union, with whom the Chinese had signed a security treaty in 1950 but with whom they had had serious difficulties. It was in America's interests, Eisenhower's critics argue, to exploit those Sino-Soviet differences rather than to push the Chinese Communists closer to the Soviet Union out of a need for Soviet protection against an aggressive America.

On the other hand, Eisenhower conducted foreign policy within a democracy and needed to protect his political base, lest he suffer the same fate as Truman and Acheson in their last years. Moreover, recent research on the policy towards China pursued by Eisenhower and Dulles has suggested that it was more complex than it was previously regarded and that the hardline policy was designed in a subtle way to deepen the divisions between China and the Soviet Union. As Dulles argued, 'It was the view of the United States that the best hope for intensifying the strain and difficulties between Communist China and Russia would be to keep the Chinese under maximum pressure rather than by relieving such pressure. There were two theories for dealing with this problem. One was that by being nice to the Chinese we could wean them away from the Soviets, and the other was that pressure and strain would compel them to make more demands on the USSR which the latter would be unable to meet and the strain would consequently increase. The United States adhered to the latter view that pressure should be maintained both politically and economically and, to the extent possible without war, military pressure should be maintained.'[35]

An even more acute crisis in the Far East arose over Indo-China. Indo-China, which consisted of Vietnam, Laos and Cambodia, had been under French colonial rule since the late nineteenth century. The Japanese had taken over Indo-China during the Second World War and following their defeat the reimposition of French rule had been resisted by independence movements, especially the Vietminh, led by Ho Chi Minh. In the 1940s, the United States had been critical of French colonialism and remained aloof from the conflict between the French and the Vietminh. With the onset of the Cold War, however, the United States began in 1950 to give economic assistance to France, a vital NATO ally, for the prosecution of the war in Indo-China and by 1954 80 per cent of the costs of the war were paid for by the United States. In the spring of 1954 a settlement of the Indo-China conflict was sought by a conference in Geneva. This was fraught with difficulties, with such problems as Chinese representation and refusal by Dulles to greet with a handshake Chinese Foreign Minister Chou En-lai or to sit at the same table as him. Even more serious was the military situation, with Vietminh guerrilla tactics wearing down the French, culminating in the encirclement of a French garrison at Dienbienphu in March, 1954.

Eisenhower's view was that the loss of Indo-China to the Communists would seriously undermine containment. As he famously put it at a press conference, 'You have a row of dominoes set up. You knock over the first one, and what will happen to the last one is the certainty that it will go over very quickly.'[36] No serious consideration was given to the idea that Ho Chi Minh was an independent, nationalistic Communist rather than a part of monolithic Sino-Soviet Communism. On the other hand, Eisenhower did not wish to have another Korea. In the weak position in which he found himself with regard to Indo-China, Eisenhower probed for a solution that might somehow prevent a Communist victory or at least deny the Communists total victory. He rejected as unrealistic the more extreme proposals, such as an American air strike with tactical nuclear weapons to save the French at Dienbienphu. Eisenhower gave covert aid to the French at Dienbienphu, with re-supply flights by the Civil Air Transport, which was secretly operated by the CIA. This was limited assistance in the circumstances, but CAT pilots flew 684 sorties and one pilot, James B. McGovern, was shot down and killed on May 7, 1954.[37] On that same day, May 7, 1954, Dienbienphu fell, weakening the Western bargaining position at the Geneva conference, which opened on May 8. Eisenhower's preferred solution was 'united action', a somewhat ambiguous proposal whose purpose essentially was to build up a coalition of powers, including Britain, Australia and New Zealand, to strengthen the French and to enable them to prevent a Communist victory. Eisenhower was insistent, however, that support should be given by Congress, which was unwilling to give support without the agreement of allies, especially Britain. Britain's unwillingness to participate in united action doomed the scheme, though Britain was willing to join the new alliance of SEATO (South-East Asia Treaty Organisation) as a collective arrangement for the longer-term security of South-East Asia. Moreover, Britain, as co-chair of the Geneva conference, used its influence to reach a settlement that denied total victory to Ho Chi Minh in Vietnam but divided Vietnam at the 17th Parallel. This was intended as a temporary military demarcation line, but it provided the United States, which had not been satisfied with the terms of the settlement and was not a signatory of the Geneva agreement, with the opportunity to support a non-Communist government in South Vietnam. Eisenhower had denied total victory to the Communists, but he had created a hostage to fortune for the United States in its support for the new régime in South Vietnam.

On the crucial issue of Vietnam, then, which had such momentous consequences for the future, Eisenhower had been torn in two directions. He foresaw the horrors that could ensue from the commitment of American troops, yet he was very fearful of the political and international repercussions of Communist triumph. 'The people who know war, those that experienced it,' he said, 'are the most earnest advocates of peace in the world.'[38] At an NSC meeting in January, 1954, 'For himself, said the

President with great force, he simply could not imagine the United States putting ground forces anywhere in Southeast Asia ... If we did so, the Vietnamese could be expected to transfer the hatred of the French to us. I can not tell you, said the President with vehemence, how bitterly opposed I am to such a course of action. This war in Indochina would absorb our troops by divisions.'[39] Yet at the same time Eisenhower felt that Communist domination of South-east Asia would seriously endanger American security interests. As he put it with feeling, 'We can't get anywhere in Asia by just sitting here in Washington and doing nothing. My God, we must not lose Asia. We've got to look the thing in the face.'[40] When the complex manoeuvring to bring about 'united action' as a deterrent against the Communists came to nothing, he resorted, with British diplomatic assistance at the Geneva conference, to the partition of Vietnam, which would involve American commitment to South Vietnam. Chester Pach and Elmo Richardson comment that 'That commitment seems by far the more significant than the temporary avoidance of war.'[41] In the short term, however, it seemed the least unsatisfactory solution to a situation in which the American position was very weak.

In the Middle East, fundamental problems in the area were becoming clear, which would create serious dilemmas for the United States. America's main interests in the Middle East were oil, protection of Israel and the prevention of Soviet intrusion into the area. As Eisenhower realised, however, these interests were mutually contradictory. The United States had had relatively little contact with the Middle East before the Second World War, and there was quite a strong tradition of anti-Semitism in America. The Holocaust, however, and a guilty conscience over American reluctance to admit many Jews as refugees in the 1930s, led to strong American support for Jews in the postwar years and in particular to support for the Zionist dream of a homeland for the Jews in Palestine. These sentiments were reinforced by political considerations, when it became clear that, although Jews numbered only six million in an American population of one hundred and fifty million, they were extremely influential in the media and in finance, especially in key states such as New York and California, which was evident in Truman's election victory in 1948. Eisenhower was even-handed in his attitude towards Jews. He had visited concentration camps in Germany after their liberation, which affected him deeply and made him sympathetic to the Jews. On the other hand, he realised the difficulties that were created by the establishment of a Jewish state in Palestine, and he resented the influence of the Jewish lobby in American politics, especially since Jews were overwhelmingly Democratic.

As Eisenhower appreciated, American support for Israel was in direct contradiction to America's other interests in the Middle East, namely, oil and the exclusion of Soviet influence. The United States was largely self-sufficient in oil, with its vast oil resources in such states as Texas and California, while New World sources in Venezuela and Mexico were also available to the United States. But American oil companies were eager to penetrate the Middle East oil market, while future energy needs in an expanding economy made the availability of Middle East supplies at a favourable price important for the American economy and vital for the economies of America's NATO allies.

The Middle East was largely an area of British influence. Eisenhower was for the most part prepared to accept continuing British dominance in the Middle East and to allow Britain to play the leading role in keeping the Soviets out of the area. On the other hand, Eisenhower realised that colonialism was the main issue that provided the opportunity for Soviet penetration into the Middle East. He was not an outspoken anti-colonialist, as Franklin Roosevelt had been, but took a more moderate, ambivalent position. He favoured the independence of colonies in principle, but, as in many matters, he was a gradualist and realised the need not to alienate the major colonial powers, who were America's allies in NATO. While the British had operated an informal empire in the Middle East through pliant monarchies, Eisenhower wished to support younger nationalist republican elements who were not Communists, such as the Young Officers Movement in Egypt. In delicate negotiations, in 1953–54, Eisenhower encouraged Britain to withdraw from its military base in Suez in 1954. Eisenhower hoped that this would ease relations with Egypt, where Gamul Abdel Nasser, the key figure in the Young Officers Movement, formally assumed power in 1954. The CIA had been in contact with Nasser since 1952. Eisenhower felt that Nasser's radicalism would moderate, especially if he received Western aid, and that he might assist in settling the Arab–Israeli conflict.

The most acute crisis in the Middle East in Eisenhower's first year in office arose in Iran. A left-wing government had come to power in Iran in 1951, led by Mohammed Mossadegh. The Anglo-Iranian Oil Company, a British oil company that controlled the Iranian oil industry, was nationalised, while Mossadegh cooperated with the Tudeh party, which was the Iranian Communist Party. The Eisenhower administration concluded that Mossadegh was either a Communist or a tool of the Communists. Mossadegh then attempted to replace the Shah of Iran as commander-in-chief of the armed forces, and he opened trade talks with the Soviet Union. In Eisenhower's view, 'Iran's downhill course toward

Communist-supported dictatorship was picking up momentum.'[42] Eisenhower therefore authorised project AJAX, a CIA plan to stir up demonstrations in Tehran against Mossadegh to bring about his downfall.

The Shah attempted to dismiss Mossadegh and to appoint in his place General Fazollah Zahedi. Mossadegh, however, refused to yield power, and the Shah left Iran for Italy on August 18. On August 19, demonstrations, financed by the CIA, led to disorder, which culminated in Mossadagh's arrest and Zahedi's assumption of the office of prime minister. On August 22 the Shah returned to Iran and resumed power. British diplomats, who observed the demonstrators of August 19, reported that 'Most of these men, although possibly inspired by royalist sentiment, had obviously been hired for the purpose.'[43] John Foster Dulles, however, told the NSC that 'the United States now had a "second chance" in Iran when all hope of avoiding a Communist Iran appeared to have vanished.'[44] The Shah protected American interests but was regarded as an American puppet. Communist influence was eliminated in Iran and a new consortium consisting mainly of major American oil companies replaced the Anglo-Iranian Oil Company. Seething resentment, however, had been created underneath the surface against the blatant manipulation of political and economic power on the part of the United States and the disrespect shown to a leading Moslem power. It was a short-term victory at a heavy long-term price.

As in the Middle East, in Latin America and in other Third World countries, Eisenhower was torn between policies based on America's ideals, especially by means of economic aid to assist such countries to develop as peaceful democracies, and policies based on realpolitik, which were designed to ensure above all that these countries did not turn towards Communism. Eisenhower felt that it was necessary to work with unsavoury leaders and to resort to morally dubious methods in order to achieve the broader goal of saving countries from Communism. Eisenhower's chief adviser on Latin America was his brother, Milton, who encouraged him to try to promote peaceful democratic development in Latin America. Congress, however, was resistant to requests for foreign aid, while Eisenhower was inclined to view left-wing régimes in Latin America as Communist. Milton, while emphasising economic aid, agreed on the dangers of Communist subversion in Latin America. 'The possible conquest of a Latin American nation today', Milton warned, 'would not be . . . by direct assault. It would come, rather, through the insidious process of infiltration, conspiracy, spreading of lies and the undermining of free institutions, one by one. Highly disciplined groups of communists are busy, night and day, illegally or openly, in the American republics, as they are in every nation of the world . . . One nation has succumbed to communist infiltration.'[45] The country to which Milton referred was Guatemala, where a left-wing reformer, Jacobo Arbenz Gutman, has been in power since 1950 and had engaged in social and economic reforms, especially land reform, including the expropriation with little compensation of 400,000 acres of the land of the United Fruit Company, a large American company.

Guatemala provides the worst example of failure on Eisenhower's part to differentiate between nationalist reform and Communist subversion. 'In Guatemala', he wrote in his memoirs, 'the Arbenz régime since December, 1950, had been attempting to establish a Communist state within the Western Hemisphere.'[46] Eisenhower's suspicions of Arbenz's pro-Communist leanings were added to by the importation of arms to Guatemala from Czechoslovakia in May, 1954. Eisenhower therefore approved a CIA plan to recruit Carlos Castillo Armas, a former Guatemalan colonel who had led a brief insurrection in 1949 against Arbenz's predecessor, to organise a force in Honduras and lead a revolt to overthrow Arbenz. On June 18, 1954, Armas crossed into Guatemala with a rag-tag army and unimpressive air cover in the form of about a dozen Second World War bombers. To provide the necessary display of military power to intimidate Arbenz, the dictator of Nicaragua, Anastas Somoza, offered to supply two modern fighter-bombers, provided that the United States would replace them. CIA Director Allan Dulles recommended acceptance of Somoza's offer, lest the revolt fail, and Eisenhower agreed. The Guatemalan army was overawed and made no effective resistance. On July 3, 1954, Armas flew into Guatemala City, accompanied by the US ambassador to Guatemala, John Peurifoy. Arbenz fled into exile. His reforms were reversed, a dictatorship was imposed and corruption and repression characterised Guatemala in succeeding years.[47]

At the outset of his presidency, as the internationally acclaimed war hero who had led the liberating armies of the Second World War, Eisenhower appeared to have the potential to project an image of America as a progressive liberator. The policies pursued in such places as Iran, Guatemala and Vietnam served instead to project the image of the ugly American. Throughout the Third World, as Eisenhower conceded, 'it was a matter of great distress to him that we seemed unable to get some of the people in these downtrodden countries to like us instead of hating us'.[48]

Overall, however, Eisenhower recorded significant achievements in foreign policy in his first two years in office. He put together a good system of foreign policy organisation, though this somewhat obscured the extent to which he was in control of it. He swiftly brought peace to Korea. He sought to maintain peace primarily through the consolidation of the Western alliance as a bulwark of freedom and strength, which would be capable of the long-term containment of Communism. He set in place a defence strategy to attain security objectives at an affordable cost, with the health of the economy regarded as a top priority within the defence programme. He had tried to promote progressive social and economic development in the Third World, but support from Congress had been limited and he had shown an inclination to regard left-wing reformers as tantamount to Communists and demonstrated a willingness to resort to undemocratic covert action to thwart left-wing reforms. In the short-term the policies seemed to have been reasonably successful. How far such policies would be successful in the longer run became more apparent in 1955–56, with such events as the Geneva summit in 1955 and the Suez crisis in 1956.

Chapter 3

Affluence and Good Feelings, 1955–56

In January, 1955, a new Congress convened, with the Democrats in the majority in both the Senate and the House of Representatives. Lyndon Johnson became Senate Majority Leader, and Sam Rayburn, like Johnson a Texan, became Speaker of the House of Representatives. Eisenhower faced a new challenge in working with a Congress in which the opposition party held a majority.

Eisenhower developed good relations with the new Democratic leaders. His relationship with Lyndon Johnson was in fact much more constructive than with William Knowland, who remained as a rather difficult Senate Minority Leader until 1958. 'In his case', Eisenhower wrote of Knowland, 'there seems to be no final answer to the question, "How stupid can you get?"'[1] Johnson, on the other hand, was extremely energetic, dynamic and ambitious, and he perfected 'the Johnson treatment' as a means of winning support in Congress for the passage of measures. Johnson in the 1950s, however, was not the extreme liberal which he became in his Great Society days as president in the 1960s.[2] Rayburn was even more so a traditional conservative Southern Democrat. Ten of the fourteen chairs of committees in the Senate and fourteen of the nineteen in the House were held by Southern Democrats. Eisenhower was well-disposed towards Southerners and broadly agreed with their ideological standpoint. Eisenhower continued his orderly process of regular meetings with Congressional leaders. At the same time, he appealed to the general public over the heads of other politicians as a non-partisan president of all the people. His communication with the people was enhanced when his weekly press conferences began to be televised from January, 1955. This helped Eisenhower to retain a very favourable public image, which was reflected in an approval rating in the polls in 1955–56 of over 60 per cent, consistent with his poll rating throughout his presidency.

Eisenhower's top priority in domestic affairs continued to be the economy. In 1955–56 the American economy boomed. There was a healthy growth rate of over four per cent, with low unemployment and low inflation. There was a large trade surplus and the dollar had a high purchasing power abroad. With Western Europe and Japan struggling to recover from the Second World War, America enjoyed a uniquely advantageous position in the world economy, with a standard of living that was well above any other country in the world. By 1955, the budget deficit had been reduced considerably since 1953, due to cuts in government spending and increased government income as a result of economic growth. Federal government spending fell from 20.6 per cent of Gross National Product in 1953 to 17.3 per cent in 1956. Eisenhower resisted attempts by Democrats to increase the defence budget. In May, 1955, Senator Henry Jackson (D. – Washington) and Senator Richard Russell (D. – Georgia) claimed that the flyby on Soviet Aviation Day in Moscow raised fears of Soviet superiority in bombers, while Senator Stuart Symington (D. – Missouri) claimed that the Soviets had gained the lead in missile development. Eisenhower rejected these claims and asserted that 'There is no magic number of dollars or of military units and weapons that would solve all our defense problems and guarantee national security . . . It is essential to have a stable long-range defense program suited to our needs.'[3] He emphasised that 'true security for our country must be founded on a strong and expanding economy, readily convertible to the tasks of war'.[4] He warned that 'There is no amount of money you can pour into bombs and missiles and planes and tanks and guns that will assure you peace. After you get to a certain point, it is a very, very emphatic case of diminishing returns.'[5] The 'great equation' of a strong economy and sufficiency in defence was a subject to which he gave constant consideration. 'Professional military competence and political statesmanship must join to form judgments as to the minimum defensive structure that should be supported by the nation,' he wrote to the Secretary of Defense. 'To do less than the maximum would expose the nation to the predatory purposes of political enemies. On the other hand, to build excessively under the impulse of fear could, in the long run, defeat our purposes by damaging the growth of our economy and eventually forcing it into regimented controls.'[6]

Eisenhower was very proud that by 1956 the budget was balanced and that he was able to project a balanced budget for Fiscal Year, 1957, which was from June 30, 1956–July 1, 1957. The accrued surplus, Eisenhower advocated, should be used for reduction of the national debt. 'Once a budgetary surplus comes definitely into sight,' he said, 'and economic conditions continue to be favourable, we should begin reducing our public debt. Such an act of fiscal integrity would signify with unmistakable clarity that our democracy is capable of self-discipline.'[7]

Social critics charged that America was not simply attaining prosperity but was also developing the worst features of a crassly materialistic society, which Eisenhower allegedly condoned or even encouraged. Writers and intellectuals, from abroad as well as in the United States, condemned the deplorable by-products of unrestrained consumerism and the rise of a repressive, homogenised mass culture. The consumerist binge of the period was exemplified by the growth of the advertising industry, which encouraged the purchase, often on credit, of consumer goods well in excess of basic needs. The irresponsible excess of the 1950s, it is suggested, was best illustrated by automobiles. Many families had several cars, which were excessively large in size and gaudy in style – multi-coloured, chrome-encrusted gas guzzlers, with a new feature added in 1955 of a sweeping, non-functional tail fin. No note was taken of the environmental consequences of the doubling of the number of cars in America in the 1950s nor of the fact that by 1953 the United States had ceased to be self-sufficient in oil and had become an oil importer. Sales of automobiles, as all other consumer goods, benefited from the expansion of the television industry. American television was controlled by business enterprise with laissez-faire attitudes. The Federal Communications Commission played only the minor role of regulation of largely technical matters, while the financing and programming of television was operated by the networks, CBS, NBC and ABC, whose values were aggressively commercial. Commercial competition led to the reduction in the standard of television programmes to the lowest common denominator, with vapid melodramas, soap operas and quiz shows interspersed with frequent, mindless commercial breaks. Television embodied and influenced the growing homogenisation of American society in the 1950s. In the great expansion in the housing market, virtually identical suburban developments became the faceless dormitories of the middle class. Standardised food, promoted heavily on television, expanded massively, illustrated by the success of Ray Kroc, who opened the first McDonald's in 1955. By 1960 the famous golden arches were visible over 285 franchises across America.

Social critics expressed their concern over the cultural aridity and uniformity in a wasteland of conformity. The sociologist, C. Wright Mills, who in *White Collar* in 1951 had written a penetrating analysis of the social and economic trends in a society with fewer industrial workers and a growing number of employees in service industries, developed further his theme of the subtly repressive nature of these trends in *The Power Elite* in 1956.[8] Combined with the influence of Cold War clichés, the homogenising trends within a society that was increasingly dominated by commerce and advertising seemed to narrow political debate and cultural expression and to encourage a self-satisfied, uncritical outlook. As David Halberstam puts it, 'In that era of general good will and expanding affluence, few Americans doubted the essential goodness of their society.'[9] Americans of the mid-1950s seemed to have developed a smug self-satisfaction, wrapped in patriotic ardour. The value of the dollar abroad created a large increase in the number of American tourists, especially in Europe, who embodied these attitudes of smug superiority. This aroused resentment against the ugly Americans, who boasted about how things were bigger and better back home. No attention was paid to the deficiencies in an economic system that left a quarter of the population in poverty and created an ever-widening gap between the rich and poor, while even less attention was paid to the widening chasm between the world's rich and poor countries.

The changing social trends produced ugly blots on the bland social structure, such as juvenile delinquency. Teenagers became prominent in American society, as they acquired purchasing power, partly from parental wealth and often from part-time jobs while at high school. This produced harmless consequences, such as the growing popularity of juke-boxes. Less socially desirable expressions of teenage independence and rebelliousness were manifested as teenagers indulged in underage drinking and went hotrodding in flashy cars. Films of the times, such as *Rebel Without a Cause* (1955), starring James Dean, the ultimate cult teenage hero, who was killed in a car crash in 1955, and *Blackboard Jungle* (1955), portrayed problems of antisocial behaviour on the part of alienated youth. The soundtrack of *Blackboard Jungle*, featuring Bill Haley and the Comets playing *Rock Around the Clock*, introduced trends in music that the established middle class found not simply entertaining but in some ways threatening. Elvis Presley exploded onto the scene, along with such figures as Little Richard and Chuck Berry, with their raucous rock 'n' roll music, with its powerful rhythms and sexual energy. This was in marked contrast to the prevailing musical trends, which had been dominated by crooners such as Pat Boone, Bing Crosby and Perry Como, singing their somewhat anaemic love songs. Teenage behaviour was regarded as a sufficient problem as to merit Senate sub-committee hearings on Juvenile Delinquency in 1955, chaired by Senator Estes Kefauver (D. – Tennessee).

Eisenhower's main concern with regard to the economy was economic stability and economic growth rather than with excesses of social behaviour that grew out of increasing prosperity. From his upbringing in modest circumstances, he welcomed a greater level of general prosperity for the great majority of people, expressing his belief that 'a high and rising standard of living brings to more of our people the opportunity for continued intellectual and spiritual growth'.[10] As a politician, particularly a Republican politician, he was well aware of the immense political benefits that followed from economic prosperity and of the dire political consequences of an economic downturn. With his admiration for business entrepreneurs and his conservative political philosophy, he was inclined to place trust in business enterprise as the means of gradually lifting more and more of the deprived out of poverty into prosperity. Environmental concerns and the issue of finite resources were not matters that were raised at the time, and Eisenhower had no inclination to be greatly concerned about them. Nevertheless, there is some validity in the argument that, to the extent that America in the 1950s had tendencies towards reversion to the Gilded Age, Eisenhower was a William McKinley rather than a Theodore Roosevelt. He did not attempt to use the 'bully pulpit' of the presidency, as TR had described it, to exercise moral leadership on the issues of the perils of prosperity and the somewhat uncritical self-glorification on the part of Americans. His presence in the White House helped to create the stability that produced the prosperity of the 1950s, so that he was consequently identified not only with the economic success but with some of the less worthy social, cultural and economic trends of the times.

On the other hand, as recent historians of the culture of the 1950s have emphasised, the 1950s were by no means as bland and uncritical as earlier writers suggested. The surface of American life in the 1950s was deceptively placid, while beneath the surface there roiled powerful currents of protest and unease. At a poetry festival in San Francisco in 1955 Alan Ginzburg read his poem, *Howl*, which excoriated America as a ravenous beast sacrificing its young on the altars of commerce and technology. In 1956 Jack Kerouac publicised *On The Road*, portraying footloose people seeking freedom and friendship outside the bonds of familial obligations. Ginzburg, Kerouac and the other Beats engaged in literary iconoclasm in which they flaunted middle-class taboos and, in place of middle-class restraint, they cultivated frenetic movement, fleeting relationships and casual sex. The Beats were on the periphery of American society of the mid-1950s, yet they were in some ways the tip of the iceberg and represented the extreme edge of widespread forces of cultural alienation, which were dissatisfied with the smug contentment of Eisenhower's America. Among earlier writers who dismissed the 1950s as bland and conformist, the novelist Norman Mailer described the 1950s as 'one of the worse decades in the history of man', while the historian Eric Goldman wrote of the years of the 1950s as 'the dullest and dreariest of all our history'.[11] A more recent cultural historian, Paul Boyer, in rejecting such a view, concludes that 'What finally impresses one more about the fifties is less its bland uniformity than its vibrant diversity.'[12] Eisenhower was open to the criticism, then, that he did not take a lead in urging more critical self-awareness. It is not true to suggest, however, that he presided over a passive, uncritical society, and this perhaps reduced the need for presidential leadership on the matter.

With regard to policy on agriculture, Eisenhower's attempted reforms in the Agricultural Act of 1954 came into force and met with stiff resistance and very limited success. The most important single reform was a change from fixed parity of 90 per cent to flexible parity of from 75 per cent to 90 per cent. Parity was a concept devised in the First World War and the 1920s to work out a balance between prices received by farmers and prices paid by them, with government programmes aiming to ensure that farmers received a fair return in comparison with their costs. Secretary of Agriculture Ezra Taft Benson introduced a modernised formula for fixing parity, which took into account costs of tools and equipment in recent years, but this proved controversial. Even greater opposition arose against flexible parity, whereby the level of government support for any commodity varied between 75 per cent and 90 per cent in accordance with the supply of the commodity. This involved Benson in endless wrangles with producers of different commodities. To reduce surpluses, the new mechanism of a Soil Bank was introduced, whereby farmers could allocate up to 50 per cent of their acreage for soil conservation and receive in return a certificate from the government that was redeemable in cash or commodities from government storage. At the same time, Benson made strenuous efforts to expand trade in agricultural goods with many trips abroad. In addition, the Agricultural Trade Development and Assistance Act of 1954, popularly known as PL480, established a system of the export of agricultural surpluses to create funds for development loans in Third World countries.

None of these agricultural programmes were very successful, however. Eisenhower stated that his programme was designed 'to bring production and consumption as nearly into line as possible'.[13] Mechanical improvements, crop-spraying and other such developments in agriculture resulted in very large increases in production, while political opposition to reductions in government supports was fierce in farm states. The Soil Bank helped the problem of surpluses to some extent, but at a very high cost. The export market was very competitive, with other countries such as Canada and Australia having similar production increases. Distribution of agricultural surpluses for foreign aid purposes was problematical. Demands were constantly made for a return to fixed parity of 90 per cent. Even in an election year in 1956, however, Eisenhower refused to bow to the political pressure. He wrote that he was 'unwilling to return to a program of increased government bribes to create a false and fleeting prosperity – and to purchase votes'.[14] His agriculture policy was undoubtedly one reason for Republican failure to regain their majority in Congress in 1956.

The most emotive and controversial issue in domestic affairs in 1955–56 was civil rights. On May 31, 1955, the Supreme Court issued its ruling on the implementation of desegregation in schools as a follow-up to Brown v. Board of Education. The Supreme Court ruled that the initiative for implementation of desegregation should come at the local level and that school districts should make a 'prompt and reasonable start towards full compliance' and do so 'with all deliberate speed'.[15] Eisenhower regarded this ruling as a recommendation for the cautious, gradual approach that he favoured. He held the Federal government conspicuously aloof from taking any positive action and he refrained from making public statements on the subject. His temporising approach had the advantage that it reduced tensions, which could have led to confrontations and violence. Its disadvantage was that it seemed to signal endorsement of Southerners who sought to delay desegregation of schools indefinitely. In 1955 White Citizens Councils were formed across the South in opposition to desegregation in schools, which put up a respectable front but which were basically a revived Ku Klux Klan. In March, 1956, the Southern Manifesto was signed by almost all the senators and representatives from Southern states, pledging themselves to work for the reversal of the 1954 Supreme Court decision. Eisenhower felt that this potentially explosive situation required delicate, diplomatic handling, while he was in any case sympathetic towards the Southerners. Eisenhower noted that the signatories of the Southern Manifesto had pledged to use 'every legal means' and that there was no threat of nullification. He pointed out that for three generations Southerners had been 'acting in compliance with the law interpreted by the Supreme Court of the United States under the decision of 1896. Now, that has been completely reversed, and it was going to take time for them to adjust their thinking and their progress.'[16] He said that 'The South is full of people of good will, but they are not the ones we now hear. We hear the people that are adamant and are so filled with prejudice that they even resort to violence; and the same way on the other side of the thing, the people who want to have the whole matter settled today.'[17] He observed that the Supreme Court had called for 'successive steps' and he stated that 'To expect a complete reversal in their habits and thinking in a matter of months was unrealistic.'[18] He stressed that 'Here is a problem . . . that is charged with emotionalism, where everybody has got to work hard with all of the strength he has; and I think that the more that that work is done privately and behind the scenes rather than charging up on the platform and hammering desks, the better and more effective it will be.'[19] His constant message was that 'If ever there was a time when we must be patient without being compla-cent, when we must be understanding of other people's deep emotions as well as our own, this is it.'[20] He argued that 'It is difficult through law and through force to change a man's heart.'[21] With regard to a time scale, he stated that 'The length of time I am not even going to talk about – I don't know about the length of time it will take.'[22]

By the end of 1956, only a very small number of school districts in Southern and border states had become desegregated. Eisenhower faced criticism over foot-dragging on the issue. His defence was, as Herbert Parmet puts it, that 'it would have been compounding the situation by forcing social realignment upon those intellectually and emotionally unprepared to make the transition. It was, moreover, a matter best left to the states'.[23]

Eisenhower took a similarly aloof approach with regard to desegrega-tion of buses, which flared up into a widely publicised issue with the bus boycott in Montgomery, Alabama, in 1955-56. Martin Luther King emerged onto the national scene, using as a focal point for civil rights protest the incident of the arrest of Mrs Rosa Parks in Montgomery in December, 1955, for refusing to move to the back of the bus in order to allow a white person to sit at the front. Eisenhower deplored the tactics of protests, marches, demonstrations, confrontations and suchlike. The events in Montgomery attracted massive national and international attention, especially due to Martin Luther King's charismatic personal-ity and his enthralling rhetoric. King spoke with deep moral passion, expressed in dramatic, cadenced tones. In contrast, Eisenhower took a legalistic standpoint. When he was asked for his reaction to the arrest in March, 1956, of black protestors in Montgomery for refusing to ride on the buses, he blandly stated that, 'As I understand it, there is a state law about boycotts, and it is under that kind of law that those people are being brought to trial.'[24] In November, 1956, the Supreme Court ruled that the Montgomery city ordinances concerning segregated seating on buses violated the Fourteenth Amendment. Thurgood Marshall, who had fought the case in court for the NAACP, commented that 'All that walking for nothing. They might as well have waited for the Court decision.'[25] Eisenhower strongly felt that orderly procedure through the courts and the political process, with patience and restraint, was the proper approach for progress in civil rights rather than the drama of boycotts, confrontations and emotional rhetoric, which was liable to produce a backlash of resentment and violence. In 1956, Eisenhower proposed a Civil Rights bill, to establish a commission to monitor progress in civil rights, to create a Civil Rights Division in the Department of Justice and to take measures to protect the voting rights of blacks. The bill's prospects of enactment, however, particularly in an election year, were slim, and it was bottled up by Southern Democrats in Congress.

Eisenhower also faced the opposition of Southern Democrats on a racial issue on which Eisenhower took a much more liberal stance than he did on civil rights for blacks, namely, statehood for Hawaii. Southern Democrats opposed the admission of Hawaii, which had been an American territory since 1898, as the 49th state, on account of Hawaii's very mixed racial population of whites, Japanese, Chinese and native Hawaiians. There was greater support for the joint admission of Hawaii along with Alaska, whose population was largely white. Eisenhower, however, felt that the population of the territory of Alaska was too small to justify statehood. Eisenhower spoke eloquently in favour of the admission of Hawaii, stating that 'In the Hawaiian Islands, East meets West. To the Islands, Asia and Europe and the Western hemisphere, all the continents, have contributed their peoples and their cultures to display a unique example of a community that is a successful laboratory in human brotherhood. Statehood, supported by the repeatedly expressed desire of the Islands' people and by our tradition, would be a shining example of the American way to the entire earth.'[26] Eisenhower steadfastly worked for Hawaii's admission as a state until this goal was achieved in 1959, though Eisenhower had to compromise and agree to the prior admission in 1958 of Alaska, whose claim for statehood seemed weaker to Eisenhower but whose population was largely white.

Eisenhower had little success in 1956 with his Civil Rights bill, which was not surprising with Southern Democrats so powerful in Congress. On most issues, Eisenhower, however, had more difficulty with conservative Republicans than with Southern Democrats. Many progressive measures that Eisenhower favoured were doomed by conservative Republican opposition, such as a Rural Development programme to help small family farms to raise their productivity, an Area Development programme to deal with pockets of unemployment, and a health insurance programme to cover catastrophic illness. Conservative Republicans also opposed the school construction programme, which Eisenhower favoured as a short-term five-year programme to provide Federal assistance for the building of schools to compensate for the diversion from school building during the Second World War. To compound the problems, liberal Democrats supported an amendment to the School Construction bill, which was introduced by Adam Clayton Powell, Representative from Harlem, to withhold Federal aid from school districts that did not desegregate. The combination of liberal Democratic and conservative Republican opposition to the School Construction bill led to its defeat. Eisenhower became very frustrated by what he regarded as the connivance of politicians.

There were, however, some successes. The most significant was the Federal Highway Act of 1956. Ever since his cross-country trip in 1919, and especially after he had seen Germany's autobahn system, Eisenhower, for both economic and military reasons, strongly supported the construction of an interstate highway system funded by the Federal government. In practice, the military purpose of the interstate system proved to be of relatively minor significance, though it complicated its construction, such as the requirement that every fifth mile should be straight, so that a plane could use it as an emergency runway. Nevertheless, the defence purpose helped to overcome the many constitutional and political obstacles to the construction of such a massive Federal project, while Eisenhower exerted skill in reaching the compromises that were essential in a scheme in which the economic stakes were extremely high. Eisenhower showed his awareness of the economic implications of the route of the interstate highway by, for example, his intervention to ensure that the route across Kansas favoured his home town of Abilene. The construction of the interstate system from the mid-1950s gave Eisenhower the flexibility to increase or decrease government spending on this very large project, depending upon the state of the economy, while it also greatly benefited economic development and facilitated military transportation.

His progress, however, even when combined with his considerable success with regard to the budget and general economic prosperity, fell far short of his goal of broadening the base of support for the Republican party to make it the natural majority party, with wide national support as a moderate, progressive party. In December, 1954, in setting out his aims for 1955–56, Eisenhower had written that 'These next two years I have just one purpose and that is to build up a strong Republican party in this country . . . If the right wing want a fight, they're going to get it. If they want to leave the Republican party and form a third party, that is their business, but before I end up, either the Republicans will reflect progressivism or I won't be with them anymore.'[27] From time to time Eisenhower toyed with the idea of forming a new party, composed of moderate Republicans and Southern Democrats, committed to 'the Middle Way'. 'It may come about that this will be forced upon us,' he wrote, 'but the difficulties are vast, and if we can possibly bring about a great solidarity among Republicans, if we can get them more deeply committed to teamwork and party responsibility, this will be much the better way.'[28] His fundamental objective was, as he wrote to his friend Swede Hazlett, 'to make certain that the policies in which I firmly believe will have younger men and abler champions when I step off the stage'.[29] In his speech accepting the renomination of the Republican party as candidate for president in 1956, Eisenhower indulged in an uncharacteristic poetic flourish with a quote from Henrik Ibsen that 'I hold that man is in the right who is most clearly in league with the future.'[30] Eisenhower's wish was for the Republican party to be regarded by the majority of Americans as the progressive force for the future. At the end of his first term in office, however, this remained on Eisenhower's wish list rather than being recognised as an achievement.

Aside from issues of policy, the most significant developments for Eisenhower in 1955–56 related to his health. On September 24, 1955, while he was on vacation in Colorado, Eisenhower suffered a heart attack.[31] He spent six weeks in hospital in Denver and the next six weeks recuperating at his farm in Gettysburg. He made a good recovery and was able to retain responsibility for government decisions during his hospitalisation and recuperation. Congress was not in session and there were no serious crises in either domestic or foreign affairs. Sherman Adams went to Denver and handled administrative matters and arranged appointments for members of the Cabinet to come to see Eisenhower. Vice-President Nixon chaired meetings of the Cabinet and National Security Council in Washington.

The public response was not only sympathy for Eisenhower but also admiration for his dedication to duty. It did, however, raise the question of his fitness to run for a second term. In June, 1956, Eisenhower suffered an attack of ileitis, an inflammation of the lower intestine, which required surgery and which was a manifestation of Eisenhower's chronic medical problems, especially relating to his heart and stomach.

In 1952 Eisenhower had felt that he would run for only one term. He had intended to state in his Inaugural Address that he would be a one-term president, but he was persuaded to omit this statement.[32] He ruminated on numerous occasions on the seductive lure to which many succumbed of staying on too long and developing a belief in their indispensability. 'I am reminded of how hard it is for older men to retire and to accept the inevitable verdict of passing years,' he noted in his diary. 'I have watched this over my life, and I continue to pray that I, in my turn, will not fall victim to the same human failing.'[33] In a letter to Swede Hazlett he wrote that 'I have seen many a man "hang on too long" under the definite impression that he had a great duty to perform and that no one else could adequately fill his particular position.'[34] He wrote to his brother Milton that 'One of my good political friends . . . said that he had "never heard of a President who didn't want a second term." Brother, if he only knew! . . . If ever for a second time I should show any signs of yielding to persuasion, please call in the psychiatrist – or better the sheriff.'[35] Eisenhower realised that if he ran for a second term this would take him to the age of seventy, in uncertain health. He observed that 'No man has reached his 70th year in the White House . . . No one has the faintest right to consider the acceptance of a nomination unless he honestly believes that his physical and mental reserves will stand the strain of intensive work.'[36] Eisenhower also made the point that the Twenty-second Amendment to the constitution passed in 1952, which limited a president to two terms, would make a president a 'lame duck' in his second term, and thus make a second term less attractive.[37]

In 1953 Eisenhower continued to assert firmly that he would be only a one-term president. 'With respect to the political campaign of 1956,' he wrote, 'my position will be exactly as I determined it would be when I gave way in '52 to the convictions and arguments of some of my friends. I shall never again be a candidate for anything . . . This determination is a fixed decision.'[38] He decided, therefore, that he would try to encourage the emergence of possible candidates to succeed him. 'Far from trying to keep young men out of the spotlight,' he wrote, 'it is my hope to push them into it and so have ready a group of young men who are not only able but who will have the publicity that a political party always seeks in its candidate.'[39] The candidates whom he most strongly favoured, however, were unrealistic as serious contenders. His favourite candidate was Robert Anderson, Under-Secretary of Defense in 1955–56, whom Eisenhower described as 'just about the ablest man that I know anywhere. He would make a splendid President of the United States, and I do hope that he can be sufficiently publicised as a young, vigorous Republican, so that he will come to the attention of Republican groups in every state of the union.'[40] Anderson, however, was a little-known figure, a technocrat rather than a politician, a former Southern Democrat who lacked a political base, political ambition or charisma. Another excellent candidate, Eisenhower felt, would be his brother, Milton. 'The man who, from the standpoint of knowledge of human and governmental affairs, persuasiveness in speech and dedication to our country, would make the best president I can think of,' Eisenhower wrote, 'is my young brother, Milton.' But Eisenhower conceded that such a candidacy was unrealistic, since 'I do not think that he is physically strong enough to take the beating,' and also since 'any effort to make him the candidate would probably be resented by our people.'[41] Eisenhower referred to more realistic candidates such as Henry Cabot Lodge, Herbert Brownell, Harold Stassen, Charles Halleck and Richard Nixon. There is little evidence, however, of much effort on Eisenhower's part to fulfil his proclaimed aim of promoting the advancement of any of these figures as a possible successor. In fact, as early as July, 1954, Eisenhower had decided that he would probably run for a second term. His Press Secretary, James Hagerty, records that on July 27, 1954, 'For the first time the President virtually told me that he would run again in '56.' Eisenhower said to Hagerty that 'Right now I kind of think that the answer will be that I will run for another term.'[42] Eisenhower did not make a public statement with regard to his intentions, but he conceded that no viable successor had emerged. 'For two-and-a-half years,' he wrote, 'I have genuinely tried to place two or three able younger men constantly before the public in the hope of giving them the publicity value that would compare favourably with their ability. The inertia and indifference that I have encountered are scarcely less than phenomenal.'[43] Public opinion, and even more so the Republican party, overwhelmingly wished Eisenhower to run for a second term. Eisenhower, for all his protestations and his reflections on the imprudence of staying on too long, was not immune, as in 1952, to persuasion of his indispensability.

Eisenhower's heart attack only briefly altered the situation with regard to a second term. Within a few days it became clear that the prospects of a good recovery from the heart attack were fair. As Eisenhower considered the alternative candidates in late 1955, he concluded, with regard to running for a second term, that 'I don't want to, but I may have to.'[44] He later somewhat disingenuously wrote that 'Had I not suffered a heart attack in September, I could have taken much more drastic steps than I did to force the Republican party to consider and accept someone else.'[45] Eisenhower was in fact very concerned that a weaker Republican candidate might lose to the Democratic nominee, who was likely to be Adlai Stevenson. The major other Democratic contender, Averell Harriman, was equally unacceptable to Eisenhower, who referred to him as 'nothing but a Park Avenue Truman'.[46] Following final medical reports on the progress of his recovery, Eisenhower announced on February 29, 1956, that he would be a candidate for a second term.

With the matter of Eisenhower's candidacy settled, the next important matter was the vice-presidential candidate. Nixon's record as vice-president seemed to have been satisfactory. He had been an effective campaigner in 1952. He had gone on many foreign trips as vice-president and performed very well. He contributed intelligently at meetings of the Cabinet and the National Security Council. Eisenhower had noted in his diary in June, 1953, that Nixon 'is not only bright, quick and energetic, but also loyal and co-operative'.[47] During Eisenhower's illness, Nixon presided at meetings with sufficient authority to win confidence and respect but also with sufficient discretion to allay fears that he was overly eager to replace Eisenhower. Moreover, Nixon maintained good contacts with the right wing of the Republican party, while in all sections of the party he was highly regarded as a tireless campaigner to whom large numbers were indebted.

Eisenhower, however, was distrustful of Nixon. The political fund and Checkers speech episode in the 1952 campaign had added to Eisenhower's wariness of Nixon as a hustling politician. For all of Eisenhower's recognition of Nixon's many assets, Eisenhower did not include Nixon among his confidants and he rarely invited him to White House social events. Eisenhower seemed to wish to replace Nixon as his running mate in 1956, but he lacked the decisiveness and ruthlessness to dump Nixon, while he also feared the political fall-out within the Republican party if Nixon was replaced. With his health problems, Eisenhower took seriously the possibility that he might die in office, and he doubted that Nixon would be a worthy replacement. 'I've watched Dick a long time,' he said to his speechwriter Emmet John Hughes, 'and he just hasn't grown. So I haven't honestly been able to believe that he *is* presidential timber.'[48] Eisenhower felt that Nixon should take a Cabinet post in a second Eisenhower administration, such as Secretary of Defense, which would give him administrative experience and enhance his qualification to be Eisenhower's successor in 1960. The vice-presidency was not, as it became after 1960, a natural stepping stone to a presidential nomination. No vice-president had gone on to the presidency, apart from successions in cases of the death of the president, since Martin Van Buren succeeded Andrew Jackson in 1836. When Eisenhower, however, suggested to Nixon at a meeting on December 26, 1955, that Nixon move to a Cabinet post in Eisenhower's second term, Nixon responded that this would not be perceived as an enhancement of his qualifications for the presidency but as a demotion and an expression of a lack of confidence in him on Eisenhower's part.[49] In January, 1956, when Eisenhower resumed his full duties, he was asked at a press conference whether he would retain Nixon as his running mate if he ran for a second term. Eisenhower spoke effusively about Nixon's qualifications, but he was equivocal with regard to his nomination as a vice-presidential candidate. 'He has my respect, my admiration,' said Eisenhower. 'Never has there been a Vice-President so well-versed in the activities of government. He has attended every important meeting. He has gone to numerous nations and been widely and favorably received in these nations.'[50] On another occasion he said that Nixon 'has been brought into the affairs of government more closely than, so far as I know, any other Vice-President that has ever been brought in. He has done everything I asked him, beautifully. So from that viewpoint, as far as efficiency, dedication to the job, loyalty to his country is concerned, I think he is as good a man as you can get.'[51] But Eisenhower said that he could not speak with regard to Nixon's renomination as vice-president 'until I know his desires, and I don't. I don't know his desires at all.'[52] Nixon's desire to be renominated as vice-president was plain, as the press was well aware. Eisenhower's equivocations added to the impression, which had been public knowledge since 1952, that Nixon did not enjoy Eisenhower's confidence and trust. In the New Hampshire primary in March, 1956, Nixon received a large write-in vote. Eisenhower responded by heaping further praise on Nixon verbally. 'Anyone who attempts to drive a wedge of any kind between Dick Nixon and me', said Eisenhower, 'has just about as much chance as if he tried to drive it between my brother and me. We are very close . . . I am happy that Dick Nixon is my friend. I am very happy to have him as an associate in government. I would be happy to be on any political ticket in which I was a candidate with him.'[53] Yet Eisenhower continued to adhere to the position that the vice-presidential nomination would be decided by the Republican convention and that he should not pre-empt its decision, while he continued to state that Nixon had not expressed his preference with regard to the matter. On April 26, Nixon had a meeting with Eisenhower at which Nixon formally stated that he wished to be the candidate for vice-president. Eisenhower expressed pleasure in receiving this news and asked Hagerty to arrange a press conference for Nixon to make this announcement. Ambiguity persisted, however, and frequent questions on the matter at press conferences made it clear that Eisenhower had left the impression that he wished to keep his options open with regard to his choice of vice-president. Eisenhower's health situation, which his ileitis attack on June 9 brought to the fore again, held the implication that a vote for Eisenhower might well be a vote for his vice-presidential candidate in the event of Eisenhower dying in office. Adlai Stevenson made this point and held up the bogey figure of Nixon in an attempt to scare voters away from support of the Republican ticket. As late as July 23, Harold Stassen met with Eisenhower and told him that a poll showed that Nixon's presence on the ticket would reduce support by five per cent, and Eisenhower did not dissuade Stassen from holding a press conference to advocate that Republicans should nominate Christian Herter, Governor of Massachusetts, as vice-presidential candidate. Eisenhower did not immediately squash this idea but left the matter hanging for a few days until Herter repudiated the suggestion and endorsed Nixon.

At the Republican convention, support for Nixon as Eisenhower's running mate was overwhelming. The Democrats nominated Stevenson, with Ernest Kefauver as his running mate, who had narrowly defeated John F. Kennedy for the vice-presidential nomination. The Stevenson–Kefauver ticket had a jaded appearance and ran a very ineffective campaign. Eisenhower, largely for health reasons, did not campaign widely but confined himself mainly to a few television addresses. The Eisenhower–Nixon ticket won by an even wider margin than in 1952, with 58 per cent of the popular vote and a 457–73 margin in the electoral college. Eisenhower's sweeping victory, however, did not produce a Republican victory in the Congressional elections. In the Senate the Democrats gained two seats to attain a majority of 49–47, while in the House of Representatives the Democrats gained one seat to give them a majority of 233–200. In the gubernatorial elections, the Democrats fared even better, adding several governorships to give them a total of twenty-nine, compared to nineteen Republican governorships. In Eisenhower's home state of Kansas, the electorate voted in a Democratic governor in 1956 for the first time in the history of the state.

Eisenhower's policies had created stability and prosperity. Some of his policies, however, had been unpopular, such as his farm policies, which cost him dearly in farm states. Moreover, he had not succeeded in his overall goal of projecting the image of the Republican party as a moderate, progressive party that would attract majority support across the nation. On election night, Eisenhower said to Nixon with regard to the Congressional and gubernatorial results, 'You know why this is happening, Dick? It's all those damned mossbacks and hard-shell conservatives we've got in this party. I think that what we need is a new party.'[54] Eisenhower issued a statement in which he boldly, and somewhat provocatively, proclaimed his election victory as a triumph for 'Modern Republicanism'.[55] Nixon recorded that 'As I had feared, many party

Chapter 4

World in Crisis, 1955–56

In 1955–56 Eisenhower faced dangerous crises in foreign policy in the Taiwan straits, Hungary and Suez. Aside from these tests of his skills in crisis management, Eisenhower continued to try to build up a solid, sustainable American foreign policy for the longer term.

In February, 1955, the Soviet leader, Georgi Malenkov, was removed from office and replaced by a joint leadership of Nikolai Bulganin, Chairman of the Council of Ministers, and Nikita Khrushchev, First Secretary of the Communist Party. This appeared to symbolise a change from Malenkov's more moderate policy to a more hardline Soviet stance. Eisenhower continued to be deeply suspicious and distrustful of Soviet policy and disinclined to pursue any new initiatives, such as a summit meeting.

In April, 1955, Winston Churchill finally retired as prime minister of Britain, to be succeeded by his long-serving Foreign Secretary, Anthony Eden. Ironically, Eden almost immediately pressed for a summit meeting with the Soviets. Eden faced a General Election in Britain within the next year and he realised that a summit meeting was popular with public opinion as a symbol of peace and a relaxation of tensions. Therefore, although as Foreign Secretary Eden had been very sceptical about the value of a summit meeting and had supported Eisenhower against Churchill on the matter, as prime minister Eden was more aware of political considerations. He was, therefore, eager to arrange a summit meeting, which would enhance his electoral prospects, while he also felt that there was the possibility, though he remained sceptical, that a face-to-face meeting with the new Soviet leadership might promote better understanding. Eisenhower had always been a great admirer of Churchill, but he had felt that Churchill had hung on too long and needed to be replaced by a younger British leader. Eisenhower had known Eden very well since the Second World War days, and wrote to Eden following his appointment that 'I cannot tell you how delighted I am that my old friend Winston has been succeeded by an equally valued friend in an office in which friendliness and genuine readiness to cooperate can mean so much to my own country.'[1] A personal correspondence began between Eden and Eisenhower, as between Churchill and Eisenhower, which continued throughout Eden's premiership and reflected a close working relationship between the two leaders, until the Suez crisis in 1956 destroyed it.

When Eden, then, somewhat to Eisenhower's surprise, suggested a summit meeting with the Soviets, Eisenhower wished to make a cooperative response towards his British ally. 'We appreciate the importance to you of this project under existing circumstances', Eisenhower wrote to Eden, 'and are naturally disposed to do everything we can to further it.'[2] He wished to assist the Conservatives to win re-election in Britain rather than risk the election of a Labour government, which would include left-wing figures, such as Aneurin Bevan. Eisenhower was wary of the domestic political hazards that he would face if he agreed to attend a summit conference. 'Americans are afraid of international conferences,' as Roger Makins, British Ambassador to the United States, noted. 'The belief that simple-minded Americans are no match for the subtle and unscrupulous foreigners and that their representatives are bound to be outsmarted dies hard. They are afraid of being trapped by the Russians, or of being led down the garden path by their allies, or both.'[3] With McCarthyism a spent force, however, Eisenhower was no longer so politically vulnerable in making a positive gesture towards the Soviets. Moreover, the Soviet Union passed one of Eisenhower's tests of good faith by agreeing to the Austrian State Treaty in May, 1955, whereby Soviet forces withdrew from Austria, which became a united, neutral state. A summit meeting between the United States, the Soviet Union, Britain and France was, therefore, arranged, which helped Eden and the British Conservatives to win re-election at the end of May, 1955, with an increased majority. The summit meeting duly took place in Geneva in July, 1955.

Over the five days of formal and informal meetings at Geneva, July 18–23, Eisenhower weighed up the personalities of the Soviet leaders. He concluded that Khrushchev was the effective leader and that Bulganin was subordinate. Eisenhower was thoroughly briefed about Khrushchev and concluded that a figure who had been close to Stalin and who remained a true believer in the inevitable triumph of Communism was a threatening adversary, who was not susceptible to any significant degree to personal charm and persuasion. Nevertheless, Eisenhower felt that the personal meeting with Khrushchev was beneficial in giving a human face to the ideological conflict. On the issues, however, Eisenhower felt that the discussions at Geneva confirmed his scepticism over the prospects of a meaningful improvement in relations with the Soviet Union. Eisenhower's major proposal was Open Skies, namely, an agreement that, in order to allay fears of surprise attack, the United States and the Soviet Union should have the right to overfly the other nation's territory and to take photographs of military installations. Khrushchev dismissed the proposal as a propaganda ploy. The Soviet Union felt that Open Skies would be of much greater advantage to the United States, since the Soviet Union easily gathered a great deal of intelligence about America's military capability in the open society of the United States, while America was effectively barred from acquiring accurate knowledge of Soviet military capability. Khrushchev argued that the American objective in Open Skies was not so much the defensive purpose of safeguarding against surprise attack as the offensive aim of gathering information about targets in the event of war. Khrushchev's rejection of Open Skies confirmed Eisenhower's fundamental suspicion of Soviet purposes. Although the summit created a 'spirit of Geneva', which suggested superficial friendliness, the follow-up Foreign Ministers conference in November, 1955, degenerated into wrangles and illustrated that no important progress had been made on issues of substance. Eisenhower had perhaps made some impression on the Soviet leaders as a man of humanity, sincerity and goodwill. However, he did not regard such matters as greatly significant but instead concentrated on policy disagreements. With the brusque Soviet dismissal of Open Skies, Eisenhower decided to resort to illegal American overflights over Soviet territory by the U-2, a risky policy that was bound to increase tension and distrust between the two nations.

A first attempt at overflights over the Soviet Union with photo-reconnaissance cameras was made in January, 1956, by means of balloons. Project Genetrix had been planned for several years, with the technical details perfected by 1955 and given Eisenhower's go-ahead in December, 1955. On January 10, 1956, and over the following few days, more than 500 balloons were launched from bases in Scotland, Norway and West Germany, to be carried by the jet stream on a three-day journey across the Soviet Union. Cameras were fitted in the gondola of these large, unmanned, polyethylene balloons, with photographs taken constantly during their journey. When the balloons exited from Soviet airspace, American C-111 transport planes from Alaska and Japan were able to rendezvous with the balloons. By means of a radio signal, the balloons were made to descend and the cameras were recovered from the gondolas by means of a grapple from the planes. The balloons flew at a height of 50,000 feet, which it was thought was beyond the reach of Soviet anti-aircraft surface-to-air missiles and interceptor planes.

Eisenhower was impressed and fascinated by the technical details of this project, but he had misgivings as to whether the intelligence that might be gathered outweighed the risks of serious repercussions with regard to relations with the Soviet Union. In fact, many of the balloons were blown off course and did not cross the Soviet Union. The film from those that completed the journey proved to be of little worth, since unmanned balloons naturally took a haphazard path. Moreover, the balloons flew at a height that was just within reach of Soviet surface-to-air missiles and interceptor planes, so that large numbers were shot down. On February 4, 1956, the Soviets lodged a diplomatic protest, and on February 9 a number of destroyed balloons were put on display in Moscow. The American cover story that this was part of International Geophysical Year was exposed as farcical falsehood, since the balloons had a clear intelligence purpose. Only 50 of the balloons were recovered by American planes. In mid-February, 1956, Eisenhower ordered the end of Project Genetrix, which had clearly not been a success. Its one benefit, however, was that it provided useful information for the potentially much more promising project, namely, U-2 flights over the Soviet Union.[4]

Eisenhower had grave misgivings with regard to the U-2. He was well aware of extreme Soviet sensitivity over intrusions by American planes across the Soviet border. At the Moscow air show on June 24, 1956, Khrushchev told US Air Force Chief of Staff, Nathan Twining, to 'stop sending intruders into our airspace. We will shoot down uninvited guests.'[5] In Eisenhower's view, a flight by a military aircraft over Soviet airspace was an act of war. Technically, this was circumvented by the operation of the U-2 programme by the CIA, with CIA pilots rather than Air Force pilots, under the cover of weather reconnaissance as the 1st Weather Reconnaissance Squadron, Provisional. The CIA Director of Operations, Richard Bissell, assured Eisenhower that the U-2 would fly at a height of 70,000 feet, which was well beyond the reach of Soviet surface-to-air missiles and interceptor planes. Indeed, Bissell stated that at such a height the U-2 would not be detected by Soviet radar. Moreover, in the event of a possible mishap, the plane had a self-destruct button and the pilot was provided with a suicide pill. There was no chance, therefore, Eisenhower was assured, of a U-2 falling into Soviet hands or a pilot falling into captivity.

The U-2 was due to be based in Britain, but in the spring of 1956 Eden became uneasy over the possibility of an intelligence operation from an

American base in Britain going wrong. Eden's fears were deepened when a British intelligence operation in April, 1956, went badly wrong. Khrushchev and Bulganin came on a visit to Britain, which was the first visit by Soviet leaders to a Western country since the Second World War. The visit was for the most part successful in helping to improve relations. Its impact was seriously damaged, however, by the detection by Soviet sailors of a British diver under the cruiser on which Khrushchev and Bulganin had sailed to Britain, while it was docked in Portsmouth harbour. The diver, Commander George ('Buster') Crabb, had been recruited by MI6, the British Secret Intelligence Service, to inspect the cruiser's sonar equipment. Following Crabb's detection the Soviets made a public protest and, especially since Crabb mysteriously disappeared, until his body was found a year later further along the south coast of England, the incident became a cause célèbre. The British government issued an implausible denial of knowledge or responsibility. Eden was furious over the episode and warned that it illustrated his point of the danger of a botched intelligence operation undermining the benefits of a diplomatic meeting between leaders.[6] He feared, with prescience, as the later events of May, 1960, proved, that a similar development could occur as the result of a U-2 flight. He therefore withdrew permission for U-2s to be based in Britain, and the U-2 programme was transferred to Wiesbaden in West Germany.[7]

Eisenhower authorised the first flight of the U-2 from Wiesbaden over the Soviet Union on July 4, 1956. Khrushchev attended an American Independence Day reception at the American embassy in Moscow while a U-2 flew over Soviet territory. Soviet radar, contrary to CIA expectations, detected the U-2 as soon as it entered Soviet airspace, and Khrushchev had been informed of the intrusion of the American plane before he went to the reception at the American embassy.[8] There were four further U-2 flights over the next week, but there was then a break of five months until three more flights took place in November and December, 1956. Eisenhower was very concerned over the risks. Although Soviet radar was capable of detecting the U-2, Soviet defences were unable to bring it down. The Soviet Union protested, in private, through diplomatic channels, over the violation of their airspace. The State Department disingenuously replied that 'no United States military planes . . . could possibly have strayed over the Soviet Union'.[9] Eisenhower was very anxious over the matter but he felt that the intelligence that was gathered was of such value, enabling him to make a much more accurate evaluation of Soviet military capability, that it outweighed the damage to relations with the Soviet Union. The Soviets were left with a sense of humiliation over their inability to defend themselves effectively against this deeply resented intrusion into their airspace.

In his concern over the tensions in US–Soviet relations, Eisenhower was well aware of the catastrophic consequences of the outbreak of a nuclear war. On the anniversary of D-Day on June 6, 1956, in offering some reflections about the devastation of the Second World War, he observed that 'There is no destruction that we saw in World War II . . . that would give a hint of what another war would bring.'[10] With the development of nuclear weapons, he said, 'War has become not just tragic but preposterous. With such weapons there can be no victory for anyone. Plainly, the objective now must be to see that such a war does not occur at all.'[11] As he expressed it pithily on another occasion, 'The only way to win World War III is to prevent it.'[12] At the other extreme, Eisenhower reiterated the enormous benefits that could follow from peace and disarmament. 'If effective disarmament could be agreed upon,' he said, 'think how the world would be transformed . . . The pall of mutual suspicion, fear and hatred that covers the earth would be swept away in favour of confidence, prosperity and human happiness.'[13] Eisenhower, however, was a realist, who did not engage in utopian dreams. He was prepared to engage in disarmament talks, such as at the United Nations Sub-Committee on Disarmament, and in 1955 he appointed Harold Stassen as Special Assistant on Disarmament. Difficulties, however, over such matters as inspection procedures, which constantly stymied disarmament talks, seemed to Eisenhower symptomatic of the basic distrust which meant that meaningful disarmament could only follow from rather than cause the eradication of the underlying political and ideological differences between the two sides. Similarly, Eisenhower toyed with proposals for a test ban as a means to curb the nuclear arms race. But America's need in the mid-1950s to test new weapons as part of the development of a reliable nuclear deterrent led Eisenhower to conclude that, like general disarmament, a test ban and the curbing of the nuclear arms race would result from rather than be itself the cause of the resolution of underlying international tensions.

Eisenhower placed his greatest faith for the preservation of peace in the strength and unity of the West. 'The security of the United States', he wrote, 'is inextricably bound up with the security of the free world.'[14] The most important element in the defence of the free world, in his view, was the NATO alliance. 'NATO has done a very great thing,' he said, 'as much in the political and moral world . . . as it has in the defensive.'[15] The key to stability and peace lay, in his view, in 'the unification of the free world, by cooperation'.[16] He strongly supported moves towards European unity. 'I just cannot overemphasize', he said, 'the importance to the security of the free world of a great economic, industrial and social connection and indeed finally some greater and better political connection between the nations of Free Europe.'[17] He was encouraged by the growing recovery of Europe not only in its economy but in its spirit. 'Morale!', he said, 'Morale is the most important thing that a human being has, whether he is tackling a job or whether he is going to war or whether he is trying to gain a peace.'[18] Substance was required, however, in addition to matters of spirit, particularly military assistance through the Mutual Security Program and liberal trade policies to assist allied countries to build up their economies. 'Mutually advantageous trade relationships', he said, 'are not only profitable, but they are also more binding and more enduring than costly grants and other forms of aid.'[19] The security of the United States, he argued, 'is dependent upon the economic strength of all free nations, for without economic strength they cannot support the military establishments that are necessary to deter Communist armed aggression. Economic strength is indispensable, as well, in securing them against internal Communist subversion.'[20]

Eisenhower felt that Eastern Europe provided the most significant area through which an impact might be made in relations with the Soviet Union. Eisenhower was prepared to give some support to clandestine programmes which were designed to undermine the régimes in Eastern Europe. His major concentration, however, was on efforts to encourage evolution towards a greater degree of independence on the part of Eastern European countries. He wished to give support to the nationalistic aspirations of East European countries against Soviet control, without stirring them up to open revolt, which would be dangerous and futile. The most promising developments were the continuing progress of Yugoslavia in maintaining its status as an independent Communist country and Khrushchev's speech denouncing Stalin at the 20th Congress of the Communist Party of the Soviet Union in February, 1956.

The Soviet Union had employed pressure and threats to try to gain greater control over Yugoslavia since the time of Tito's break with Stalin in 1948. The United States had given aid and encouragement to Yugoslavia, despite its Communist status, to preserve Yugoslavia as a model for Eastern European nations to develop towards as a first, non-provocative step towards the ultimate goal of throwing off Soviet control and Communist rule. Eisenhower was pleased to observe Soviet moves towards reconciliation with Yugoslavia, illustrated by the visit of Khrushchev and Bulganin to Yugoslavia in 1955 and Tito's visit to Moscow in 1956. Evidence of a more liberal Soviet stance was more dramatically presented by

Khrushchev's speech to the 20th Congress of the Communist Party of the Soviet Union in Moscow in February, 1956. Khrushchev denounced the crimes of Stalin and outlined a more progressive, tolerant form of Communism. The speech was secret to the Congress, but the CIA obtained a copy and ensured its wide distribution, especially in Eastern Europe.

Eisenhower felt that events in Poland were a reflection of the promising new directions in Eastern Europe. In June, 1956, Polish workers in Poznan protested over working conditions, but the protest developed from a labour dispute into a political protest. In October, 1956, Wladyslaw Gomulka, a more progressive Communist, came to power. The Soviets appeared to be very threatening towards the new Polish régime and seemed to be on the point of military intervention, which was encouraged by the Polish Minister of Defence, General Konstantin Rokossovsky, who was a Soviet citizen. But the Soviets then backed down and appeared to acquiesce in the more nationalistic, progressive régime in Poland. Rokossovsky was removed from his post and repatriated to the Soviet Union.

Eisenhower was well aware, however, of the limitations of American power in the Soviet sphere of influence in Eastern Europe, which was tragically and dramatically illustrated in the Hungarian Revolution of October–November, 1956. Encouraged by developments in Poland and Yugoslavia and by Khrushchev's denunciation of Stalin, Hungarians pressed for the removal of the repressive dictator, Matyas Rakosi, and his replacement by the liberal Communist, Imre Nagy. Nagy became prime minister on October 23, 1956, but a protest march by students and workers led to violence and the death of many protestors at the hands of the Hungarian Secret Police and Soviet troops. Violence continued over the next few days, but Nagy then appeared to reach agreement for the withdrawal of Soviet forces from Hungary and the introduction of liberal reforms, including multi-party elections. The Soviet Union seemed to accept these changes, withdrawing Soviet troops from Hungary and issuing a proclamation on October 30 upholding peaceful coexistence between the Soviet Union and socialist states 'on the principles of complete equality, of respect for territorial integrity, state independence and sovereignty, of non-interference in one another's international affairs'. There were, however, strong differences of opinion within the Kremlin as to whether Hungary could be allowed such a degree of freedom. On October 31, at a crucial meeting of the Soviet Politburo, it was decided that the loss of Hungary might lead to the collapse of the Soviet empire in Eastern Europe and that the Hungarian Revolution must be put down by force.[21] On November 4, Soviet troops moved back into Hungary and brutally crushed the Hungarian Revolution. Janos Kadar, a Soviet puppet, was installed as prime minister, while Nagy was arrested and later executed. American impotence was evident as pathetic radio messages were broadcast, 'This is Hungary calling,' asking for assistance from the West. Eisenhower was aghast by the brutality and treachery of Soviet action in Hungary, but he was very conscious of the dangers of escalation of the conflict, which American intervention would produce. He refused to allow the CIA to air-drop arms and supplies to Hungarian Freedom Fighters. Despite strong American sympathy for the people of Eastern Europe, Eisenhower realised that intervention in an armed revolt by an Eastern European country against the Soviet Union was liable to lead to world war. Eisenhower reluctantly accepted that the preservation of peace regrettably necessitated acquiescence in Soviet assertion of control in their East European satellites. American fury and frustration over the Soviet suppression of the Hungarian Revolution, in which 40,000 died and large numbers were driven into exile, brought a final end to the thaw in US–Soviet relations that had begun at the Geneva summit.

In the Far East, Eisenhower faced in early 1955 the climax of the crisis over Quemoy and Matsu. The Chinese Communists continued to shell Quemoy and Matsu on a daily basis to force the Nationalists to withdraw. Eisenhower would have preferred if Chiang Kai-shek had agreed to withdraw. Chiang, however, adamantly refused, insisting that such a withdrawal would demoralise the Nationalists on Taiwan and lead to the collapse of Nationalist rule and the Communist takeover of Taiwan. Eisenhower backed Chiang and took a determined stand to face down the Communist aggression. On January 28, 1955, Congress passed the Formosa Resolution, giving the president discretionary authority to commit US armed forces to the defence of Taiwan and, rather ambiguously, to 'such related positions and territories of that area now in friendly hands'.[22] Ominously, veiled threats were sent to the Chinese that the United States might be prepared to use nuclear weapons against China in response to a Chinese invasion of Quemoy and Matsu. Eisenhower said at a news conference, for instance, with regard to tactical nuclear weapons, that 'in any combat where these things can be used on strictly military targets and for strictly military purposes, I see no reason why they shouldn't be used exactly as you would use a bullet or anything else'.[23] Allies, such as the British, were alarmed by Eisenhower's stance. Churchill wrote to Eisenhower that 'a war to keep the coastal islands for Chiang would not be defensible here'. Churchill argued that Formosa must, of course, be defended. But Churchill wrote that 'I cannot see any decisive relationship between the offshore islands and the invasion of

Formosa. It would surely be easy to drown any Chinese would-be invaders of Formosa whether they started from Quemoy or elsewhere.'[24] Eisenhower replied that 'if the Chinese Nationalists got out of Quemoy and Matsu, . . . this retreat, and the coercion we would have to exert to bring it about, would so undermine the morale and the loyalty of the non-Communist forces on Formosa that they could not be counted on.' Hence, Eisenhower argued, weakness over Quemoy and Matsu would lead inevitably to the loss of Formosa and to further falling dominoes in Asia. 'There comes a point where constantly giving in only encourages further bullying,' he wrote, 'I think we must constantly be careful not to pass that point in our dealings with China.'[25] The crisis continued for several months, with constant shelling of Quemoy and Matsu from the Chinese mainland. In April, however, the Chinese Foreign Minister, Chou En-lai, sent a peaceful signal, saying at a meeting of non-aligned powers in Bandung, Indonesia, that the Chinese people were friendly towards the American people. Dulles sent a message expressing America's willingness to negotiate, and the shelling of Quemoy and Matsu came to an end.

Eisenhower's critics, such as Chester Pach and Elmo Richardson, suggest that 'The peaceful resolution of the crisis arose more from good fortune than shrewd diplomacy.'[26] Pach and Richardson argue that 'It is hard to be dazzled by policy that brings the world to the brink of nuclear war over territory whose value to American – or for that matter Taiwanese – security was close to nil.'[27] Gordon Chang is even more critical, arguing with regard to Eisenhower's policy that 'The ambiguity of his stand on the offshore islands . . . might well have allowed the Communists to miscalculate American intentions and thus have invited an attack . . . That war had been avoided was due more to Chinese Communist caution and to luck rather than to the diplomatic skills of President Eisenhower.'[28] On the other side, Robert Divine argues that the offshore islands had become a vital symbol of American credibility and that 'The beauty of Eisenhower's policy is that to this day no one can be sure whether or not he would have responded militarily to an invasion of the offshore islands and whether he would have used nuclear weapons.'[29] Stephen Ambrose goes further, arguing that 'Eisenhower's handling of the Quemoy-Matsu crisis was a *tour de force*, one of the great triumphs of his long career.'[30] Ambrose perhaps engages in hyperbole, but overall, given the complex range of considerations that Eisenhower had to take into account, relating to domestic politics, relations with allies, maintaining confidence and stability, as well as narrow calculations of national security, Eisenhower demonstrated impressive statesmanship in his successful diffusion of the crisis.

In the other major crisis area in the Far East, Vietnam, matters became deceptively quiet in 1955–56, after the dramatic events of 1954. The superficial appearance of progress and stability in South Vietnam was misleading. As David Anderson writes, 'Ignorance and confidence bred an illusion of success that trapped Eisenhower . . . in a frustrating and futile effort to define and defend US interests in Vietnam.'[31] The United States had taken a firm stand in aiming to build up South Vietnam as a bulwark against the expansion of Communism in Asia. Yet, as George Herring puts it, 'Had it looked all over the world, the United States could not have chosen a less promising place for an experiment in nation-building.'[32] Eisenhower, as well as some leading Democratic politicians, such as John F. Kennedy and Senator Mike Mansfield (D. – Montana), placed great faith in Diem. 'The President and his advisers believed', as Robert Schulzinger writes, 'that Diem expressed a genuine nationalism that could deny Ho Chi Minh the fruits of victory won by his fighting in the war against the French.'[33] Diem made progress in a number of areas. The flood of nearly a million refugees from North Vietnam, many of whom were Catholic, were absorbed into South Vietnam. The army was reorganised and, with the assistance of large-scale aid from the United States, there were improvements in such fields as transportation. A National Assembly was elected and Diem was confirmed as head of state in a referendum. The North Vietnamese régime was fully occupied with internal consolidation and received little support from the Soviet Union or elsewhere in its protest over Diem's refusal to honour the terms of the Geneva Agreement of 1954 that an all-Vietnam election should be held in 1956. Eisenhower optimistically stated that the Communists 'were stopped finally in the northern part of Vietnam; and Diem, the leader of the Southern Vietnamese, is doing splendidly and is a much better figure in that field than anyone ever dared to hope'.[34]

Beneath the façade of relative stability and progress, however, Diem's régime was characterised by repression, corruption and nepotism. In October, 1955, Diem won the referendum to replace Bao Dai as head of state with 98 per cent of the vote – a manifestly rigged election result. In the elections to the National Assembly, dissenting figures were disqualified as candidates, which ensured a pliant legislature. In January, 1956, Diem issued a decree that effectively banned political opposition. Thousands of opponents were sent to 're-education' camps, while clamps were imposed on the press. Diem ran a closely controlled régime, along with his brothers, Ngo Dinh Nhu and Ngo Dinh Can, while Ngo Dinh Nhu's wife, Madame Nhu, exercised considerable influence. 'Austere, politically inept and fundamentally disdainful of democracy,' Robert Mann writes, 'Diem was inherently unsuited to lead his nation's fight for demo-cratic self-rule.'[35] Beneath the superficial orderliness and progress of Diem's government, then, serious problems were developing.

While Eisenhower was willing to engage in almost any means in his opposition to Third World figures whom he regarded as Communists, he tried to give support to progressive nationalists who were not Com-munists. In Egypt, for example, although the Americans were wary of Colonel Gamal Abdul Nasser, they were prepared to support his nation-alistic aspirations and to offer economic and military aid, especially in the hope that Nasser would be cooperative with regard to a settlement with Israel. This led to differences with the British, who were much more suspicious of Nasser. The British agreed with the Eisenhower administra-tion, however, that Western support for progressive reform throughout the Third World was the best means of keeping Third World countries out of the Communist camp. Britain combined, therefore, with America in supporting financial assistance to Egypt for the construction of the Aswan Dam, a grandiose project to build a massive High Dam at Aswan, which would control the flood waters of the Nile, generate large amounts of electricity and provide an enormous benefit to the Egyptian economy. Nasser, however, proved to be awkward and untrustworthy in negotia-tions over the terms of the loan from Britain and America for the con-struction of the Aswan Dam. Although he was not a Communist, Nasser flirted with the Soviet Union and played off East against West. In Sep-tember, 1955, Nasser imported large quantities of arms from Czechoslo-vakia. In May, 1956, he extended diplomatic recognition to Communist China, which was provocative to the Americans. Meanwhile, American opposition to support for the Aswan Dam grew among Southern Con-gressmen, who had no desire to help Egypt to boost production of cotton in competition with the American South. On July 19, 1956, therefore, Dulles informed the Egyptian ambassador that the United States was withdrawing financial support for the construction of the Aswan Dam. In retaliation, as a means of raising an alternative source of revenue for the Aswan Dam as well as an act of defiance of the West, the Egyptian government decided to nationalise the Suez Canal. On July 26, 1956, in a heated speech in Alexandria, Nasser announced the nationalisation of the Suez Canal.

The British response to Nasser's action was to prepare for immediate military intervention to retake the Suez Canal and to overthrow Nasser. To Britain, the Suez Canal was not only important economically as a short route to India and for the transportation of oil from the Persian Gulf to the Mediterranean, but even more so symbolically as a symbol of the might of the British Empire. The British, especially Eden, regarded Nasser as a treacherous upstart, who had been responsible for terrorist activity against British troops and civilians and who had haughty ambitions to become the new Saladin, uniting the Arabs against the West. Eden warned against a policy of appeasement towards Nasser, referring to the appeasement of the 1930s and arguing that if Nasser was allowed to succeed in his bold action it would lead to further acts of aggression, which would end in widespread instability and world war.

Eisenhower did not agree with his British ally. Throughout the Suez crisis Eisenhower demonstrated steady, moderate and generally enlightened leadership. He sent Dulles to London to seek a peaceful solution by means of compromise. This led to lengthy negotiations in August and September, 1956, with two international conferences in London of nations with an interest in the Suez Canal and a complicated proposal for a Suez Canal Users Association. Nasser did not accept any of the proposed solutions that emerged from the conferences and negotiations. Eisenhower hoped, however, that the process of negotiation would allow tempers to cool and make it possible for a compromise solution to be reached, while delay until autumn and winter would also allow weather conditions in the Mediterranean to rule out military action. Meantime, in an exchange of letters with Eden, Eisenhower presented a very lucid statement of the case against the use of force. He stressed to Eden 'the unwisdom even of contemplating the use of military force at this moment'.[36] He argued that 'the use of force would, it seems to me, vastly increase the area of jeopardy'. Eisenhower agreed with Eden's characterisation of Nasser as an untrustworthy menace, who could allow the Soviets greater opportunities to extend their influence in the Middle East, but 'I am afraid, Anthony', Eisenhower wrote, 'that from this point onwards our views on this situation diverge.' If a military solution was attempted, Eisenhower argued, 'The peoples of the Near East and of North Africa and, to some extent, of all of Asia and of Africa, would be consolidated against the West to a degree which, I fear, could not be overcome in a generation.'[37]

Eden, however, decided to go behind Eisenhower's back and to collude with France and Israel in a scheme for the use of force against Egypt. Eisenhower became suspicious in October, 1956, when letters from Eden ceased and in almost every way there was silence in Anglo-American communications. Eden was secretly arranging with France and Israel that Israel would invade Egypt across the Sinai Desert. Britain and France, feigning no foreknowledge of the Israeli attack, would send in a supposedly peacekeeping force to keep the Israelis and Egyptians apart and to protect the Suez Canal but whose real purpose was to regain control over the Suez Canal and to bring down Nasser. On October 29, 1956, the Israelis duly began their invasion and swept across the Sinai Desert to the Suez Canal. Britain and France expressed shock and surprise and on October 30 Britain and France sent an ultimatum to the two sides, Israel and Egypt, to move back to lines ten miles from each side of the Suez Canal. When Egypt refused to do so, British planes on October 31 destroyed the Egyptian air force on the ground. Meanwhile, British forces sailed from Malta for a landing in Egypt.[38]

Eisenhower was aghast and furious over this turn of events. Within days American intelligence sources provided Eisenhower with details of the collusion between Britain, France and Israel and of British military moves, as British forces made their way in a week-long journey from Malta to Egypt. Eisenhower was dismayed that his closest ally, Britain, could have acted so deceptively and so foolishly. On November 2, Eisenhower wrote to Swede Hazlett that this was 'a sad blow because, quite naturally, Britain not only has been, but must be, our best friend in the world'.[39] Eisenhower outlined to Hazlett all the arguments that he had advanced to try to dissuade the British from pursuing a military course. 'All these thoughts I communicated to Eden time and again,' he wrote. 'It was undoubtedly because of his knowledge of our bitter opposition to using force in the matter that when he finally decided to undertake the plan, he just went completely silent.'[40]

Vigorous protests were made to Britain, France and Israel and the matter was taken to the United Nations, where the United States sided with the Soviet Union against Britain and France. A United Nations resolution was passed on November 3 for the formation of a UN peace-keeping force to be sent to Egypt to restore peace between Israel and Egypt and to keep the two sides apart. Britain and France accepted the UN resolution but argued that until the UN force was sent, which would take several weeks, British and French forces should, as planned, move into Egypt. On November 5, British troops landed at Port Said and French troops at Port Faud and engaged in hostilities that resulted in large-scale Egyptian civilian and military casualties, as well as a number of British and French casualties. The Soviet Union threatened a missile attack against Britain and France if they did not withdraw from Egypt, and Bulganin sent a letter to Eisenhower proposing the formation of a joint US–Soviet force to intervene against the British and French. Eisenhower dismissed these Soviet intrusions as unwelcome and dangerous. He put massive pressure on Britain and France to agree to an immediate ceasefire and withdrawal. The Suez crisis had produced a run on the pound, which left Britain completely dependent on American financial support, while

Britain also faced an oil boycott by all Arab countries in retaliation against Britain's attack on Egypt, which left Britain dependent on the United States for oil from the New World. Eisenhower used these American weapons of financial power and control over access to oil to pressurise Eden into an immediate ceasefire and an agreement to withdraw. On November 6 a ceasefire was declared. By the end of November a UN force had been deployed in Egypt and Anglo-French forces had withdrawn. Nasser remained in control of the Suez Canal and his overall position had been strengthened. Eden was humiliated. His health deteriorated and he resigned on January 9, 1957.[41]

When the immediate crisis passed, with the ceasefire on November 6, 1956, Eisenhower at once took immediate steps to begin to repair the damage to Anglo-American relations. Even at the height of the crisis, Eisenhower had said to an aide, 'Those British – they're still my right arm.'[42] When Eden suggested on November 7 that he should come to Washington, Eisenhower agreed, before reluctantly changing his mind on the advice of Dulles and the Anglophobic Under-Secretary of State Herbert Hoover, Jr, who pointed out that an Eden visit so soon after the crisis might suggest to Arab countries that the United States had fundamentally been on the side of Britain and France.[43] More realistically, Eisenhower looked to Eden's successor for a restoration of warm Anglo-American relations. Eisenhower was very pleased to learn that the leading contender for the succession to Eden was Eisenhower's old friend from wartime days in North Africa, Harold Macmillan. Eisenhower described Macmillan as 'a straight, fine man ... the outstanding one of the British he served with during the war'.[44]

Eisenhower's leadership and use of American power and influence throughout the Suez crisis seems highly commendable in almost every respect. His analysis of the situation was intelligent, especially with regard to the dangers of the imprudent use of force. When his allies deceived him and resorted to force nonetheless, his response was decisive and highly effective. When the crisis was over, he took immediate steps to repair the damage that had been caused to relations with his allies, especially his closest ally, Britain. As Cole Kingseed puts it, Eisenhower 'remained unflappable in the face of dissenting allies, contentious military chiefs and political opposition in a presidential election year. Though he failed to keep the crisis from escalating, he, more than any other statesman, restored peace to the troubled region. It was a splendid performance.'[45]

Particularly pleasing to Eisenhower was the response of Third World countries to his stance over Suez. Eisenhower had found it frustrating that, despite all the efforts of the United States to project its image as a progressive democracy that sought the best interests of the developing Third World and despite the large amounts of American aid to Third World countries, the Communists nevertheless seemed to be winning the propaganda battle in the Third World. As the British ambassador to the United States observed, 'Americans are puzzled and distressed by the example of India, which has received overwhelmingly more aid from America than from Russia, but whose public sympathies appeared to be swinging nevertheless in favour of the latter.'[46] Following the Suez crisis, however, Henry Cabot Lodge, US ambassador to the United Nations, wrote to Eisenhower at the end of December, 1956, that 'I continue to get enthusiastic reactions from Afro-Asian nations about your policy here in the Near East crisis. They feel that it was "an honorable act performed in a clear cut way" . . . and that it was in the best traditions of the Declaration of Independence and Abraham Lincoln . . . You have given us a position of moral *authority* which in turn created a degree of *respect*.'[47]

Aside from Eisenhower's anger over the deception over Suez by his allies in general, he was particularly furious that the resort to force was not at least postponed until after the American elections on November 6. One of Eisenhower's main planks in his re-election platform was that he was a man of peace, who had ended the Korean War and kept America at peace in tense and dangerous times. The Soviet invasion of Hungary on November 4, followed by the Anglo-French landing in Egypt on November 5, meant that the election on November 6 took place in an atmosphere of widespread international violence rather than peace. In fact, however, the explosion of these crises into violence was to Eisenhower's electoral advantage rather than to his disadvantage. With turbulence and fear arising from revolution and war, a large majority of Americans were eager to keep Eisenhower's hand at the helm. There were various areas in which Eisenhower's record in his first term were deemed to have been deficient, as the increased Democratic majorities in Congress reflected. But with regard to leadership in a crisis, Americans felt reassured by Eisenhower's presence in the White House, which was reflected in his overwhelming re-election victory in the presidential election in 1956.

Chapter 5

Domestic Doldrums, 1957–58

On January 20, 1957, Eisenhower was inaugurated for a second term as president. With a landslide victory in the 1956 presidential election and a rating in the opinion polls of nearly 80 per cent, he seemed to be in a very strong position. In fact, however, the following two years proved to be the most difficult of Eisenhower's presidency. The economy ran into serious recession in 1957–58. The launch of the Soviet satellite, Sputnik, in October, 1957, dealt a severe blow to American self-confidence and raised demands for large increases in defence spending, which would upset Eisenhower's budget plans. In September, 1957, the crisis at Little Rock in Arkansas created the type of confrontation over civil rights that Eisenhower had sought to avoid. In November, 1957, Eisenhower suffered from a stroke, which added to the question marks over his health. In 1958, a scandal led to the resignation of his trusted assistant Sherman Adams. The result of the difficulties was made apparent in the Congressional elections in 1958, in which the Republicans suffered severe losses.

'The air rings with the song of our industry,' Eisenhower said in his second Inaugural address, 'rolling mills and blast furnaces, dynamos, dams and assembly lines – the chorus of America the beautiful.'[1] The economy had boomed in 1955–56 after the recession in 1953–54. Eisenhower was increasingly confident that his policies of fiscal conservatism, mingled with a degree of flexibility where necessary, were the correct policies for America. He was disinclined to change economic policy to any significant extent, even in the face of a Congress with an increased Democratic majority.

In 1957 George Humphrey was replaced as Secretary of the Treasury by Robert Anderson. Eisenhower regarded Anderson as one of his brightest protégés, whom Eisenhower favoured as his successor as president. Although much less flamboyant in style than Humphrey, Anderson did not differ in policy from his predecessor. As a Texan, however, he was more inclined to work more closely with his fellow Texans, Lyndon

Johnson, the Senate Majority Leader, and Sam Rayburn, Speaker of the House of Representatives. At the head of Council of Economic Advisers, Arthur Burns was succeeded by Raymond Saulnier, who was less close to Eisenhower personally but who was more conservative than Burns, reinforcing Eisenhower's trend to a more conservative position.

Eisenhower continued to regard scrutiny of the budget as one of his most important duties. 'I think nothing is more necessary in our domestic affairs', he wrote to George Humphrey, 'than to examine each day our economy, as well as our government receipts and expenditure, and to act prudently.'[2] He sought to keep down government expenditure and he was disappointed when heads of departments whom he had appointed as economisers became converts to the spending demands of their departments. Albert Cole, for example, who had opposed liberal housing measures as a Republican congressman from Kansas, 1947–53, fought against cuts in urban renewal funds as head of the Housing and Home Finance Agency in the late 1950s. Eisenhower continued to adhere to the philosophy of government encapsulated in Abraham Lincoln's dictum that government should do only the tasks that individuals and local communities were not able to do for themselves. Eisenhower conceded, however, that 'That is a very hard line sometimes to determine.'[3] The Democratic majority in Congress pressed to push the line further in the direction of adding to the responsibilities of government, with the fiscal consequences that this entailed. The majority of Democrats in Congress, however, were Southern Democrats, so that Congressional pressures were not too strongly liberal. Public opinion, however, was increasingly demanding of government but unwilling to pay the cost of those demands in increased taxation. 'One thing bothers me,' Eisenhower wrote to Harold Macmillan, 'it is the seeming desire of the people of this country to depend more and more upon government. They do not seem to understand that more government assistance inevitably means more government control.'[4] Eisenhower was concerned that 'What to do to benefit the present and not harm the future economy presents one of the toughest problems I have had in a lifetime of difficult ones.'[5]

Eisenhower worked constantly to restrain government activities and government costs, but he felt that it was necessary to demonstrate a degree of flexibility in his thinking. Eisenhower supported, for example, a five-year Federal school building programme. Such support for Federal aid to education seemed contrary to his constitutional principles. But he accepted the argument that, owing to Second World War restrictions on civil construction, short-term Federal assistance was needed to overcome the critical shortage of schoolrooms, since many states and school districts had restrictive laws that made it difficult for them to engage in the extensive amount of school construction that was necessary. Eisenhower insisted, however, that 'The Federal role should be merely to facilitate – never to control – education.'[6] Similarly, Eisenhower supported the extension of unemployment insurance to employees of small firms and wider minimum wage protection to cover additional categories of workers.

Eisenhower's main goal, however, was a balanced budget. This was achieved in 1956 and 1957. Eisenhower regarded this as one of his proudest accomplishments. Credit for this achievement, however, was marred somewhat by the battle over the budget in early 1957 when right-wing Republicans assailed spending levels as too high and the Democrats tried to make political capital by proposing a number of cuts in the budget. The political in-fighting obscured the basic point that the budget had been brought into balance by 1957, with small surpluses for reduction of the National Debt. The most significant single reason for the attainment of a balanced budget was the maintenance of relatively low levels of defence expenditure. In his State of the Union message in 1957 Eisenhower stated that 'Beyond a wise and reasonable level, which is always changing and is under constant study, money spent on arms may be money wasted on sterile metal or inflated costs, thereby weakening the very security and strength we seek.'[7] He warned that 'Once you spend a single dollar beyond adequacy, then you are weakening yourself ... The Communists' objective is to make us spend ourselves into bankruptcy.'[8]

Greater flexibility in economic policy and willingness to accept a budget deficit became necessary, however, with the onset of a recession in August, 1957. The recession, which lasted until April, 1958, was of shorter duration than in 1953–54, but it cut deeper, with unemployment rising to 7.6 per cent, the highest unemployment rate since 1941. Eisenhower was well aware of the need for a Republican president to avoid being tarred as another Herbert Hoover in a time of deep recession. Eisenhower had said that 'From the very time I agreed to enter politics, one of the questions that has been put at me most is "What would you do to prevent a depression of the character that we experienced in the thirties?" My answer has always been, I would do everything that was constitutional and the Federal Government could do.'[9] He suggested that 'you might see signs of a depression coming on ... you might begin to apply moderate means, and then more, and if it finally keeps going, you would go into every single thing, and very quickly ... that would correct the situation.'[10] In fact, however, Eisenhower was only prepared to take moderate corrective measures during the recession of 1957–58. He resisted the more sweeping proposals of the Democrats in Congress. He was prepared to add some stimulus to the economy, but not at the expense of fiscal prudence. He felt that recovery from the 1953–54 recession had illustrated that moderate measures were sufficient and were less likely to damage business confidence. 'The 1953–54 experience,' he said, 'demonstrated that, when consumer and business confidence is maintained, timely public policies can help keep recessionary tendencies in check.'[11] In February, 1958, Eisenhower announced several anti-recession measures, such as an increase in Federal highway expenditure, an acceleration of defence contract awards and the modernisation of post offices. In March, 1958, unemployment benefit was extended from twenty-six to thirty-nine weeks. But Eisenhower rejected more extensive Democratic proposals, and he opposed a tax cut. 'My honest conviction', he wrote, 'is that the greatest service we can do for our country is to oppose wild-eyed schemes of every kind. I am against vast and unwise public works programs . . . as well as the slash-bang kinds of tax cutting from which the proponents want nothing so much as immediate political advantage.'[12]

The economy recovered from recession by April, 1958. Nevertheless, the severity of the recession seriously damaged the Republicans in the Congressional elections in November, 1958. Eisenhower was widely criticised for moving too slowly and in too restrained a manner in dealing with the recession. Also, he was charged with placing too much emphasis on regulating the fluctuations of the business cycle rather than in realising the potential of the American economy. The economy grew at a rate of 4.7 per cent in 1953–56, but a slower growth rate of 2.25 per cent in Eisenhower's second term produced a swelling chorus of criticisms from Democrats, such as John F. Kennedy, that Eisenhower was old-fashioned and unsophisticated in his economic management and was consequently retarding America's economic growth.

Agriculture continued to be a major problem. The Soil Bank proved to be very expensive. The Acreage Reserve Program, which was the major part of the Soil Bank programme, was discontinued in 1958. Exports did not make a sufficient contribution to an increase in the market outlets of the American farmer. Production levels reached a new record high in 1958, creating further problems with low farm prices and very large surpluses and government storage costs. Benson's forthright, somewhat sanctimonious manner exacerbated the difficult underlying problems. Dissatisfaction over agriculture policy was strongly expressed in the farm states and seriously damaged the Republicans in the 1958 Congressional elections.

Debate over the economy, however, as well as over all aspects of American life, were dealt a stunning jolt on October 4, 1957, when the Soviet Union launched Sputnik, the first satellite from earth into space. This was followed by the launch of a second satellite on November 3, 1957, with a dog, Laika, on board. This suggested a step in the direction of a manned flight by the Soviets, although the poor dog was doomed not to return. On December 6, 1957, the test of an American Vanguard rocket failed, with the rocket exploding on its launch pad at Cape Canaveral in Florida.

Sputnik created a hysterical reaction in America. Sputnik demonstrated, it was alleged, not only the superiority of Soviet science and technology but basic weaknesses in American society, especially an inadequate system of education, complacent political leadership and over-absorption in materialistic consumerism. Above all, Sputnik raised fears of American vulnerability to nuclear attack, on account of assumed Soviet superiority in missile technology. This produced panic and a demand for increased defence spending, including the construction of nuclear fallout shelters.

Eisenhower evaluated the implications of Sputnik in a measured, calm fashion. He was rather taken back by the popular American overreaction. 'Most surprising of all', he later wrote, 'was the intensity of public concern.'[13] Many historians have made the same point. 'What baffled Eisenhower, and remains puzzling today', William L. O'Neill writes, 'was the readiness of so many Americans to attribute to Russia a level of excellence that it simply did not possess.'[14] Eisenhower pointed out that the United States had developed the capability to launch a satellite by 1955 but had chosen not to launch the military satellite that was then possible but instead to emphasise the peaceful purposes of space exploration by the construction of a scientific satellite for a launch during International Geophysical Year in 1958. Eisenhower congratulated the Soviets on their achievement and conceded that this illustrated impressive development on the part of Soviet science and technology. He pointed out, however, that the Soviets achieved this goal by an excessive concentration of resources on one area, to the neglect of most other areas. The successful launch of an American satellite on January 31, 1958, gave some substance to Eisenhower's reassurances. He spoke out against a panicky overreaction, especially in the form of demands for increased expenditure on space exploration and on defence, warning against 'hysterically devised crash programs and propaganda stunts'.[15] Eisenhower realised that space exploration had a fascination that was appealing to the popular imagination and involved American prestige in a contest to be ahead of the Soviets, but he emphasised the massive expense involved and wished matters to be kept in proper perspective. At a meeting with Republican Congressional leaders, it was noted that 'The President was firmly of the opinion that a rule of reason had to be applied to those space projects and that we couldn't pour unlimited funds into these costly projects.'[16] He wished to avoid a space race with the Soviet Union, which he felt would be immensely costly and would divert resources into a prestige project to the neglect of more deserving needs.

Eisenhower was even more concerned that Sputnik was seized upon by the many groups who were constantly pressing for higher levels of defence spending. In April, 1957, Eisenhower had reluctantly agreed to the establishment of a panel of experts, chaired by H. Rowan Gaither, former head of the Ford Foundation, to report on issues of civil defence, particularly fallout shelters. Eisenhower was suspicious that the Gaither Committee would not stick to its brief but would conduct a broad examination of overall strategy, especially since the Gaither Committee included several prominent figures with a well-known disposition to stress America's strategic vulnerabilities, such as Albert Wohlsetter of the RAND Corporation and Paul Nitze, the author of NSC-68 in 1950, which had advocated very large defence increases in 1950. The Gaither Committee decided that instead of focusing upon the passive issue of civil defence, it should examine the alternative of improvements in deterrent power to prevent an attack, which would remove the need for civil defence. The Gaither Report gave a doomsday warning about the vulnerability of America's nuclear forces to a Soviet first strike, portrayed Soviet military strength as superior to the United States and recommended a comprehensive overhaul of America's defence policy, with increases in expenditure of over $40 billion over five years.[17]

Eisenhower agreed with some parts of the Gaither Report, but he dismissed its alarmist tone and its call for a crisis response. He rejected the far-fetched worst case scenarios with regard to American vulnerability to a Soviet first strike. He emphasised the actualities of the formidable strength of America's defences rather than the theoretical capabilities of Soviet military power. As always, Eisenhower emphasised the need for a defence policy that was economically sustainable over a long period, not panic measures that would cause serious economic damage and disruption.

One source of Eisenhower's greater faith in the adequacy of America's defensive strength was secret information from intelligence sources, especially the U-2. From the radar listening post at Kiyarbakir in Turkey, the United States gained a great deal of information about the main Soviet missile testing site at Kapustin Yar, 600 miles away across the

Soviet border. When the Soviets built a second missile test site at Tyuratam, near the Aral Sea, it was a destination for many U-2 flights. From these intelligence sources, the Eisenhower administration had known by the late summer of 1957 of the impending launch of a Soviet satellite. More significantly, intelligence sources revealed that Soviet advances in missile technology were not so great as fear-mongers in America suggested. In August, 1957, the Soviets announced the test of an ICBM (Intercontinental Ballistic Missile). Eisenhower made it clear, however, that although the Soviets had tested an ICBM before the United States and may well be a little more advanced in missile technology than the United States, there were very considerable problems for the Soviets to overcome with regard to such matters as guidance and re-entry before the Soviet ICBM would be a useable weapon. From U-2 flights and other sources, Eisenhower knew that Soviet progress in missile deployment was much slower than many in the West suggested. The number of Soviet ICBM tests in 1957–58, for example, were very few, and the large size of their SS-6 missile created great difficulties. Eisenhower, however, could not compromise those intelligence sources by revealing this information to the public, though it would have given greater weight to his reassurances. As he wrote to Swede Hazlett, 'You can understand that there are many things that I don't dare to allude to publicly, yet some of them would do much to allay the fears of our own people.'[18]

Popular fear was increased, however, by leaks from the Gaither Report, which was intended to be confidential, and by statements by Democratic politicians such as Senator Stuart Symington (D. – Missouri) and Senator Henry Jackson (D. – Washington) and other advocates of increased defence spending. In November, 1957, Lyndon Johnson held hearings on satellite and missile programs before the Senate Preparedness sub-Committee, which Johnson chaired. The sub-Committee report criticised the administration for allowing the Soviets to gain the lead in satellites and missile development and thereby endanger American security. The Rockefeller Brothers Fund, under its director Henry Kissinger, drew up a report by a panel of experts, who concluded that America had fallen behind the Soviet Union and needed to boost defence spending by a large amount. Eisenhower, however, stood firm against all of these pressures to respond to Sputnik with large-scale increases in defence spending. Stephen Ambrose writes that 'In his response to Sputnik and the uproar it created, he reached one of the finest points . . . The Ford Foundation, the Rockefeller Brothers, the JCS, Congress, indeed all of "The Establishment" clamored for more defense spending. But Eisenhower said no . . . It was one of his finest hours.'[19]

Eisenhower argued his case in radio and television addresses to the people and in meetings with Congressmen and Cabinet members. 'Although the Soviets are quite likely ahead in some missile and special areas,' he said, 'the overall military strength of the free world is distinctly greater than that of the Communist world.'[20] He laid out the massive build-up of America's nuclear arsenal since the early 1950s, not only bombers but also Titan, Thor, Jupiter and Atlas missiles, to be succeeded by Minuteman and Polaris missiles. He said to Neil McElroy, who had succeeded Charles Wilson as Secretary of Defense, that this expansion was so excessive that 'we are apparently planning to kill every Russian three times in the development of our forces for massive retaliation'.[21] He emphasised the need for selectivity in defence spending. 'We cannot,' he said, 'on an unlimited scale, have both what we must have and what we would like to have. We can have a sound defense and the sound economy on which it rests – if we set our priorities and stick to them.'[22] He pointed out that after the Soviet Aviation Day flyby in Moscow in 1954 Congressional and Air Force critics had claimed that there was a bomber gap between the United States and the Soviet Union in the Soviet's favour, but that subsequent developments had shown this to be untrue. He suggested that the allegations with regard to a missile gap were in the same category. Critics such as John F. Kennedy warned of an impending missile gap that would 'place us in a position of grave peril' and which resulted from the 'complacency' of policies that put 'fiscal security ahead of national security'.[23] Eisenhower dismissed such statements as politically motivated, ill-informed and irresponsible. He accepted that Sputnik illustrated the advanced nature of Soviet military power. 'But this does not mean', he said, 'that we should mount our charger and try to ride off in all directions at once.'[24]

Eisenhower realised, however, that he could not simply take a defensive, negative stance over Sputnik. He responded with a number of positive initiatives, some of which he strongly favoured and others that he accepted more reluctantly. He established a new post of Special Assistant to the President for Science and Technology, to which James R. Killian, the president of the Massachusetts Institute of Technology, was appointed. Killian proved to be an excellent appointment and he became a very valued and important adviser to Eisenhower. The Department of Defense was reorganised, with a new post created of Director of Defense Research and Engineering, whose main task was to prevent duplication by the different branches of the armed services in the enormously expensive matter of missile development. Herbert York, who was appointed to this post, likewise proved to be an excellent appointment.

Eisenhower was much less enthusiastic over the creation of a civilian space agency. He wished space activity to be kept under the control of the Pentagon, with major expenditure on projects with a clearly useful purpose, especially reconnaissance satellites, and with low expenditure on scientific projects that, however worthy and educational, were not high priority. He was successful in retaining top priority status and a high level of expenditure for reconnaissance satellites, which he wished to replace the vulnerable and diplomatically dangerous U-2. He was unsuccessful, however, in his opposition to the creation of a civilian space agency. He was compelled to bow to the popular demand for the establishment in April, 1958, of NASA (the National Aeronautical and Space Agency), whose budget, Eisenhower feared, was bound to swell, as it engaged in space spectaculars in undisguised competition with the Soviet Union.

Eisenhower was even less enthusiastic about the National Defense Education Act, which was passed in 1958. The assumption underlying NDEA was that Sputnik had demonstrated the deficiency of American education in general and education in science and technology in particular. NDEA established a Federal programme of grants and loans to promote the teaching of science, mathematics, and foreign area studies and graduate fellowships in subjects relating to national defence. Eisenhower was in principle opposed to Federal involvement in education, while he did not accept the basic premise of the deficient nature of the American system of education. He was, moreover, wary of the over-emphasis on science and technology. The need, he said, 'is not just for engineers and scientists, but for people who will be able to keep their heads and, in every field, leaders who can meet intricate human problems with wisdom and courage'.[25]

Above all, Eisenhower was reluctant to accept the need to compromise over the defence budget and to accept some increases. Nevertheless, in October, 1957, he authorised McElroy to seek a supplemental $1.2 billion for defence and he increased the 1959 defence budget from $38 billion to $39.8 billion. He agreed to acceleration of the development of ICBMs and IRBMs (Intermediate Range Ballistic Missiles), such as an increase in the number of Thors and Jupiters from 120 to 180. He accepted the need for greater dispersal of B-52s, including the air alert programme of keeping a number of B-52s in the air at all times armed with nuclear bombs. He felt, however, that most of these increases were, as he put it, 'more to stabilize public opinion than to meet the real need for acceleration'.[26] He resisted large-scale increases in defence spending. He referred to 'the truism that security is more important than a balanced budget. The difficulty with this, as with most aphorisms, is that the problem is not so simple as the statement implies. I refer again to the fact that our plans must be based upon the probability of their lengthy prolongation. We face, not a temporary emergency, such as a war, but long-term responsibility.'[27]

Nelson Rockefeller, who succeeded C. D. Jackson in the mid-1950s as Special Assistant for Psychological Warfare, had warned Eisenhower that the first launch of a satellite would make a deep impact as a symbol of scientific and technological superiority. Given Eisenhower's longstanding interest in psychological warfare, it is perhaps surprising that he did not pay more heed to this warning and take measures to put an American satellite into space before the Soviets. At least in retrospect, failure to do so would seem to have been a serious error. In other respects, however, Eisenhower's handling of the Sputnik crisis seems highly commendable in almost every way. Stephen Ambrose concludes that 'Eisenhower's calm, common-sense, deliberate response to Sputnik may have been his finest gift to the nation.'[28] Robert Divine agrees that 'The passage of time has confirmed the wisdom of the president's response. He believed that American science and American education was much sounder than critics charged and, above all, he was confident that the United States held a commanding lead over the Soviet Union in strategic striking power.'[29] Divine, however, makes the criticism that 'Eisenhower, for all his prudence and restraint, failed to meet one of the crucial tests of presidential leadership: convincing the American people that all was well in the world.'[30] This would seem to be an unrealistic requirement, beyond the reaches of the power of any president, and a good case can be made for Eisenhower's strategy of letting hysteria run its course, while he presented a reassuring case to the public and took prudent actions rather than engaging in panic measures. Nevertheless, Divine is correct in suggesting that, however sensible Eisenhower's conduct may have been, the political impact of Sputnik was very damaging for Eisenhower. 'Democratic leaders, and many others', as Pach and Richardson observe, 'cried that the nation had suffered a scientific Pearl Harbor.'[31] As Divine puts it, 'Contemporaries saw his calm reaction as proof of his complacency, if not senility, and condemned him for lack of leadership.'[32]

Almost contemporaneous with the launch of Sputnik, Eisenhower faced another severe crisis over school desegregation in Little Rock, Arkansas. Since the Supreme Court rulings in 1954 and 1955, he had constantly reiterated his view that the law must be obeyed but that gradualism, consensus and local initiative were the appropriate watchwords rather than swift enforcement. Open defiance of the law in Little Rock and the outbreak of mob rule forced him to engage in the type of Federal intervention with the use of force that he had sought very hard to avoid.

In 1957 School Board officials in Little Rock drew up a plan for the very gradual integration of the schools in the city over a seven-year period, beginning with the admission of nine black students into Little Rock Central High School in September, 1957. White segregationist groups filed suit to block the admission of the nine black students, but a Federal judge issued an injunction against all who were seeking to interfere with the process of integration. The governor of Arkansas, Orval Faubus, who had been regarded as a moderate on race but who was looking towards re-election in 1958, ordered units of the Arkansas National Guard to maintain law and order by preventing the black students from entering Central High School. A Federal judge charged Faubus with obstructing a Federal court order. Faubus took the matter to Eisenhower, who was on vacation in Rhode Island. Eisenhower asked Faubus to come to Rhode Island, and on September 14 a compromise seemed to have been reached that Faubus would allow the admission of the black students but would save face by keeping the National Guard in place but change their instructions from blocking admission to the black students to maintaining order during their admission. On his return to Little Rock, however, Faubus went back on this agreement and withdrew the National Guard altogether. On Monday, September 23, an angry mob of about 1,000 milled around outside Central High School to keep out the black students, who slipped in by a side door but who were later sent home for their own safety. Eisenhower was furious over Faubus' action. On September 24 he sent 1,000 US Army paratroopers to Little Rock to restore order and to enable the black students to attend school, and he federalised the Arkansas National Guard and ordered the Guard to perform the same duties as the army troops. The crisis gradually eased, and by the end of October the black students could attend Central High School without a military escort. The troops were gradually withdrawn and the National Guard de-federalised. In 1958 Faubus closed the public schools in Arkansas and re-opened them as private institutions, which could practice segregation. In 1959 the Federal District Court invalidated this schools closure policy and Little Rock Central High School re-opened as an integrated school, with a small number of black students.

Eisenhower's action over Little Rock was, as recorded by his assistant, Sherman Adams, 'a constitutional duty which was the most repugnant to him of all his acts in his eight years at the White House'.[33] Eisenhower felt that the use of force was essential to uphold the constitution and the rule of law but that it was gravely damaging to the process of gradual acceptance and reconciliation, which in his view had to be at the heart of a solution to the delicate and sensitive problem of school desegregation. 'Moderation, decency, education', he said, 'have to go hand in hand with application of law.'[34] He pointed out that 'law alone, as we found out in the prohibition experiment, does not cure some of the things it set out to cure'.[35] He said that at 'the very core of my political thinking' was the belief that 'it has got to be the sentiment, the good will, the good sense of a whole citizenry that enforces law. In other words, you have got to win the hearts and minds of men to the logic and the decency of a situation before you are finally going to get real compliance.'[36]

Moreover, Eisenhower realised that Little Rock was a propaganda disaster for the United States. As Mary Dudziak has argued, 'Safeguarding the image of America was behind Eisenhower's involvement.'[37] In a radio and television address on the day he sent the troops to Little Rock, Eisenhower said that 'Our enemies are gloating over this incident and using it everywhere to misrepresent our whole nation.'[38] Henry Cabot Lodge, American ambassador to the United Nations, reported that 'Here at the United Nations I can see clearly the harm that the riots in Little Rock are doing to our foreign relations.'[39] Eisenhower's firm action in sending troops to Little Rock to enforce the rule of law mitigated only to a slight extent the international condemnation of America's racial practices, which were considered to render hollow America's claims with regard to democracy, freedom and justice.

Awareness of the damage to America's international reputation on account of its record on race relations was one reason for Eisenhower's support for a Civil Rights Bill. In 1957 he revived the bill that had been pigeon-holed in 1956. The bill was intended, he said, in keeping with his emphasis on moderation, 'to preserve rights without arousing passions and without disturbing the rights of anybody else'.[40] The bill's provisions were that a bipartisan Civil Rights Commission should be set up, a Civil Rights Division should be established in the Department of Justice and that the Attorney-General should be empowered to obtain an injunction in instances of denial of the right to vote on the grounds of race. These measures were of a mild nature, especially when the Southern Democrats added an amendment that weakened the powers of the Attorney-General in the enforcement of voting rights. Eisenhower was basically opposed to a Civil Rights Act on the grounds of constitutional principle as unwarranted interference by the Federal government in the affairs of the states. He was persuaded, however, to support a mild measure, which had symbolic significance as the first Civil Rights Act since Reconstruction and as a sign that the Eisenhower administration was not wholly negative on civil rights at a time when the issue attracted widescale national and international attention. Moreover, the opportunity to pass a Civil Rights Bill presented itself on account of the presidential ambitions of Lyndon Johnson. As Majority Leader and a leading Southern Democrat, Johnson was in a pivotal position to win passage for the bill. Johnson was inclined to do so partly out of conviction but also due to his need to establish his national credentials in his bid to win the Democratic nomination for president in 1960 rather than being regarded only as a regional Southern Democrat.[41] The Civil Rights Act of 1957 therefore won passage, but in practice its impact was very limited.

Civil rights leaders pressed Eisenhower to take an outspoken stance on civil rights, but he played a very muted role on the issue. At a rare meeting with prominent civil rights leaders in June, 1958, Martin Luther King urged him to make a strong presidential statement endorsing desegregation as a moral issue. Eisenhower rejected such an approach. As he said in a speech to black leaders in May, 1958, 'In such problems as these, there are no revolutionary cures . . . We must be patient.'[42]

Adding to Eisenhower's difficulties in the autumn of 1957, he suffered a stroke on November 25, 1957. He made a swift recovery, but, following his heart attack in 1955 and ileitis in 1956, his stroke seemed an ominous sign. His doctors ruled that his health was generally good and that he was quite capable of fulfilling his duties, with the exception of a slight reduction in some ceremonial duties. In fact, although his health problems were not sufficiently severe as to impair his basic conduct of the presidency, his virtually chronic health problems, especially relating to his heart and stomach, meant that he was functioning at a level significantly below full health. This added to his irritability over political problems.

One serious political problem that arose in 1958 was the scandal surrounding Sherman Adams. In June, 1958, the House sub-Committee on Legislative Oversight reported allegations that Bernard Goldfine, a New England textile manufacturer, had given gifts to Adams, such as payment of hotel bills and the gift of a vicuna coat to Adams' wife, in exchange for Adams' assistance in using his influence on Goldfine's behalf with the Federal Trade Commission and the Securities and Exchange Commission. Adams stated that Goldfine was an old friend and that the exchange of gifts between the families was longstanding, while his enquiries to regulatory commissions were not significantly different from enquiries that he not infrequently made about the status of investigations.[43] Under scrutiny, however, it was revealed that Goldfine had given gifts to various figures and written them off as business expenses. With an election looming in November and memories still fresh of the accusations in 1952 of venality and influence-peddling in the Truman administration, including gifts of racoon coats, Adams' position became untenable. Moreover, his abrasive personality had won him few friends. He had, however, been a loyal and useful member of Eisenhower's team, so Eisenhower was reluctant to dismiss him. Eisenhower wrote that 'Nothing has had a more depressive effect on my normal buoyancy and optimism than has the virulent, sustained demagogic attacks made upon him . . . He is not only honest, effective and dedicated, but in most cases, *his attackers knew this to be true* . . . I grow to despise political expediency more every day. The whole affair has added a heavy burden upon me.'[44] Indirect attempts through Nixon and others to persuade him to go of his own accord were slow to take effect, and Adams hung on until September 17, when he finally resigned.

The Adams scandal was the last straw in the long list of burdens that weighed down the Republicans as they faced the 1958 Congressional elections. In 1957 the new chairman of the Republican National Committee, Meade Alcorn, a moderate from Connecticut, had declared his goal of projecting the image of modern Republicanism as 'enlightened conservatism'.[45] This was very much in accordance with Eisenhower's outlook. He said that 'Our party is not a many-splintered party', and he urged party members to 'lead the defeatists away from the wailing wall. Time has proved right this Administration's confidence in the American economy . . . And I believe the American voter is going to be grateful that we have overcome the economic challenge without risking the certain dangers of unnecessary big deficits and the snares of a hastily devised patchwork of costly public works.'[46] In fact, however, in 1957–58 the Republicans presented an image of deep division, while they paid a high political price for the recession of 1957–58, farm policies, Sputnik, Little Rock and Sherman Adams. Eisenhower and the Republicans were on the defensive and proved unable to exploit divisions and weaknesses within the Democrats.

The battle over the budget in 1957 had revealed the divisions in the Republican party, with right-wing Republicans, such as Barry Goldwater and Styles Bridges, assailing Eisenhower's spending plans as watered-down New Dealism, while liberal Republicans, such as Nelson Rockefeller, criticised Eisenhower for unimaginative concentration on the goal of a balanced budget and failing to produce a higher economic growth rate. In Congress, Republican divisions were compounded by ineffective leadership. In the Senate in particular, Knowland's weakness as Minority Leader became increasingly apparent, especially after his announcement in early 1957 of his intention not to seek re-election to the Senate in 1958 but to run for governor of California. Meanwhile, Little Rock destroyed any hope of developing a Republican Southern strategy to build on Eisenhower's success in winning four Southern states in the presidential election in 1956. Sputnik had an overall effect politically of undermining faith in Eisenhower's leadership. Above all, the recession had aroused fears of uncaring Republicans in a time of economic hardship. Many Republicans, such as Nixon, argued that Eisenhower needed to show greater awareness of the political impact of the recession rather than concentrating on the economic aspects. Iwan Morgan writes that through the 1957–58 recession 'The president had shown far greater concern for fiscal prudence than partisan interest.'[47] John W. Sloan suggests that in his second term Eisenhower demonstrated an 'increasingly rigid moral conservatism'.[48] Neither Eisenhower himself nor the Republican party in general proved able to project an image of enlightened, dynamic conservatism, offering a vision of prudent fiscal policies and limited Federal powers as the most appealing and responsible path to prosperity and good government. Attempts to label the Democrats as the spendthrift party, who would produce debt, inflation and high taxes, had little success, while the wide divisions within the Democratic party, especially between the North and South, were not brought out to the same extent as Republican divisions. Eisenhower wrote to Harold Macmillan that the Democrats, 'while representing the extremes of the political spectrum can always unite for the election battle'.[49]

Eisenhower had not intended to campaign very extensively in 1958, especially on account of his health. In the event, however, he made many campaign trips, though far fewer than in the Congressional elections in 1954. His popularity had, however, fallen somewhat. His Gallup Poll rating, which had been 79 per cent in February, 1957, had fallen to 48 per cent in April, 1958, rising only to 52 per cent in November, 1958. His intervention in the Congressional elections proved to be ineffective. He made several trips to California to campaign for Knowland for governor and for Goodwin Knight for senator, but both Knowland and Knight were defeated. The results across the country were a disaster for the Republicans. The Democrats gained thirteen seats in the Senate and forty-nine in the House to attain a majority of 64–34 in the Senate and 282–154 in the House. In the gubernatorial elections the Democrats gained five governorships, including California, which had surpassed New York as the largest state in the union, to attain a majority of 35–14 governorships. There were some successes for moderate Republicans, such as Mark Hatfield's election as Governor of Oregon and John Lindsay's victory in the House contest in the Manhattan district in New York. Most

Chapter 6

Waging Cold War, 1957–58

As Eisenhower began his second term in office, the international scene seemed menacing, and the next two years were characterised by crises and strained relations with adversaries. The aftermath of the Hungarian Revolution, followed by the Soviet launch of Sputnik in 1957 and the Berlin crisis in 1958, made these years a period of difficult relations with the Soviet Union. The offshore islands issue over Quemoy and Matsu blew up again in 1958, making even less likely than ever any changes in America's estranged relationship with China. In the Middle East the United States became the leading power following the Suez crisis, but America's exercise of power in the region proved problematical. Throughout the Third World, America continued to fail to project an image of a progressive, liberating force, but instead was perceived as a regressive, domineering power.

The Hungarian Revolution had produced a reassertion of repressive Soviet control over the East European satellites. The United States continued its policy of encouraging any nationalistic or liberalising tendencies within East European countries, but the Eisenhower administration accepted that the prospect of inducing any significant change in the immediate aftermath of the Hungarian Revolution was very limited. The United States continued to make protests over Hungary at the United Nations, without much effect. Eisenhower was appalled when in June, 1958, Imre Nagy and several close associates, who had been kept in prison in Romania since November, 1956, were brought back to Budapest, given a swift trial and were summarily executed.

Eisenhower had a lengthy exchange of letters in 1957–58 with Bulganin, who was the official head of the Soviet government as Chairman of the Council of Ministers. The tone, however, was accusatory and propagandistic and held out little hope of a significant improvement in relations. On March 27, 1958, Bulganin was removed from his post by Khrushchev, who continued as First Secretary of the Communist Party as well as taking over as Chairman of the Council of Ministers and was thus clearly the undisputed leader of the Soviet Union. Nevertheless, Khrushchev needed always to be wary of his domestic position, lest he suffer the same fate of removal from office that he had participated in meting out to colleagues such as Malenkov and Bulganin. This reinforced Khrushchev's tendency towards bombastic assertiveness, which led him, for example, to exploit the propaganda opportunities of Sputnik to the hilt, to Eisenhower's chagrin. Although Eisenhower realised that Khrushchev was a mercurial character and that he had some liberalising tendencies, for the most part Khrushchev seemed to Eisenhower a dangerous, regressive figure who was bent on exploiting every opportunity to further his goal of expanding Communism. Eisenhower and Khrushchev exchanged letters, but the tone was even sharper and less conducive to an improvement in relations than in Eisenhower's correspondence with Bulganin. 'I was frankly surprised by your letter of June 11,' Eisenhower wrote to Khrushchev in July, 1958, for example. 'The Soviet Government has disrupted our discussions in Moscow by taking upon itself to publish with bare hours of warning and no attempt at consultation the documents between it and the Western powers . . . This action is scarcely consonant with the spirit of serious preparation in which the Western powers entered into these discussions.'[1] In this atmosphere, the prospects of détente in US–Soviet relations seemed dim.

On the Soviet side, however, an ongoing source of deep grievance was the continuation of U-2 flights over Soviet territory. After a six-month interlude, a U-2 flew over the Soviet Union on June 19, 1957. The United States was particularly concerned to gain information about the development of a Soviet ICBM. In August, 1957, in Operation Soft Touch, the most concentrated cluster of flights in the entire U-2 programme took place, with eight U-2 flights between August 4 and August 28, 1957. The flights were from Pakistan and Turkey, mainly over southern USSR. On August 5, a U-2 located the new Soviet ICBM testing site at Tyuratam and the missile impact area at Klyuchi. On August 21, the Soviets announced the first successful test of an ICBM. A U-2 flight on August 28 brought back excellent photographs of the Tyuratam missile site. A flight on September 10 went over the other main Soviet test site at Kapustin Yar, and a flight on September 15 photographed the Klyuchi missile impact area, to which test missiles from Tyuratam were fired. On October 12 a U-2 flew from West Germany over north-west USSR, but no flights then took place until March 1, 1958, when a U-2 flew from Japan over Siberia. Thereafter Eisenhower ended U-2 flights until April, 1959. Eisenhower was deeply concerned over the risk of a U-2 being shot down and the disastrous diplomatic consequences that would ensue. Nearly all U-2 flights were picked up on Soviet radar and tracked closely. MIG fighters were sent up towards the U-2 but were unable to climb to the U-2's altitude of 70,000 feet. SAM missiles were sometimes fired, which likewise could not reach the U-2's altitude. Following almost every flight, a Soviet note of protest was sent through diplomatic channels, providing a detailed flight path of the U-2's journey. The US State Department replied with denials that any American plane had followed such a route. After the State Department's usual bland denial in response to the Soviet protest note following the March 1, 1958, flight, the Soviets sent a further, very strong note of protest on April 21, 1958, which strengthened Eisenhower's conviction that there should be no further U-2 flights over the Soviet Union for the foreseeable future.[2] As Curtis Peebles writes, 'Eisenhower's fear of the political consequences of the loss of an aircraft remained strong, as did his assessment that the Soviets were much weaker than the United States and his belief that the value of the intelligence did not equal the political price that would have to be paid.'[3]

In the summer of 1958, Eisenhower agreed to a further attempt to use balloons as a safer alternative to the U-2 as a means to gain photographic intelligence. The US Air Weather Service discovered that for six weeks over the summer the jet stream underwent a direction change, turning upwards to 100,000 feet over the Bering Sea and flowing east to west. This would allow a balloon to fly at a height at which it probably would not be seen and to drift across the Soviet Union to Europe, where it would be recovered. After the Genetrix fiasco in 1955, Eisenhower's first reaction was to dismiss out of hand the suggestion of another experiment with the use of balloons. His desire to find an alternative to the U-2 led him, however, to agree to the launch of three WS-461L reconnaissance balloons in July, 1958. The balloons duly traversed the Soviet Union at a great height. They were, however, detected by the Soviets and, even more disastrously, they came down before they reached Western Europe, landing in Eastern Europe, where they were handed over to Soviet authorities. Eisenhower was incandescent with rage over the incompetence displayed in this episode. Of greater significance, the Soviets were deeply aggrieved by this further unauthorised American intrusion into their air space.[4]

With relations with the Soviet Union in a state of strain and tension, at the heart of Eisenhower's policy was, as always, a firm belief in containment and the need to preserve Western unity and strength. 'Eternal vigilance and free world military power, backed by combined economic and spiritual strength,' he said, 'provide the only answer to this threat until the Soviet leaders themselves cease to consume their resources in warlike and expansionist purposes and turn them to the well-being of their own peoples.'[5] In December, 1957, Eisenhower took his first trip to Europe as president to attend the NATO meeting in Paris. He was buoyed by the evidence of Europe's economic recovery and its growing unity, manifested, for example, by the establishment of the Common Market in 1957. America's relations with France were difficult after the Suez crisis and became even more strained when Charles de Gaulle returned to power as president of France in 1958. But America's relationship with her most important ally, Britain, was restored to close friendship. Harold Macmillan, with an American mother and a pro-American inclination, and with a longstanding good relationship with Eisenhower since wartime days in North Africa in 1942, was very eager to repair the damage of the Suez crisis and to restore close Anglo-American relations. Macmillan was, of course, motivated not only by sentiment but by Britain's self-interest. Eisenhower, with his wartime association with British military and political leaders, was a strong Anglophile, who was equally eager to move on from the divisions and disagreements of the Suez affair. Eisenhower's motives, like Macmillan's, were not based simply on sentiment and desire for an Anglo-American special relationship based on common language and traditions. Eisenhower appreciated the importance of close relations with other powers as well as Britain, such as West Germany, and he did not wish a relationship with Britain that might appear to be in any way exclusive. Eisenhower's policy was based on national self-interest as much as on sentiment. He regarded a close Anglo-American relationship as the bedrock of America's international involvement and the key link to other alliances, which created the bulwark of the containment of the Soviet Union. He therefore changed American policy with regard to the supply of atomic information to Britain, enabling Britain to receive nuclear information that had been denied since the McMahon Act in 1946, and he negotiated the emplacement of Thor IRBM missiles in Britain in 1958, with a dual key arrangement, requiring joint British and American agreement to the firing of these missiles.[6]

A vital part of the strength of the West, in Eisenhower's view, was the Mutual Security Program. Eisenhower described America's Mutual Security Program as 'of transcendent importance to the security of the United States'.[7] It was, he said, 'one of the main imperatives of security and peace'.[8] He advocated, as always, a high level of economic and military assistance to allies through the Mutual Security Program. 'The common label of "foreign aid" is gravely misleading,' he said, 'for it inspires a picture of bounty for foreign countries at the expense of our own. No misconception could be further from reality. These programs serve our own basic national and personal interests.'[9] He battled endlessly against Congressmen who took a parsimonious view of aid to other countries. 'Every time another year comes around', he said, 'the Mutual Security Program is compelled to engage in a life-and-death struggle for its very existence. The attack is based, not on the record, not on the facts. It is based on slogans, prejudices, penny-wise economy.'[10] In 1957 and 1958, as in other years, Mutual Assistance was reduced by Congressional budget-cutters, whom Eisenhower described as 'ostrich-like opponents of mutual security'.[11] Despite such cuts, annual appropriations of almost $3 billion enabled the Eisenhower administration to disperse very large sums in military and economic assistance to many nations to build up the strength of America's allies worldwide. Such a position of strength, in Eisenhower's view, was the most important mainstay of peace. Although Eisenhower was deeply suspicious of Soviet intentions, he believed that Soviet leaders had a strong sense of desire for self-preservation, so that, faced with firm Western resolve and solid military, economic and spiritual strength, the Soviet leaders would be very unlikely to initiate a conflict.

Eisenhower's standpoint on containment, however, was not wholly passive and negative. He was very sceptical with regard to a summit meeting, but he favoured people-to-people contacts, such as the Cultural Agreement of 1958 for the exchange of students and artistic perform-ances. The numbers involved in such exchanges were so small, however, and the bureaucratic restrictions so considerable, that their impact was bound to be slight. Of much greater significance was Eisenhower's inter-est in disarmament and an atomic test ban. Despite the unpromising general state of US–Soviet relations, Eisenhower was very interested in exploring any possible avenue to a reduction in the colossal expenditure on weapons, with their terrifying increase in explosive power and the health hazards involved in testing nuclear weapons. In the 1956 election campaign Eisenhower appeared to be dismissive of the suggestion of a test ban, but this had largely been due to the feeling that this was too complex an issue to be reduced to the simplicities of an election cam-paign. Once re-elected, Eisenhower gave more sympathetic consideration to the idea of a test ban as the most hopeful first step towards disarma-ment. The Pentagon and the Atomic Energy Commission (AEC) strongly opposed a test ban on the grounds that national security required tests to perfect new weapons and that tests were vital to the credibility of deterrence, which was the key to peace. Proponents of a test ban were dismissed as political innocents, the equivalent in the nuclear age of the appeasers of the 1930s. As for the health hazards from nuclear tests, these were dismissed as infinitesimal, no greater for the average citizen than the exposure in a chest x-ray, while it was claimed that tests helped to develop cleaner bombs, with less radioactive fallout. At the other extreme, supporters of a test ban argued that sufficient information about nuclear energy for weapons had already been obtained, making further tests superfluous, while the health hazards were alleged to be very considerable and insidious, creating an increase in the incidence of leukaemia, for example, in future generations as well as in the present population. Eisenhower's position was somewhere between these two extremes, initially closer to the more hawkish position but moving gradually to a much more flexible position. Eisenhower's initial standpoint was that a test ban could only be part of an overall disarmament programme, which must include ironclad inspection procedures. A test ban would, therefore, be the last step in the process, a reward if the other steps were taken. Since inspection procedures proved to be an insuperable obstacle in disarmament negotiations, this doomed the possibility of a test ban. Gradually, however, Eisenhower became more attracted to the concept of a test ban as a feasible first step to break the disarmament logjam, which might lead to more substantial steps. Also, a test ban did not involve the same problems of inspection as other disarmament proposals, since nuclear tests could be detected by radioactive fallout, which was carried by the wind. On the health issue, Eisenhower felt that the views of scientists were at such variance that it was difficult to judge the truth of the matter, but he concluded that, if possible, the risks should be removed by ending tests. Matters were complicated in 1957 when the United States conducted the first successful underground test. This had the advantage that it eliminated the hazards of radioactive fallout, but it made the detection of tests more difficult. Underground tests could be detected only by seismographic devices, which could not distinguish between earthquakes and nuclear tests.

Eisenhower's position became clearer in 1957 in his instructions to AEC Director Lewis Strauss to keep tests to a minimum. In July, 1958, a conference of technical experts was held in Geneva to explore the practicalities of verification procedures and other such matters, which produced agreement on a number of possibilities. The outcome was that in August, 1958, Eisenhower proposed a moratorium on tests for a year, provided that the Soviets did likewise. This was intended as a goodwill gesture to encourage progress at a conference of all the nuclear powers, which was due to open in Geneva on October 31.[12]

Eisenhower was also well aware of the propaganda issues surrounding a test ban and disarmament. He felt that the Soviets blatantly exploited the issues for propaganda purposes, especially when on March 31, 1958, at the end of a series of Soviet tests and just as a previously announced American series was about to begin, Khrushchev announced a unilateral Soviet ban on further tests. 'It seems peculiar', Eisenhower wrote to Khrushchev, 'that the Soviet Union, having just concluded a series of tests of unprecedented intensity, should now, in bold headlines, say that it will not test again, but add, in small type, that it may test again if the United States carries out its already long announced and now imminent series of tests.'[13] Eisenhower hoped that his proposals of August, 1958, would not be regarded as merely a propaganda ploy but that they would be treated as a serious effort to initiate a process that could stem the arms race and begin a reduction in the arsenals of each side. Harold Macmillan noted in August, 1958, that Eisenhower was 'unusually excited' about the plans for a test moratorium.[14]

Eisenhower realised, however, that discussions on a test ban and disarmament were bound to be influenced by developments or crises in any other aspects of US–Soviet relations. In November, 1958, the Berlin crisis sharply heightened tensions in US–Soviet relations. Berlin was a running sore to the Soviets, in its situation of being politically part of West Germany but geographically located in the middle of East Germany. The Soviets and their East German allies chafed over the flow of East German migrants into West Berlin, the use of West Berlin for intelligence purposes and the propaganda benefit of the presentation of West Berlin as an island of prosperity and freedom in the midst of grey, dreary Communist gloom. Khrushchev therefore decided in November, 1958, that he would sign a peace treaty with East Germany in six months and give control to the East Germans of the access routes from West Germany to West Berlin. This was in violation of the rights of the United States, Britain and France under Second World War agreements and was clearly an unacceptable, provocative action. The crisis was gradually defused over the next year, but it meant that at the end of 1958 relations between the United States and the Soviet Union were at one of their low points of the Cold War.

In the Far East, relations with Communist China remained at an impasse. In August, 1958, the resumption of the shelling of Quemoy and Matsu from the mainland created another serious crisis over the offshore islands. Chiang Kai-shek had not reduced troop levels on Quemoy and Matsu, as he had agreed at the end of the 1954–55 crisis, but instead the Nationalist Chinese garrison had been increased substantially. Nevertheless, Eisenhower felt that he could not back down under duress, but he did not wish to encourage Chiang's ambitions. On September 4, Dulles issued a statement that the United States might regard the seizure of the offshore islands by the Chinese Communists as grounds for American retaliation under the authority granted by Congress under the Formosa Resolution of 1955. Khrushchev's ambivalence in his support of the Chinese Communists in the crisis made Eisenhower more willing to take a firmer stand. At the same time, Eisenhower appreciated how potentially very dangerous the crisis could become and that it damaged America's relations with allies in Europe, who had little sympathy for Chiang and who felt that the offshore islands were in no way worth a war.

In the absence of diplomatic relations with China, the United States had begun the practice of holding meetings between the American and Chinese ambassadors to Poland. A meeting of the ambassadors in Warsaw led to some progress, while Dulles flew to Taiwan and extracted an agreement from Chiang to announce a reduction in the Nationalist garrison on the offshore islands and a renunciation of any intention to mount an invasion of the mainland from Quemoy and Matsu. On October 6 a seven-day truce was announced. This was followed by a somewhat bizarre situation when the Chinese Communists bombarded Quemoy and Matsu every second day, while on alternate days the shelling was suspended and the Americans were allowed to re-supply the Nationalists on the offshore islands. Eisenhower, as he later wrote, 'wondered if we were in a Gilbert and Sullivan war'.[15] By early November the Chinese shelling ceased and the crisis passed. Eisenhower's familiar tactics of firmness, delay and obfuscation had produced a peaceful end to the crisis. Estrangement with China, however, had grown even greater.

In the other area of serious crisis in the Far East, namely, Vietnam, developments were deceptively quiet in 1957–58. Ngo Dinh Diem's régime appeared to be making good progress. By the end of 1957, however, the weaknesses of Diem's régime were beginning to become more apparent and opposition to his rule became stronger. In May, 1957, Diem visited the United States. Eisenhower acclaimed his achievements in South Vietnam. In fact, however, these successes were illusory. As David Anderson puts it, 'The United States successfully achieved its objectives of creating an ally for itself in Vietnam. Once established, however, the Saigon régime proved to be an unruly and impotent client whose requirements for survival trapped its patron in ever-increasing costs and risks.'[16] The American ambassador to South Vietnam, Eugene Dubrow, became increasingly concerned over the repression and lack of social progress in South Vietnam and sought to put pressure on Diem to engage in reform. But American efforts to influence Diem had limited impact, especially since Diem responded to threats of reduction in American aid with the argument that this would weaken his régime and allow the Communists to come to power. Opposition to Diem grew within South Vietnam, particularly to the administrators appointed by Diem in villages in rural areas. In 1957 opposition groups, some Communist and some non-Communists, formed the Viet Cong, who engaged in guerrilla tactics, especially assassinations of village chiefs.

Eisenhower was as afraid of the loss to Communism of Laos as much as of Vietnam. In the very confused situation in Laos, which was Vietnam's small neighbour, with a population of only two million people, the King was pro-Western but had weak powers. Three factions developed, namely, the Communist Pathet Lao, who, with the assistance of the North Vietnamese, gained control of two northern provinces; the neutralists, led by Prince Souvanna Phouma; and the conservatives, who formed a new party, the Rally of the Laos People (RLP), led by Prince Phoui Sananikone. In December, 1956, Souvanna was prime minister and decided to form a coalition government with the Pathet Lao, which would enable the government to regain control of the two northern provinces. The process of formation of this coalition took place over the next eighteen months, until elections were held in May, 1958, in which a number of Pathet Lao representatives were elected. The United States was afraid that the Pathet Lao would act in the same way as Communists had done in other countries to undermine the government and to seize power. The United States used its influence, including activity by the CIA, to bring about a government in Laos that would not include Communists. The political situation, however, became increasingly unstable, with army support for the conservatives and with the outbreak of violence and guerrilla warfare in several parts of the country.

In the Middle East, the discrediting of Britain and France in the Suez crisis left a vacuum, which Eisenhower feared would be filled by the Soviet Union. Nasser was not a Communist, but his brand of radical Arab nationalism led him to play off the East against the West, which provided opportunities for the Soviet Union to make inroads in the Middle East. The Soviets began work on the Aswan Dam, which involved the presence of large numbers of Soviet engineers and military personnel in Egypt. In Syria, Soviet influence grew with the importation of Soviet arms into Syria in 1957. In January, 1958, Syria united with Egypt to form the United Arab Republic, headed by Nasser. In Jordan, pro-Nasser elements gained strength in the parliamentary elections in 1957, and when the pro-Western King Hussein dismissed the prime minister, Hussein's position came under threat. In Iraq, the pro-Western régime was overthrown in a coup on July 14, 1958, in which King Faisal, Crown

Prince Abdullah and Prime Minister Nuri-as-Said were killed and power was seized by the pro-Nasser army commander, General Abdul Karim Kassam.

From early 1957 the United States moved to fill the vacuum created by the humiliation of Britain and France in the Suez crisis. On March 9, 1957, Congress passed the Eisenhower Doctrine, which not only granted the president discretionary authority to disburse $200 million in economic and military aid in the region of the Middle East but, more controversially, granted approval to the president to send American troops to any nation that requested assistance when threatened with 'overt armed aggression by any country controlled by international communism'.[17] Eisenhower sought to bolster friendly Arab régimes in such countries as Saudi Arabia and Lebanon, and he encouraged the British to assist Hussein in Jordan. Eisenhower was increasingly worried by Nasser's ambitions, which seemed to endanger Western access to oil as well as to create opportunities for Soviet penetration. Eisenhower said to Nixon that 'since 1945 we have been trying to maintain the opportunity to reach vitally needed petroleum supplies peaceably', but difficulties had been created 'by the struggle of Nasser to get control of these supplies – to get the income and the power to destroy the Western world'.[18]

The underlying tensions led to a crisis in Lebanon in July, 1958, when the Eisenhower Doctrine was invoked and American marines landed in Lebanon. Disagreements had developed between the Muslims and the Maronite Christians in Lebanon, with sporadic violence kept under control with difficulty. A crisis arose in 1958 when the Maronite Christian president, Camille Chamoun, sought to amend the constitution to enable him to seek a second term as president. At the same time the Muslims claimed that the parliamentary elections in 1957 had been fraudulent. In the midst of the tensions that had arisen, the coup in Iraq on July 14, 1958, aroused fears that radical Muslims in Lebanon would seize power. Chamoun therefore asked for American intervention. Eisenhower responded on July 15 by sending in 15,000 marines from the US Sixth Fleet, which had been sent to the Eastern Mediterranean. The marines met with no opposition. On the contrary, bemused sunbathers on the Beirut beaches were puzzled by the appearance of an American invasion force, and the purpose of the intervention seemed difficult to explain. On July 18, Under-Secretary of State Robert Murphy was sent to Beirut and a compromise agreement was reached, whereby General Faud Chehab, the Maronite Christian commander of the Lebanese army, succeeded Chamoun as president, while Rashid Karami, the Sunni Muslim insurgent leader, became prime minister. The US marines began to withdraw in early August and by the end of October the last American troops had left Lebanon. Eisenhower claimed that the show of force in Lebanon had provided reassurance of American support to friendly Arab régimes and demonstrated American willingness to use its military power as an expression of support. Eisenhower later wrote that the American intervention in Lebanon had given Nasser 'food for thought' and brought about 'a definite change in Nasser's attitude towards the United States'.[19] Eisenhower's critics suggested that the intervention was misguided, damaging American prestige, which had risen after the Suez crisis, and confirming the impression that American action arose from hegemonistic tendencies and from the simplistic misperception of crises with complex social and religious roots as Communist plots. On this issue, Eisenhower's critics seem to have the stronger case.

The other major problem in the Middle East was Israel. Eisenhower realised that the American need to support Israel meant that 'We are laboring under an inherent disadvantage in this area.' He observed that 'Except for Israel we could form a viable policy in the area. In his mind, the question is how to take a sympathetic position regarding the Arabs without agreeing to the destruction of Israel.'[20] After his re-election in 1956 Eisenhower was not under strong domestic political pressure, which enabled him to follow his inclination to be even-handed towards Israel and the Arabs. Moreover, he had been deeply offended by Israel's deceptive collusion with Britain and France in the Suez crisis. Eisenhower thereafter took the Arab side on a number of issues, particularly relating to the settlement of the Suez affair. Israel refused to withdraw from Gaza or from Sharm-El-Sheik at the southern tip of the Sinai peninsula, as required by the terms of the agreement at the end of the Suez crisis. Eisenhower, despite opposition from Lyndon Johnson and other Democrats in Congress, threatened to support a United Nations resolution banning either government or private aid to Israel by member states of the United Nations, unless Israel withdrew from these territories. Such a ban would have caused Israel serious financial problems, cutting off private contributions from Americans. In March, 1957, Israel withdrew from these territories. A United Nations peacekeeping force was sent in to establish a peace line between Israel and Egypt, which remained in operation until the outbreak of the Six Day War in 1967.

In early 1957 Henry Cabot Lodge reported from the United Nations that as a consequence of American policy in the Suez crisis, 'The standing of the United States – notably, among the Asian powers – is at a brand new high.'[21] Eisenhower hoped to project an image of the United States as a liberating, progressive force worldwide. 'Only in respecting the hopes and cultures of others', Eisenhower said in his Second Inaugural Address in January, 1957, 'will we practice the equality of all nations.'[22] He expressed an empathy with the rising spirit of nationalism in emerging countries, especially former colonies. 'The spirit of nationalism,' he wrote, 'coupled with a deep hunger for some betterment in physical conditions and living standards, creates a critical situation in the underdeveloped areas of the world.'[23] Eisenhower strongly supported economic aid to developing countries, both as a means to keep them out of the Communist camp and as a desirable social and moral goal in itself. In 1953, the Eisenhower administration placed strong emphasis on liberalised trade as the preferable means for assisting the developing countries rather than direct economic aid – trade, not aid, as the slogan put it. At the beginning of his second term in office, however, Eisenhower set his administration to work on what Burton Kaufman describes as 'the most searching review of the US foreign aid program since the Marshall Plan'.[24] The outcome of this review was a new policy of trade *and* aid instead of trade, not aid. A Development Loan Fund was introduced in 1957 to facilitate the distribution of foreign aid and, despite Congressional cuts that reduced foreign aid to less generous levels than Eisenhower proposed, vast amounts of American foreign aid were dispersed to developing countries, while a number of regulations were changed to liberalise trade with less developed countries. Eisenhower totally rejected a policy of working with colonial powers. From his experience in the Philippines he wrote that independence brought people 'fierce pride and personal satisfaction', and he expressed the view that 'almost any one of the newborn states of the world would far rather embrace Communism or any other form of dictatorship than to acknowledge the political domination of another government, even though that government brought to each citizen a far higher standard of living'.[25]

Yet, in spite of all these efforts, America's image in the Third World was increasingly negative. Afro-Asian support as a result of American policy over Suez proved to be fleeting. More typical as an expression of Third World opinion of the United States was the treatment of Vice-President Nixon when he went on a tour of some Latin American countries in 1958. Nixon's car was surrounded by a mob in Caracas, Venezuela, who yelled abuse against America and endangered Nixon's safety. The United States sponsored the Inter-American Bank as a channel for US aid to Latin America, but the image of the United States in Latin America, as throughout the Third World, was of a domineering, capitalist nation bent on the exploitation of poorer and weaker countries. In the propaganda war in the Third World, the Communists were more successful than the

United States in winning support from so-called neutralist countries, such as India, Egypt and Indonesia. Foreign policy issues had relatively little impact on the Congressional elections in 1958. The poor performance of the Republicans in the 1958 elections, together with a lack of much progress in foreign policy, meant that the end of 1958 was the lowest point in Eisenhower's presidency. The onset of the Berlin crisis in November, 1958, ended the year on a low note for Eisenhower. As a 'lame duck' president without a Congressional majority, with an awkward and aggressive adversary in the Soviet Union in the person of Khrushchev, and with seemingly intractable problems in many areas in the world, the prospects for progress in the last two years of Eisenhower's presidency did not seem good.

Chapter 7

Domestic Revival, 1959–60

As Eisenhower entered his final two years in office, he seemed to face great problems and obstacles, which were liable to foredoom his remaining period as president to stalemate and ineffectuality. His power was limited as a 'lame duck' president, the first who was constitutionally barred from seeking a third term. The Democratic majority in Congress had been considerably increased, with the significant consequence that Southern Democrats, with whom Eisenhower had been able to work quite constructively, were now outnumbered by more liberal Democrats from the North and West. Also, the temper of the times in America began to change, with a growing dissatisfaction with passivity and with a rising sense of expectancy on the part of a new generation with a new explanation. As Arthur Schlesinger put it, 'The Eisenhower era ... was drawing to its close, and a new time – a time of affirmation, progressivism and forward movement – impended.'[1]

Despite these gloomy predilections and critical evaluations by liberal historians, Eisenhower in fact demonstrated a renewed vigour and determination from the beginning of 1959, which pulled his presidency out of the doldrums of 1957–58 into a much more positive outlook in 1959–60. Partly this was due to an improvement in his health. The British ambassador to the United States, Harold Caccia, noted this improvement in Eisenhower's health and purposefulness, writing in his Annual Report for 1959 that 'The "new Ike" of 1959 is a more inspiring figure than the sick and unhappy president of 1957 and 1958 ... This has probably been the best of Mr Eisenhower's years as President.'[2]

Eisenhower's top priority in domestic policy in his last two years as president was the attainment of a balanced budget. The recession in 1957–58 had resulted in a $12.4 billion deficit in FY1959 (July 1, 1958–June 30, 1959). In January, 1959, he proposed a budget with a slight surplus for FY1960 and in January, 1960, his budget proposal for FY1961 was for a surplus of $4.2 billion, which was to be used to reduce the National Debt.

Eisenhower adhered to basic economic principles, which were accepted by John Maynard Keynes, that deficits were acceptable in times of recession but that compensatory surpluses should be achieved in better years. 'In times of prosperity, such as we anticipate in the coming year,' he said in his Annual Budget Message in January, 1960, 'sound fiscal and economic policy requires a budget surplus to help counteract inflationary pressures, to ease conditions in capital and credit markets and to increase the supply of savings available for the productive investment so essential to continued economic growth'.[3] As always, Eisenhower felt that these relatively technical financial reasons for attaining a balanced budget were only one part of the matter. Even more important was the symbolic impact of a balanced budget as a mark of America's resolution to adhere to its fundamental values, which were moral and spiritual as much as political and economic. 'A balanced budget', he said, 'will enhance the confidence of people all over the world in the strength of our economy and our currency and in our individual and collective ability to be fiscally responsible.'[4] He denounced persistent deficits as 'the cowardly habit of passing our own obligations as mortgages to our children'.[5] The budget, he argued, was an indication of the common purpose of all Americans, designed for the national welfare. 'The Budget is not designed for special interests,' he said. 'The real purpose is to promote the good of all America.'[6] He told the Cabinet that 'We seem to have an hysterical approach, from health programs to welfare programs and grants to the states, to everything: to where we are going to "cure it all" in two years, or five years, by putting in a lot of money . . . We must keep our expenses down and we must put our emphasis on productivity.'[7]

Eisenhower's fiscal policy, however, came in for increasing criticism as old-fashioned, unimaginative and regressive. Proponents of the New Economics, such as John F. Kennedy, denounced Eisenhower's conservative economic policies as reactionary, uncaring and retarding economic growth and social progress. Many Democrats argued that New Economics would create more dynamic economic growth, which could have prevented the unnecessary 1957–58 recession or at least have brought about more than a sluggish recovery, which was followed by another recession in 1960–61. Instead of an economic growth rate of 2.5 per cent in the late 1950s, Democrats argued that a more modern, imaginative approach, instead of Eisenhower's ossified conservative approach, could produce an economic growth rate of 5 per cent.[8] Eisenhower was highly sceptical of such ideas and pointed to successes, such as a very low rate of inflation and the necessity for measures to address the growing balance of payments deficit in America's trade.

Eisenhower strongly resisted pressure for increases in defence spending, which would have unbalanced the budget. He expressed his deep resentment against Democrats, such as Stuart Symington, Lyndon Johnson and John F. Kennedy, who charged that American security was endangered by the allegedly too low level of defence spending. 'These people that are trying to make defense a partisan matter', said Eisenhower, 'are doing a disservice to the United States.'[9] Eisenhower vigorously defended his position, stating that 'I get tired of saying that defense is not to be made an excuse for wasting dollars. I don't believe we should pay one cent more for defense than we have to. But I do say this: our defense is not only strong, it is awesome, and it is respected everywhere.'[10] He said that 'Just as the Biblical Job had his boils, so we have a cult of professional pessimists, who, taking counsel of their fears, continually mouth the allegation that America has become a second rate military power.'[11] He referred again to the 'great equation' between adequate defence and a sound economy. 'Just spending money does not make us stronger,' he said. 'Indeed, if you spend too much, you will make us weaker. That is when the nicety of judgment comes in – what we need; get that; get that by all means, and get no more.'[12] As to who was best able to make this judgement of what was essentially required and what was not, he said that 'I think possibly this is the first time I ever violated my own conception of humility and modesty: I think I am more able than any of those individuals of whom you speak to make an overall decision on behalf of the United States in this vital matter.'[13] He reiterated his strong feelings on the diversion of resources into arms. 'We are constantly plagued with this,' he said. 'We are putting more of our sweat, our toil and our man hours into these negative things we call armaments for no reason whatsoever, no constructive thing.'[14] He dismissively brushed aside the argument that the American economy was sustained by arms spending and that substantial disarmament would send the economy into a tailspin. 'We are now scratching around to get money for such things as school construction,' he said. 'I see no reason why the sums which now are going into these sterile, negative mechanisms that we call war munitions shouldn't go into something positive.'[15]

In the defence budget some cuts were made in the army, with a reduction in personnel of 97,000 between June, 1958 and June, 1959. Eisenhower promised, however, that there would be no further cuts in the Army or Marines. He wished to retain sufficient ground troops for small conflicts, such as Lebanon. In the 1960 election campaign John F. Kennedy proclaimed a new approach to defence of flexible response instead of massive retaliation. Eisenhower had, in fact, despite the very large reductions in the Army since the introduction of the New Look in 1953, always realised the need for ground troops for small conflicts. The main development with regard to the defence budget by 1959–60 was the continuing adjustment to the requirements of the ballistic missile age. Many weapons, especially missiles, were entering the most expensive phase of production and deployment. To keep defence spending under control, cuts were required in other parts of the defence budget. There were some reductions in the Navy, which fell to 812 ships in 1960 from 1,113 in 1954, with some new developments postponed, such as a second nuclear-powered aircraft carrier. The main cuts, however, were in the Air Force, which had benefited from the increases in earlier years. The Air Force was reduced to 96 wings in June, 1960, from 118 wings in June, 1958. The B-52 was not replaced but was retained as the mainstay of SAC, with work on a successor, the B-70, continued only at a minimal level of research and design. Other projects, such as a nuclear-powered bomber and an anti-missile system, were virtually eliminated. In terms of defence policy, Eisenhower successfully pursued his objectives of modernising America's defence, especially with new missiles, yet restraining expenditure. As Peter Roman puts it, 'Eisenhower manipulated his administrative machinery to produce defense budgets that remained stable, yet still expanded missile production to keep pace with and ultimately overtake the Soviet Union – truly a remarkable feat of presidential policy making.'[16]

In the public perception and in the political arena, however, Eisenhower encountered great difficulties over defence policy. With a presidential election looming in 1960, the missile gap succeeded in 1959–60 from the Sputnik debate in 1957–58, raising a great deal of heat in the political arena. Eisenhower was, of course, aware that several of the main critics of his defence policy were leading contenders for the Democratic nomination for president. Andrew Goodpaster recorded that 'The President expressed his deep concern over what men like Senator Symington or Senator Kennedy might do as President. In his opinion those men lack the judgment for such responsibilities.'[17]

Eisenhower derided the esoteric views of defence intellectuals and newspaper columnists, such as Albert Wohlsetter, Hanson Baldwin and Joseph Alsop, who advocated large increases in defence to guard against far-fetched, worse case scenarios. Eisenhower said that 'he had spoken out before about self-appointed military experts' but that he was 'considering making another statement about neurotics – either honest or dishonest neurotics'.[18] With regard to the possibility that the Soviet Union could in a surprise attack destroy all of America's retaliatory capability before it could be used, Eisenhower conceded that a dictatorship, such as the Soviet Union, had a greater opportunity to engage in a surprise attack than a democracy. He pointed out, however, that through such means as wider dispersal of bases and improved early warning systems, the United States was better prepared to deal with such a possibility. Above all, he dismissed as quite unrealistic the concept of a Soviet first strike that could comprehensively knock out America's retaliatory forces. 'If we are going to assume that our entire forces were going to be wiped out instantly, so that we would be helpless,' he said, 'how many of those missiles are they going to send off in one volley all over the world to immobilize us? There finally comes such a thing as just a logical limit to capability, and we know that there is not that kind of capability existing in the world today.'[19] He said that the Pentagon was 'getting into an incredible position – of having enough to destroy every conceivable target all over the world, plus a threefold reserve'.[20] George Kistiakowsky, who replaced James Killian as Science Advisor in 1959, records that at an NSC meeting in April, 1960, when the Pentagon proposed a build-up in ICBM production to 400 per month, Eisenhower 'remarked in obvious disgust, "Why don't we go completely crazy and plan on a force of 10,000"?'[21]

Eisenhower felt that much of the pressure for increased defence spending came from special interests, especially arms manufacturers and military figures, who had lobbied for pet projects, which had been underfunded or had been refused funding. He told Republican legislative leaders that, when he saw advertisements for Boeing and Douglas, he was 'getting sick of the lobbies of the munitions makers ... You begin to see this thing isn't wholly the defense of the country, but only more money for some who are already fat cats.'[22] He commented that 'the munitions makers are making tremendous efforts towards getting more contracts and in fact seem to be exerting undue influence over the senators.'[23] He was particularly suspicious of Symington, who had close contacts with Convair, the prime contractor for Atlas missiles. Thomas Lanphier, for example, a vice-president of Convair, was a former Symington aide.[24]

Eisenhower's position in the debate on defence spending was weakened by his inability to reveal intelligence information. He was contemptuous and furious over 'the way irresponsible officials and demagogues are leaking security information and presenting a misleading picture of our security situation to our people. Some of our senators in particular are doing this.'[25] Eisenhower was hamstrung by his inability to use intelligence sources to refute these arguments, especially information from U-2 flights. The number of U-2 flights over the Soviet Union in 1959–60 was severely restricted, owing to Eisenhower's fear of a mishap. Nevertheless, there were four flights in 1959 and two in the spring of 1960, before the fatal last flight on May 1, 1960, when the U-2 flown by Francis Gary Powers was shot down. These U-2 flights helped to confirm Eisenhower's suspicion that Soviet ICBM production was much less advanced than the proponents of the Missile Gap suggested. Eisenhower constantly reiterated his case that, although in some areas of missile development and satellites the Soviets had a temporary lead, this was not strategically significant. He argued that after a slow start in the early 1950s, American missile production had, since the mid-1950s, been very rapid and impressive, which should be a source of pride, not of a 'hangdog attitude of humiliation'.[26] He totally rejected the need for a crash programme of increased defence spending. 'We must guard against feverish building of vast armaments to meet glibly predicted moments of so-called "maximum peril",' he said. 'The threat we face is not sporadic or dated: it is continuous.'[27] He constantly stated not only the adequacy of America's defence but its formidable power. 'We have got a much more variegated, balanced style of defensive organization than they have,' he said, 'and we believe that with the dispersal of our planes and supported as they are with the missiles that we have developed, that we have a very splendid posture today in the whole security field.'[28] Yet, however forcefully Eisenhower presented his case and however reassuring he tried to be, he remained vulnerable to the charges of his critics that he was sacrificing the nation's security on the altar of a balanced budget.

Restraining defence spending was, in Eisenhower's view, crucial in maintaining American prosperity. Despite the recession of 1957–58 and 1960–61 and the accusations of Democrats of a lower than necessary growth rate, the overall perception of America in the late 1950s was of a very affluent society. Eisenhower had earlier said that 'No government can inoculate its people against the fatal materialism that plagues our age. Happily, our people, though blessed with more material goods than any people in history, have always reserved their allegiance to the kingdom of the spirit, which is the true source of that freedom we value above all material things.'[29] By the end of the 1950s, there was an increasing sense of unease and guilt over the great affluence of the vast majority of Americans. There was not yet the discovery of poverty that occurred in the early 1960s, especially with the publication in 1962 of Michael Harrington's book, *The Other America*.[30] There was a vague sense at the end of the 1950s that all was not as well as it should be. Eisenhower did not respond very directly to this development. He was sceptical over allegations of a growing sense of malaise and a loss of national purpose.

'I am not concerned about America losing its sense of purpose,' he said. 'We may not articulate about it, and we may not give daily the kind of thought to it that we should. But national purpose is deeply rooted in American traditions dating back to the Declaration of Independence and the Constitution, which give the nation a justified basic confidence in its values and its direction.'[31] His main goal was to maintain a healthy economy, with low inflation, low unemployment and a balanced budget. He felt that a steadily growing economy, which encouraged thrift and enterprise, provided the best avenue of assistance to the socially deprived. He felt, moreover, that private initiative at the local level was the proper source for providing aid for deep-seated social problems rather than the Federal government.

Eisenhower demonstrated a similar reluctance to involve the Federal government in the field of civil rights. After the high drama of the Brown decision in 1954, the Montgomery bus boycott in 1955 and Little Rock in 1957, civil rights faded somewhat into the background in the later 1950s. By 1959, however, there was a worrying increase in the number of violent incidents, particularly the burning down of churches, which were often the centre of black protest, and the murder of civil rights activists. In February, 1960, a sit-in was organised at the lunch counter at Woolworth's in Greensboro, North Carolina, which attracted widescale publicity and triggered off the spread of the sit-in as a form of direct action to bring about an end to racial segregation and discrimination. New Civil Rights organisations had developed, such as SNCC (Student Non-Violent Coordinating Committee), which added a sharper cutting edge to the Civil Rights movement.

Eisenhower's inclination was not to involve the Federal government and not to attempt a solution by means of new legislation or government programmes. As always, he favoured local initiatives and a gradualist approach. 'Coercive law is powerless', he wrote to Ralph McGill, the editor of the Atlanta *Constitution*, 'when in any extensive region the mass of public opinion is in bitter opposition.'[32] Yet, Eisenhower realised that the danger of social disorder and the grave damage to America's reputation internationally made it incumbent on the Federal government to take action of some kind. In February, 1959, Eisenhower sent a Special Message on Civil Rights to Congress, proposing a Civil Rights bill, including a range of measures. The FBI, it was proposed, should be given additional investigative authority in cases of the destruction of churches or schools and the flight of fugitives who were involved in such crimes from one state to another should be made a Federal offence. The powers of the Attorney-General to inspect voting records were to be broadened.

Financial assistance was to be given to states as they adjusted to school desegregation. A Commission on Equal Job Opportunities under Government Contracts was to be established, while the Civil Rights Commission, which had been created by the Civil Rights Act of 1957, was to have its life extended by a further two years. Opposition in Congress from Southern Democrats made it unlikely that a Civil Rights bill including all of these measures would be passed. Lyndon Johnson, however, was keen to pass another Civil Rights bill. The Civil Rights Act of 1957 had been deemed to have been ineffective, and Johnson wished to demonstrate Federal government support for civil rights, both as a point of principle and also as a boost to his chances of winning the Democratic nomination for president in 1960. A Civil Rights Act was, therefore, passed in 1960, though its provisions were quite limited. The shipping of explosives across state lines for use against churches or schools was made a Federal offence. The life of the Civil Rights Commission was extended for two years, and the power of the Attorney-General to inspect voting records was increased. The Act made little substantial impact, though it carried some symbolic significance.

The symbolic action that made the deepest impact in the field of civil rights in the last years of the Eisenhower administration, however, occurred during the 1960 presidential election campaign. On October 19, 1960, Martin Luther King was arrested in Atlanta, Georgia, for participation in a sit-in at a department store. Since he had been given a suspended sentence previously for a traffic violation, he was denied bail and sent to prison. The Attorney-General, William Rogers, who was a close ally of Richard Nixon, ordered a statement to be drafted protesting against King's unjust treatment and declaring that the president had directed the Justice Department 'to take all the proper steps to join with Dr. Martin Luther King in appropriate action for his release'.[33] Before the bureaucratic process of gaining presidential approval for this statement had been completed, however, the Kennedy campaign had seized the opportunity. John F. Kennedy phoned Coretta King, Martin Luther King's wife, to express his sympathy. Robert Kennedy, John F. Kennedy's brother and campaign manager, phoned the judge in Martin Luther King's case to state his objection to the denial of bail in a case of misdemeanour. The next day King was released. The episode received massive media coverage. Martin Luther King's father, Martin Luther King, Sr, a highly respected black clergyman, announced that he was switching his vote from Nixon to Kennedy. The increased black voters that Kennedy gained in the 1960 election as a result of the King episode was, especially in marginal states such as Illinois, crucial to Kennedy, who, unlike, for example, Hubert Humphrey, had no previous history of commitment to the cause of civil rights.[34]

Aside from civil rights, Eisenhower's greatest problems arose in trying to mould the Republican party in his image and in grooming a successor who could win the presidential election in 1960 and would continue his policies. With Knowland's departure from the Senate to contest unsuccessfully the governorship of California, Everett Dirksen became the Senate Majority Leader. In the House of Representatives, Charles Halleck successfully challenged Joseph Martin for the post of House Minority Leader. Eisenhower's relations with Dirksen and Halleck were much better than with Knowland and Martin. Eisenhower enjoyed the weekly meetings with legislative leaders much more in 1959–60 than previously, and he found them more constructive. Also, with the domineering, austere figure of Sherman Adams gone, replaced by the very personable Jerry Persons, Eisenhower conducted more personal meetings with political figures himself and spoke to them more frequently on the telephone. Nevertheless, Eisenhower continued to make little progress in achieving party unity behind his vision of modern Republicanism. Nelson Rockefeller, who had emerged as the champion of East coast liberal Republicanism and who had won election as Governor of New York in 1958, favoured high levels of defence expenditure and more liberal fiscal policies, which were designed to achieve a higher economic growth rate. At the other extreme, Barry Goldwater, senator for Arizona, emerged as the most articulate spokesman for right-wing conservatism. Goldwater denounced the 'dime store New Deal' of modern Republicanism. He criticised Eisenhower's failure to reduce spending on domestic programmes. In Goldwater's radical view, Federal responsibilities in social welfare, education, housing and urban renewal should be transferred entirely to the states, while the Tennessee Valley Authority and all other public power projects should be privatised and farm subsidies brought to an end.

Eisenhower denied the charge, made against him in his last two years, that he was moving away from a centrist position to a more conservative position. His adamant insistence on a balanced budget perhaps made him seem more conservative, since in other respects he was very far from a conservative such as Goldwater. 'I do not see any difference as far as I am concerned', he said, 'between Modern Republicanism or another term that I liked, Theodore Roosevelt's, which was "Progressive Republicanism".'[35] But Eisenhower made little effort to heal the rift between moderate and conservative Republicans. Indeed, his insistent emphasis upon his standpoint as a Modern Republican created, as David Reinhard argues, 'a good deal of internal ill-will. It implied that old-fashioned, regular, unhyphenated Republicanism was not good enough, and it made the Republican party an object of abuse by its own leader. Conservative Republicans, especially, resented this.'[36] His rhetoric tended to be undiplomatic and provocative to the right-wing rather than soothing and conciliatory in an attempt to create a consensus. Most people, he said, for example, 'like the broad highway stretching before them and they understand here is where human progress is achieved. Those that would insist on making the gutters of the extremes of the right and the left are, in the long run, always refuted.'[37]

In the Congressional elections in 1960, the Republicans recovered some of the ground that they had lost in 1958, picking up two seats in the Senate and twenty-four in the House of Representatives. But the Republican party was clearly the minority party, with thirty-six Republicans and sixty-four Democrats in the Senate and 178 Republicans and 259 Democrats in the House. Republican prospects had not been helped by internal divisions nor by Eisenhower's inability to project an appealing image of modern Republicanism, which would win majority support in the country. Eisenhower had hoped to achieve the type of success attained in Britain by his close friend and ally, Harold Macmillan, who won a resounding re-election victory in 1959 at the head of a Conservative party that seemed to be modern, progressive and the natural party of government. Eisenhower felt that he had quite clear principles and that his viewpoint should attract wide support. There appeared, however, to be serious deficiencies in communication. 'For a long time', he said, at the beginning of 1959, 'I have been calling together people from the Republican party and friends of the party to ask them to undertake very earnest studies of exactly what we should do to get on a better road of explaining what we are about, and what we are doing.'[38] As it came across to the general public, however, 'Modern Republicanism amounted to little more than a smorgasbord of liberal and conservative offerings,' as David Reinhard puts it. 'It lacked philosophical backbone. Nor did Ike make any real effort to build up Modern Republicanism or attend to state and local political affairs in order to bring about such a change in his political party.'[39]

Even more so, Eisenhower failed to groom a successor as president to try to ensure a continuation of his policies. Nixon seemed to be the clear heir apparent, especially after Rockefeller withdrew from the race in December, 1959. Yet Eisenhower let known his reservations about Nixon, which were highly publicised and which dealt a severe blow to Nixon's candidacy. The 1960 presidential election was extremely close, with

Kennedy winning by a very narrow margin. In such a race, any one of a number of factors can be alleged to have determined the outcome. One such factor was undoubtedly the perception of ambivalent support for Nixon on Eisenhower's part. It is not inaccurate to state that Eisenhower cost Nixon and the Republicans the presidential election in 1960.

Eisenhower made statements of strong support for Nixon on numerous occasions. 'Mr. Nixon has been close to me for something over seven years,' he said, for example, in February, 1960. 'In all that time, I know of no occasion when he has been excluded from any important group in conferring for the making of policy or deciding upon matters and never once I know of has Mr. Nixon been at any major variance with me. I think I've made clear many, many times the great respect I have for his capacities and his character.'[40] Such statements were received with scepticism, however, by the press and public. It was widely known that Eisenhower had seriously considered dropping Nixon from the ticket in 1956. It was true that Nixon had been included in discussions of all matters of policy, since Eisenhower took very seriously his responsibility to prepare the vice-president for succession to the presidency in the event of the president's death. Eisenhower was highly critical of Franklin Roosevelt's cavalier approach to this matter, which had resulted in a quite unprepared Harry Truman being plunged into the presidency in 1945. But Nixon had not been brought into the inner councils of Eisenhower's confidants and Eisenhower did not even have close social contacts with Nixon.

Eisenhower took the public position that Nixon's nomination should not be regarded as a foregone conclusion but that it was proper and in the best interests of the Republican party that the door should be left open for the emergence of any other candidates, in order to provide the strongest possible field. 'I am not dissatisfied with the individual that looks like he will get it,' Eisenhower said, 'not by any manner of means. I just simply say that there's a number that could perform the duties of the office with distinction.'[41]

With Rockefeller too much of an East Coast establishment liberal for Eisenhower's taste and Goldwater the champion of the extreme far right, which Eisenhower detested, Nixon was in fact not only the available man and the virtually inevitable candidate, but he was also ideologically as close to Eisenhower's position as Eisenhower was likely to find. Nixon showed some inclination towards supply side economics, as he demonstrated in a speech at Harvard University in 1958, and he was a little more inclined towards higher defence spending than Eisenhower. But these were disagreements of detail and emphasis, not basic ideological differences. Also, as his vice-presidential candidate Nixon chose Henry Cabot Lodge, who not only balanced the ticket very well, with Nixon from California and Lodge from Massachusetts, but who was personally close to Eisenhower and who was ideologically, as David Reinhard puts it, 'a high priest of Modern Republicanism'.[42] Nixon had shown considerable skill in keeping channels open to both the liberal and the conservative wings of the Republican party, while his conduct of affairs, such as during Eisenhower's illness or on his trips abroad, marked him as a very well-qualified candidate for president. Eisenhower's seemingly tepid support for Nixon, however, culminated in his gaffe at a press conference on August 26, 1960, when, in response to a question on Nixon's role as vice-president, which asked for 'an example of a major idea of his that you have adopted', Eisenhower replied, 'If you give me a week, I might think of one. I don't remember.'[43] In context, Eisenhower's curt remark came at the very end of a press conference, at which he had already twice been asked a similar question about Nixon's role and he had given a measured response on the issue of influence on presidential decisions.[44] It was, moreover, not uncommon for Eisenhower at press conferences to state that he would look up the matter and give an answer the next week. If the incident had been an isolated case, it might be thought that these were hastily-delivered words, which the press unfairly put out of context. The episode, however, seemed to be part of a pattern in Eisenhower's relations with Nixon. Eisenhower later phoned Nixon to apologise over his unfortunate remarks, but the damage had been done. As Charles Alexander puts it, 'Once more, Eisenhower, whose capricious streak seemed most evident when the subject of Nixon came up, had left the impression that he did not really respect the man.'[45] Furthermore, not only during the election campaign but throughout his last year in office Eisenhower had refused to make compromises in economic policy that Nixon had wanted for political reasons in order to lower unemployment and to ease credit in the run-up to the election.

Eisenhower was fairly inactive during the 1960 presidential election campaign, initially by mutual agreement with Nixon, so that Nixon did not appear in Eisenhower's shadow but showed his ability to stand on his own feet and demonstrated his readiness to assume the nation's highest office. In the late stages of the campaign, Eisenhower's health limited his role, at the particular insistence of Mamie Eisenhower.[46] With regard to Eisenhower's overall role in Nixon's bid for the presidency, however, Stephen Ambrose concludes that 'Eisenhower's contribution to Nixon's campaign was worse than unhelpful – it actually lost Nixon votes, and probably the election.'[47]

One reason for Eisenhower's ambivalent support for Nixon, it might be suggested, was Eisenhower's regret that he was not the candidate himself. Opinion polls indicated that if Eisenhower had been a candidate in 1960 he would have been easily re-nominated and re-elected. Eisenhower had made many statements about the seduction of power and the illusion of indispensability leading other figures to hang on too long. There is clear evidence, however, that if the Twenty-second Amendment to the constitution barring a third term had not been introduced in 1952, he would probably have run again in 1960, despite his age and uncertain health. He said, with regard to the third term amendment, that 'On balance it was an unwise amendment.'[48] On another occasion he said that 'I would rather see it repealed than be kept.'[49] When asked directly at a news conference, 'Had there been no third term amendment, would you now be considering in your mind running for a third term,' he replied that 'The answer . . . is "no".'[50] In private, however, he was much less definite. When Everett Dirksen and Charles Halleck at a meeting of Republican legislative leaders broached the subject of repeal of the Twenty-second Amendment, Eisenhower said, not altogether in jest, 'You won't hurt my feelings if you speak to repeal – and maybe if I read some of your eloquent speeches I'd be convinced!'[51] He came to modify his views on the Twenty-second Amendment, saying that 'I'd see some advantages and disadvantages on both sides . . . I don't feel too strongly about it.'[52] By the end of the presidency, he concluded that 'Finally, I came, on balance . . . to decide that I believe that the two-term amendment was probably a good thing.'[53] Nevertheless, Sherman Adams records that some of Eisenhower's aides had felt that, but for the Twenty-second Amendment, Eisenhower would have run for a third term, and Adams agrees with this opinion.[54] Michael Beschloss writes that 'His son John privately agreed with other members of the White House staff that, had the Twenty-second Amendment not barred him a third term, the President would probably have run for re-election in 1960.'[55] Stephen Ambrose writes more definitely that 'Had the Twenty-second Amendment not prevented him from running again, he would surely have done so.'[56]

When the election returns came in, Eisenhower felt very low. Kennedy's margin of victory was just over 100,000 votes. A switch of 32,000 votes in Texas and Illinois would have given the victory to Nixon. There were rumours of voting irregularities in both these states. Eisenhower called Attorney-General William Rogers on November 30, 1960, saying that 'he was much disturbed about continuing allegations of fraud in the election' and asking Rogers to look into the matter.[57] Rogers replied that Nixon felt that a challenge could produce constitutional paralysis and that the matter should not be pursued, and Eisenhower accepted this.[58]

Eisenhower was depressed by the election result not only because the Democrats had won power but also because he regarded the 1960 election as a referendum on his presidency. Eisenhower held a low opinion of John F. Kennedy. As Robert Dallek writes, 'Ike saw the Kennedys as arrivistes and Jack as more celebrity than serious public servant, someone who had done little more than spend his father's money to win political office, where, in the House and Senate, he had served without distinction.'[59] The Republican defeat and Eisenhower's sense of failure and rejection arose not only from issues of domestic affairs but also to an important degree from some very significant and dramatic issues of foreign policy.

Chapter 8

Détente and Disappointment, 1959–60

The freeze in the Cold War that had existed since the Hungarian Revolution continued into early 1959, especially with the Berlin crisis. Khrushchev continued to display flamboyant arrogance, which seemed threatening and dangerous. By the spring of 1959, however, a thaw began to appear in the Cold War. Eisenhower, especially after Dulles' death in April, 1959, seemed more open to new approaches in foreign policy. Like Churchill in his last days in office, Eisenhower became eager to break the deadlock in international tensions by personal diplomacy, particularly summit meetings and goodwill tours. Khrushchev began to be seen as a mercurial figure, whose blustering boastfulness was viewed as a sign of an impetuous nature rather than a mark of unrelenting hostility. The rising swell of hope and goodwill in 1959 and the spring of 1960 was set to culminate in a summit meeting in Paris in May, 1960, followed by a visit by Eisenhower to the Soviet Union in June, 1960. All of these hopes, however, were shattered by the U-2 incident in May, 1960, when the U-2 flown by Francis Gary Powers was shot down on May 1, 1960. Moreover, closer to home, the revolution in Cuba led by Fidel Castro was seen by Eisenhower as an expansion of Soviet-backed Communism into Central and South America rather than as an indigenous social revolution, and plans were laid for a CIA-backed overthrow of Castro. Meantime, there were increasing difficulties in Vietnam as well as elsewhere in the Third World. The Eisenhower presidency ended, therefore, in an atmosphere of tension and crisis rather than détente and goodwill, which had seemed possible from mid-1959 to mid-1960.

In January, 1959, the Soviet Union drew up a draft peace treaty with East Germany, to give substance to Khrushchev's threat of November, 1958, that unless a settlement was reached on Berlin within six months he would sign a peace treaty with East Germany, which would give control over the access routes from West Germany to Berlin to the East Germans. Eisenhower took a firm, unequivocal stance in defence of

Western rights with regard to Berlin. He was well aware of the enormous symbolic significance of Berlin. 'Not only the integrity of a single city', he said, 'but the hope of all free peoples is at stake.'[1] On the other hand, he rejected proposals to take military measures, which would seem provocative or an extreme overreaction, such as an increase in American ground troops in West Germany or a highly-publicised emplacement of new IRBMs in West Germany or the threat to send an armed column down the autobahn from West Germany to Berlin if control of access routes was given to East Germany. Likewise, he rejected hastily-devised, somewhat vague proposals for a change in the status of West Berlin to become a 'free city'. Berlin, he said, was 'a symbol of freedom', but 'its name has come to symbolize, also, the effort of Imperialistic Communism to divide the free world, to throw us off balance, and to weaken our will for making certain of our collective security'.[2] As he put it more colloquially, 'Let's not make everything such a hysterical sort of a proposition. We ought to keep our steadiness.'[3] At a meeting with the Congressional leaders, John S. D. Eisenhower noted that 'The President stressed the necessity to avoid overreacting. In so doing we give the Soviets ammunition. The President stressed that Khrushchev desires only to upset the United States . . . They would like us to go frantic every time they stir up difficulties.'[4] In February, 1959, Harold Macmillan went on a visit to Moscow and reported to Eisenhower that Khrushchev's deadline on Berlin was not really an ultimatum. On March 2, 1959, the Soviets sent a note that was more conciliatory and suggested a four-power Foreign Ministers conference. It became apparent that Khrushchev wished to be invited to visit the United States and also to have a four-power summit meeting, so that these were bargaining chips that could be used to persuade Khrushchev to relax the May 27 deadline on Berlin. As William L. O'Neill writes, 'The main issue was not so much settled as talked to death. Russia kept putting back the deadline until it disappeared, as did the crisis.'[5] Khrushchev was invited to the United States and the tension of the Berlin crisis eased. 'Eisenhower's wise and firm leadership', as Chester Pach and Elmo Richardson put it, 'helped turn a moment of danger into an opportunity to improve Soviet-American relations.'[6] As even post-revisionists concede, then, Eisenhower had demonstrated impressive statesmanship in the successful defusion of a potentially explosive crisis.

The harsh tone of US–Soviet exchanges began to ease by the spring of 1959, while the number of visits and personal meetings increased. In early 1959 Eisenhower used such expressions as 'the obviously, palpably intransigent attitude of Mr Khrushchev'.[7] With regard to Berlin, Eisenhower said that 'last November the Soviets announced that they intended to repudiate these solemn obligations. They once more appear to be living by the Communist formula that "Promises are like pie crusts, made to be broken".[8] Yet, Berlin, Eisenhower suggested, was not an isolated instance but was typical of Soviet behaviour. 'We have lived and continue to live', he said, 'in a period when emergencies manufactured by the Soviets follow one another like beads on a string.'[9] By the spring of 1959, this abrasive tone of expression began to be modified. At the same time, in the first half of 1959 there were several visits by leading Soviet figures to the United States and by Americans to the Soviet Union. Eisenhower supported this development, since it helped, he believed, to 'get behind each other's facial expressions and to see what we are really thinking'.[10]

In January, 1959, First Deputy Premier Anastas Mikoyan visited the United States, and in June, 1959, First Deputy Chairman of the Council of Ministers Frol Kozlov came to America. In May, 1959, Averell Harriman, who had been American ambassador to the Soviet Union during the Second World War and more recently Governor of New York, 1955–58, visited the Soviet Union and met leading Soviet figures, including Khrushchev. Most visibly, Vice-President Richard Nixon visited the Soviet Union in July, 1959, to open the American International Exhibition in Moscow, where he engaged in his famous Kitchen Debate with Khrushchev, which was a mixture of banter and barbed comment about the strengths and weaknesses of Communism and capitalism. The culmination of these exchanges of visits came with the invitation to Khrushchev to visit the United States in September, 1959. Eisenhower had come to believe that an informal meeting with Khrushchev might be helpful in melting some of the ice of the Cold War and in allowing by means of personal interchange a better mutual understanding on the part of the leaders of the United States and the Soviet Union. While Dulles had been Secretary of State, his stern demeanour and the impression that Soviet leaders had of his controlling influence on American foreign policy undermined the potential asset of the projection of American foreign policy in the much more human, attractive embodiment of Eisenhower as a straightforward, decent, democratic leader of goodwill. Harriman reported that Khrushchev had said to him about the Geneva summit in 1955 that 'It was most embarrassing if not unpleasant to note the manner in which Mr. Eisenhower had behaved at Geneva, not as a maker of policy but as an executor of Mr. Dulles' policies. Mr. Dulles, sitting on his right during the conference, had simply passed Eisenhower notes which the latter had then read out without contributing anything of his own.'[11] Khrushchev expressed this point in more graphic terms in his memoirs, writing that 'That vicious cur Dulles was always prowling around Eisenhower, snapping at him if he got out of line.'[12] With Dulles' resignation and death in early 1959 and his replacement by the less domineering figure of Christian Herter, Eisenhower, though he greatly missed Dulles' expertise for which he had great respect, felt something of a sense of liberation in his ability to conduct personal diplomacy, especially as he realised that his time in office was drawing to a close.

Khrushchev's visit to the United States and his personal meetings with Eisenhower were more successful than Eisenhower had expected. In a ten-day tour of the United States, Khrushchev was portrayed as a jovial, somewhat eccentric, cuddly bear type of figure rather than as a threatening grizzly, while his personal meetings with Eisenhower were cordial. Eisenhower liked to entertain guests at his farm at Gettysburg and in particular to show off his herd of Angus cattle. While most guests displayed little interest in the cattle or the farm, Khrushchev, who was of peasant stock, shared Eisenhower's enthusiasm over every small detail about the herd of cattle and other matters on the farm. This helped to strike up a bond, which was further developed over cocktails in the lounge at the farm as well as during a weekend at Camp David. These good personal relations created the so-called 'spirit of Camp David'. Whereas the 'spirit of Geneva' in 1955 had been ephemeral and insubstantial, the spirit of Camp David had promising embodiment. It was agreed that Khrushchev's visit to the United States should be reciprocated by a visit by Eisenhower to the Soviet Union in June, 1960, preceded by a four-power summit meeting in Paris. Most substantially, on the final day at Camp David, Khrushchev agreed to withdraw the threat regarding Berlin, bringing the Berlin crisis to an end.

In the autumn of 1959, Voice of America broadcasts to the Soviet Union ceased to be jammed. In January, 1960, Khrushchev announced a cut in the Soviet military of over a million personnel. Eisenhower announced in his State of the Union message in January, 1960, that 'Recent Soviet deportment and pronouncements suggest the possible opening of a somewhat less strained period in relationships between the Soviet Union and the Free World.'[13] Eisenhower's scepticism with regard to a summit meeting gave way to hopeful anticipation. In March, 1959, Eisenhower had said to Harold Macmillan with regard to a summit conference that 'Neville Chamberlain went to such a meeting and it is not the kind of meeting with which he intended to be associated.'[14] He had always rigidly adhered to the view that a summit conference would have no value unless progress was made at a lower level, such as at a Foreign Ministers' meeting, and he looked with a jaundiced eye at the barren results of Foreign Ministers' meetings throughout the 1950s. 'If those foreign ministers cannot prepare the ground and sow some of the seed for accord,' he said, 'then I see no use whatsoever for trying to have a harvest when there is no planting and no tilling.'[15] Progress appeared to be being made at the lower level by the spring of 1960, however, so that when Macmillan visited Eisenhower in March, 1960, he found that, in contrast to a year earlier, Eisenhower appeared to be caught up in summit enthusiasm. Eisenhower took Macmillan on a tour of the battlefield at Gettysburg, as he often did with guests, and talked optimistically about the possibility of regular summit conferences, frequent ministerial meetings and an expansion of cultural agreements.[16] Eisenhower also looked forward to his visit to the Soviet Union in June, with its itinerary of visits to the Kremlin in Moscow, the Hermitage in St. Petersburg, Kiev, and finally a return to Moscow, where he was to be given an honorary degree at Moscow State University.

At the same time, prospects were becoming much more promising with regard to a nuclear test ban. By early 1959 Eisenhower had become convinced that the health hazards from nuclear tests in the atmosphere constituted a matter of significant concern. He felt, moreover, that a ban on atmospheric tests was a more achievable goal than a comprehensive test ban. He shifted, therefore, from his position of insistence upon a comprehensive, verifiable test ban to a more flexible position of an atmospheric test ban as a first step. Diplomatic negotiations and technical investigations produced good results by the spring of 1960, making it seem possible to reach agreement on more than only an atmospheric test ban. A treaty was drafted for a ban on all tests except small underground tests. A few final details needed to be agreed upon, with regard to inspection and to the duration of the treaty, but it was hoped that those matters could be resolved at the Paris summit. Eisenhower became optimistic that a significant agreement could be reached on a test ban, which could lead on to his dream of substantial disarmament, with a significant reduction in the resources and skills that were diverted from peaceful purposes to the production of devastating weapons of massive destruction. He wrote to Harold Macmillan that 'All of us – including Mr. K. – seem in accord on one subject: the need for progress in controlled disarmament . . . I would derive tremendous satisfaction out of seeing some specific practical step agreed upon at the Summit, and initiated as soon as practicable. Such an accomplishment would be tangible evidence of some progress in a knotty problem that has engaged your effort and mine for a number of years. It would be a ray of light in a world that is bound to be weary of the tensions brought about by mutual suspicions, distrust and arms races.'[17]

Looming in the background, however, was an issue with the potential to blow all of those plans apart, namely, overflights of the Soviet Union by U-2 aircraft. U-2 flights had been suspended in April, 1958, but they were due to be resumed in 1959. Eisenhower was very uneasy over the matter. His son, John, recorded that 'The President is very reserved on the request to continue reconnaissance flights on the basis it is undue provocation. Nothing, he says, would make him request authority to declare war more quickly than violation of our air space by Soviet aircraft.'[18] Eisenhower was only prepared to accept that 'while one or two flights might possibly be permissible he is against an extensive program'.[19] Moreover, no flights were permitted while the international situation remained tense as a consequence of the Berlin crisis. Secretary of Defense McElroy pointed out, however, that at a closed session of the Senate Foreign Relations Committee on January 16, 1959, he had been unable to blunt Congressional attacks with regard to comparative US and Soviet missile capabilities. Nathan Twining, chairman of the Joint Chiefs of Staff, also pressed for renewed overflights to obtain up-to-date information, especially with regard to Soviet ICBMs. Eisenhower tried to weigh up intelligence needs and diplomatic interests. He pointed out, as his son, John, noted, 'the close relationship between those reconnaissance programs and the crisis which is impending in Berlin . . . The President believes it would be most unwise to have world tensions exacerbated by our pursuit of extensive air reconnaissance flights over the territory of the Soviet Union.'[20]

On April 6, 1959, despite considerable reservations, Eisenhower acceded to the request of CIA Director Allen Dulles for a resumption of U-2 flights. The next day, however, April 7, 1959, Eisenhower called in Richard Bissell, CIA Director of Operations, and Secretary of Defense McElroy to inform them that he had decided not to go ahead with U-2 flights, at least in the immediate future. Eisenhower based this decision on the grounds that the United States no longer needed further detailed information for targeting in the event of a war with the Soviet Union, that U-2 flights undermined the possibilities of an improvement in relations through diplomacy, that world opinion would be against the United States in the event of discovery of these flights and that in the near future reconnaissance satellites would be able to provide photographic intelligence information, without the same problems over violation of air space. Eisenhower agreed on the difficulties that were created by the need for information on Soviet missile production, which, he said, was 'highlighted by the distortions several senators are making of our military position relative to that of the Soviets, and they are helped in their "demagoguery" by our uncertainties as to Soviet programs'. But Eisenhower 'was concerned over the terrible propaganda impact that would be occasioned if a reconnaissance plane were to fail'.[21] Pressure to resume U-2 flights continued, however, from the CIA and the Defense Department. Eisenhower sought the opinion of the new Secretary of State, Christian Herter, who responded that 'the intelligence objective in his view outweighs the danger of getting trapped'. Eisenhower, therefore, warily decided that 'in view of the unanimous recommendation of the officials having the operating responsibility, he would assent to the operation being conducted'.[22]

The U-2 flight that took place on July 9, 1959, brought back excellent photographs from Tyuratam and other sites. Eisenhower did not permit further U-2 flights over the summer of 1959, with Nixon's visit to Moscow and Khrushchev's visit to the United States in September. Significantly, Khrushchev did not raise the subject of the U-2 in his conversations with Eisenhower during his visit, perhaps due to reluctance to admit that the Soviet Union was powerless to prevent these flights. On December 6, 1959, and on February 10, 1960, U-2s were flown over the Soviet Union by RAF pilots, authorised by Harold Macmillan. Bissell had been keen to involve Britain in the U-2 programme in order to share the burden of responsibility and to provide moral support to help to ease Eisenhower's grave misgivings. On April 9, 1960, an American pilot flew a U-2 over the area around Pletesk, 600 miles north of Moscow, where the Soviets were making progress on the development of an operational ICBM. The Pentagon and CIA were eager to gain further details about this development, which would indicate the rate of progress of Soviet ICBM deployment.[23] With the impending Paris summit due to meet on May 15, Eisenhower was extremely reluctant to give permission for another U-2 flight. He agreed, however, to give permission, provided that the flight took place no later than May 1. A date of April 25 was set, but due to weather conditions the flight was delayed until the very last permissible date, May 1.

On May 1, 1960, the fateful, final flight of a U-2 over the Soviet Union took off from Peshawar, Pakistan, piloted by Francis Gary Powers. Codenamed Operation Grand Slam, it was the most ambitious U-2 flight that had been attempted. It was the first U-2 flight scheduled to traverse the Soviet Union rather than to return to its starting point. It was due to fly 3,800 miles, with 2,900 miles over Soviet territory, in nine hours and land in Bodo, Norway. It was tracked by Soviet radar from its entry into Soviet airspace. Soviet detection of flights had steadily improved as well as, more ominously, Soviet air defences. The range of surface-to-air (SAM) missiles had extended from 50,000 feet to 60,000 feet, with the ability to reach 70,000 feet but with a loss of accuracy at such a height. In the vicinity of Sverdlovsk, a SAM missile exploded near the plane, causing incapacitating damage but did not injure or kill the pilot or destroy the plane. This was a much worse outcome from the US point of view than a direct hit that killed the pilot and destroyed the plane. The pilot, however, had been provided with the means to take his own life, though he was not directly ordered to do so in this eventuality. The cruder means of a cyanide pill, which had been provided on earlier flights, had been updated by a pin smeared with algal, an extremely lethal shellfish toxin, with which the pilot could prick himself and cause instant death. Powers opted against suicide and bailed out. There was, however, a self-destruct device that would blow up the plane seventy seconds after bail-out, but, due to the damage caused by the SAM missile, Powers was unable to reach the button to activate this device. The plane therefore crashed to the ground but it did not disintegrate, revealing its surveillance equipment and making evident the purpose of the flight. Powers descended by parachute, where he was apprehended and handed over to Soviet authorities.

When Powers failed to arrive at Bodo, the American authorities assumed that the plane had gone down, but they also assumed that Powers would be dead and that the plane would have been blown to pieces. Eisenhower was informed, and the prepared cover story was issued that a weather plane had gone off course and strayed over Soviet territory. The Soviet response was, as Khrushchev gloatingly announced, that they had recovered the fuselage of the plane and inspected its surveillance equipment and that they had taken the pilot into custody. Eisenhower's worst nightmare had come to pass. Khrushchev denounced the blatant act of espionage by intrusion into Soviet airspace and ridiculed the ludicrous false cover story of the weather plane. Khrushchev chose to seek maximum propaganda advantage from the incident. He left open to Eisenhower the opportunity to deny personal knowledge of the operation and to place the blame on unauthorised underlings, while Khrushchev demanded an apology from Eisenhower and an assurance that there would be no recurrence. Eisenhower decided to take full responsibility, since to place the blame on unauthorised subordinates would not only be false but would create the impression that Eisenhower was not firmly in control of the US government. Eisenhower was willing to give assurance that there would be no recurrence of a U-2 flight over Soviet territory, but he refused to apologise. He stated that Soviet rejection of Open Skies had meant that the United States had been vulnerable to the danger of surprise attack, which had necessitated reconnaissance flights to gain information on Soviet offensive capabilities.

The U-2 incident clearly endangered the Paris summit meeting. Khrushchev did not immediately cancel Soviet participation but tantalised the West over two weeks by maintaining the possibility that the summit conference might still proceed. Khrushchev came to Paris and dominated the headlines with flamboyant denunciations of American espionage. When the summit conference convened on May 16, Khrushchev delivered a scathing speech condemning America, and the Soviet delegation then walked out of the meeting. When the Soviets did not appear for the session on the morning of May 17, Charles de Gaulle, as host of the summit meeting, sent a note to Khrushchev stating that the Soviet delegation should attend the afternoon session or give a written explanation. The Soviet reply was that the Soviet delegation would attend only if the Americans agreed 'to condemn the treacherous incursion of American military aircraft into Soviet airspace, publicly express their regrets for this intrusion, punish those responsible and give assurance that in future there will be no further incursions'.[24] Eisenhower refused to accept these terms. The summit therefore broke up and the invitation to Eisenhower to visit the Soviet Union was withdrawn.

The Cold War reverted to freeze. On June 27, 1960, the Soviets walked out of the test ban talks in Geneva, destroying any hope of progress on a test ban or disarmament. On July 1, an American RB-47, which was flying over international waters at least thirty miles from the Soviet Union, was shot down and two crewmen who bailed out were taken into Soviet custody. In September, Khrushchev came to New York to attend the meeting of the General Assembly of the United Nations. On September 22, during a speech by Harold Macmillan, Khrushchev made noisy interruptions from the floor and then proceeded to take off a shoe and banged it on his desk. The presiding officer, in an attempt to restore order in this extraordinary situation, pounded his gavel so hard that its head broke off and flew into the air. Eisenhower's quest for peace and détente had ended not only in tragedy but in farce. His efforts to reduce tensions and to create greater stability in East–West relations were, as one historian has put it, 'given a finale more appropriate to a musical comedy'.[25]

Eisenhower was deeply depressed by the turn of events. His Science Adviser George Kistiakowsky records that at the end of May, 1960, Eisenhower 'began to talk with much feeling about how he had concentrated his efforts in the last few months on ending the Cold War, how he felt that he was making big progress and how the stupid U-2 had ruined all his efforts. He ended very sadly that he saw nothing worthwhile left for him to do now until the end of his presidency.'[26] To rub salt in the wound, on August 19, 1960 – ironically, the day on which Gary Powers was sentenced to imprisonment for espionage in a court in Moscow – photographic intelligence was successfully received for the first time from a reconnaissance satellite. Covering a wider swathe than an aircraft, the satellite covered wide areas of territory and gathered vast amounts of intelligence, without the problems of intrusion into another country's airspace. Satellite reconnaissance became the mainstay of American intelligence on the Soviet Union. Eisenhower had achieved Open Skies after all, but the U-2 disaster had taken the gloss off this success.

Richard Bissell later wrote, rather lamely, that 'There is now no doubt we should have been more sensitive about planning a flight so close to the summit date.'[27] The U-2 programme had undoubtedly produced invaluable evidence, which above all had confirmed Eisenhower's suspicions that Soviet missile development was less advanced than Soviet propaganda and American proponents of the missile gap claimed. 'As Eisenhower had suspected', Curtis Peebles writes, 'Khrushchev had exploited Soviet missile and space achievements to create the illusion of great missile strength.'[28] Yet, given Eisenhower's great wariness over the risks and dangers involved in U-2 flights, his authorisation of the fatal last flight, on May Day, so close to the summit meeting, against his better judgement, was the most ill-advised decision of his presidency, for which he paid an extremely heavy price.

Meanwhile, closer to America's shores, in Cuba, a serious new aspect of the Cold War was developing. In the American view, the Cuban revolution began with much promise but then turned sour and dangerous. On January 1, 1959, Fidel Castro drove into Havana in a tank and brought to an end the tyrannous, corrupt rule of Fulgencio Batista, under which Cuba had suffered for decades. Castro had great mystique as a romantic revolutionary – a young, bearded, Jesuit-educated son of the middle-class, who had fought with courage and organised with determination to rid his country of an appalling régime. As for its replacement, however, Castro sent a mixed message, with references to liberal as well as to left-wing figures as his sources of guidance and inspiration. Once in office, some ominous signs appeared. Revolutionary tribunals held widespread trials, with large numbers of summary executions. No elections were held. Many liberal figures were removed from office, while the Communist party was legalised and a number of Communists were given positions in the government. In April, 1959, Castro visited the United States. He was fêted by the press and public, who treated him like a star.

Eisenhower was sufficiently disturbed by events in Cuba, especially the executions, that he decided not to meet Castro. Instead, Castro met Nixon, who concluded that Castro was not a Communist but that he was politically naïve and was liable to be manipulated by the Communists.

Castro enacted agrarian reform, including the expropriation of large estates and prohibition of ownership of land by foreigners. By late 1959 most American direct investment in Cuba had come under threat. An ominous turning point came in February, 1960, when Castro hosted a Soviet trade fair and negotiated a commercial treaty whereby the Soviet Union agreed to purchase one million tons of Cuban sugar over the next five years and to provide $100 million in credit to Cuba for the purchase of Soviet goods. Cuba began to import Soviet oil, but American oil refineries in Cuba were ordered by the US government not to process crude oil that was imported from the Soviet Union. Castro retaliated by taking control of American oil refineries, which, like many other American companies, were nationalised. Castro appeared to be moving steadily into the Communist camp. Many commentators and historians suggested that it was American policy that drove Castro in that direction. Stephen Rabe, however, in his well-balanced evaluation, argues that 'Throughout most of 1959, the administration did not deliberately provoke Castro or try to undermine the revolution. Key officials . . . wanted to work with Castro. Indeed, they seemed fascinated by the bearded revolutionary.'[29] Rabe concludes that 'U.S. actions probably influenced the *pace* of revolutionary change in Cuba rather than its ultimate direction.'[30] In September, 1960, when Khrushchev came for his infamous visit to the United Nations, he held a highly-publicised meeting with Castro, whom he enveloped with a bear hug and a huge smile. US–Cuban relations continued to deteriorate through the autumn of 1960. A trade embargo was imposed by the United States, and on January 3, 1961, the United States broke diplomatic relations with Cuba.

By early 1960 Eisenhower had concluded that Castro was a serious threat to American interests, not only in Cuba but as a potential instigator of the spread of Communism throughout Latin America. Harold Macmillan suggested to Eisenhower that if it came about 'that an increasingly powerful movement was growing up in and outside the country, bent on restoring the revolution to its intended course, it might not be wiser to let the yeast rise of its own accord. Or at least for them to be very unobtrusively supported from the United States.'[31] Eisenhower, however, planned much more direct, behind-the-scenes action. In February, Eisenhower instructed Allen Dulles to make plans for Castro's removal. The CIA devised a variety of schemes, many of which, as the Church committee in 1975 revealed, were quite bizarre and which included plots to assassinate Castro. There is no evidence that Eisenhower knew of these assassination plans, and Eisenhower in any event believed that if Castro was assassinated he might be succeeded by an even more radical figure, such as Ché Guevara. Eisenhower wished a well-planned covert operation, based on CIA support for a well-prepared counter-revolutionary force, which would not only remove Castro but firmly establish a government that was favourable to American interests. In his State of the Union message in January, 1960, Eisenhower stated that 'The United States has no intention of interfering in the internal affairs of any nation.'[32] He had, of course, every intention of interfering in the internal affairs of Cuba, as he had done in Iran in 1953 and in Guatemala in 1954. On March 17, 1960, Eisenhower approved a CIA plan to build up the Cuban opposition and to undermine the Castro régime. CIA Director of Operations Richard Bissell was instructed to create a programme to develop a paramilitary exile force and a Cuban government-in-exile and to beam anti-Castro propaganda into Cuba. By August, 1960, a 500-strong exile force had been established in Guatemala, and plans were laid that an invasion of Cuba by this force would receive support from air strikes by the US Air Force from bases in Nicaragua. The build-up of the exile force continued through the autumn of 1960, increasing in number to 700. Eisenhower was concerned that no government-in-exile was agreed upon and that the exile force was a motley collection of very disparate anti-Castro elements. Moreover, the presence of the training camp in Guatemala was well-known locally, so that it had to be assumed that Cuban intelligence was aware of it. Nevertheless, although Eisenhower had not taken a final decision on the matter, plans for an invasion of Cuba by the exile force were well advanced by the end of the Eisenhower administration. As Mark Gilderhus puts it, 'The unsolved Cuban problem, a kind of diplomatic tiger trap, awaited the untested new administration of John F. Kennedy.'[33]

Aside from the negative approach of covert action, however, Eisenhower developed more fully a positive response to the threat of Castroism in the form of devoting more attention to Latin America and increasing American economic aid, while encouraging Latin American social and economic reform. Eisenhower became more responsive to the idea that had been advanced since the early 1950s by experts on Latin America, especially his brother, Milton. In the early 1960s Eisenhower had been prepared to be content to accept complacently any Latin American régime that was reasonably pro-American, whether it was a military dictatorship or otherwise ideologically unsuitable. It had been considered unrealistic for the United States to attempt to encourage social, political and economic reform by means of a Marshall Plan for Latin America or any such ambitious programme of American economic aid, which Congress would not be willing to fund. By 1959–60, however, Eisenhower had developed more progressive policies in relation to Latin America, and the challenge of Castroism sharpened the focus of his attention in this matter.

In early 1960 Eisenhower went on a goodwill tour to Argentina, Brazil, Chile and Uruguay. He was warmly welcomed in all of these countries and pressed for higher levels of loans to Latin American countries through the Inter-American Development Bank, which had been established in 1958. Even more so, he strongly supported the Social Progress Trust Fund, which was an imaginative new scheme introduced in July, 1960, to underwrite reform in Latin American countries that qualified for aid by introducing progressive developments in health, education and land reform. Eisenhower's objective was not only the promotion of social and economic development but also an enticement to Latin American governments to reform unjust social and political structures, which would make them less susceptible to overthrow by a Castroite revolution than authoritarian, socially unjust régimes.

Eisenhower's policy towards the rest of the Third World followed a similar pattern to his policy towards Latin America. He was willing to use covert action in a ruthless fashion, but at the same time he devoted more personal attention to Third World countries and supported an increase in economic aid for the Third World. In the Congo, where Patrice Lumumba appeared to be shaping into a Castro type of figure, who might win widespread support for his left-wing radical views throughout Africa, Eisenhower took no steps to restrain the CIA's plans to remove Lumumba, which ended in his assassination. At the same time Eisenhower gave a higher priority to personal contact with the leaders and peoples of Third World countries as well as allies. In December, 1959, Eisenhower undertook an extensive tour to Rome, Ankara, Karachi, Kabul, New Delhi, Tehran, Athens, Tunis, Madrid and Casablanca. The tour was extremely successful, with a warm welcome from large crowds at every stop on the way. Eisenhower had somewhat belatedly discovered the very valuable asset for American foreign policy of his appeal worldwide. As the British ambassador to the United States reported, 'the administration has exploited the President's personal popularity'.[34] The tour not only made Eisenhower re-assess the value of personal diplomacy, but it also convinced him to a greater extent of the need to assist Third World countries. In areas such as the Middle East, the Eisenhower Doctrine was quietly dropped, while foreign aid to Egypt was increased in 1960 to $153 million.

A not dissimilar policy was pursued, though with somewhat different results, in the potentially extremely dangerous situation in Vietnam. Eisenhower used covert action to try to destabilise the North Vietnamese government, but by 1959–60 this was quite ineffective. Massive economic aid continued to be poured into South Vietnam, but its impact was limited. At a time, however, when Vietnam was given little attention compared to crisis areas such as Cuba and Berlin, the American view of events in South Vietnam continued to be based on illusory wishful thinking. A report by a sub-committee chaired by Senator Mike Mansfield, for instance, concluded that the American aid programme to Vietnam should be 're-shaped' in order 'to make it more efficient and eventually to bring about a termination of the need for it as Vietnam achieves a reasonable means of economic self-sufficiency'.[35] The reality, however, was a seriously deteriorating situation in Vietnam. Opposition to Diem's régime became increasingly extensive. Moreover, ominously, North Vietnam became involved and began not only to give training in guerrilla warfare tactics to Viet Cong who went to North Vietnam but also sent North Vietnamese cadres to South Vietnam to fight alongside the Viet Cong. Diem attempted to improve the situation with the introduction of 'agrovilles', whereby, like the strategic hamlets introduced by the Americans in the 1960s, South Vietnamese in the countryside were brought into guarded compounds. The programme, which was very unpopular and drove many South Vietnamese to join the Viet Cong, was abandoned in 1960. Diem survived an assassination attempt in 1960, but it led him to be even more reclusive and authoritarian. In January, 1959, Eisenhower said in a speech that 'The loss of South Vietnam could, as it progressed, have grave consequences for us and for freedom.'[36] By the end of 1960, however, the situation in Vietnam had deteriorated to the extent that the loss of South Vietnam to Communism seemed virtually certain unless a drastic change of policy took place both within South Vietnam and in American policy towards South Vietnam.

Eisenhower was just as concerned over the possible loss to Communism of Laos as of South Vietnam. Indeed, the crisis in Laos at the end of Eisenhower's administration was even more acute than in Vietnam. In 1959 confusion had continued in Laos. The conservative Phoui Sananikone became prime minister and, with the support of and interference from military factions, ruled without Pathet Lao representation in government. This drove the Pathet Lao into violent opposition, so that by 1960 there was widespread guerrilla activity and virtual civil war. The King attempted to achieve a political settlement by bringing back as prime minister Souvanna Phouma, who again formed a coalition with the Pathet Lao.

Conclusion

Following the election on November 8, 1960, Eisenhower remained in office in the period of interregnum until his successor's inauguration on January 20, 1961. The transition was reasonably smooth and orderly. Eisenhower met Kennedy twice for a briefing, on December 6, 1960, and on January 19, 1961, the day before Kennedy's inauguration. Although Eisenhower had many reservations with regard to Kennedy, he was gracious and dignified, so that there was no hint of the awkward, embarrassing atmosphere of Eisenhower's transition with Truman (with whom Eisenhower was finally reconciled after meeting at Kennedy's funeral in 1963).

Eisenhower's one other major task during the interregnum was his Farewell Address on January 17, 1961. 'In the councils of government', he warned, 'we must guard against the acquisition of unwarranted influence, whether sought or unsought, by the military industrial complex.'[1] He had coined a memorable new phrase, 'the military industrial complex', which entered the language and helped to make his Farewell Address receive greater attention than perhaps any Farewell Address since George Washington's in 1797. Yet, although the phrase was new, the idea was certainly not. Rather, it was a brief, eloquent statement of the theme that he had emphasised since the beginning of his presidency, as was the case with regard to the other themes of his Address. He stressed the need for a mature appreciation of the long-term nature of the ideological conflict. 'We face a hostile ideology – global in scope, atheistic in character, reckless in purpose and insidious in method,' he said. 'Unhappily the danger it poses promises to be of indefinite duration. To meet it successfully, there is called for, not so much the emotional and transitory sacrifices of crisis, but those which enable us to carry forward steadily, surely and without complaint the burdens of a prolonged and complex struggle.'[2] He regretted that the danger of a catastrophic war was still very real. 'As one who has witnessed the horror and the lingering sadness of war,' he said, 'as one who knows that another war could utterly destroy this civilization which has been so slowly and painfully built over thousands of years, I wish that I could say tonight that a lasting peace is in sight. Happily, I can say that war has been avoided.'[3] His dream of turning swords into ploughshares had, therefore, attained no fulfilment. 'Disarmament, with mutual honor and confidence, is a continuing imperative,' he said. 'Together we must learn how to compose differences, not with arms, but with intellect and decent purpose. Because this need is sharp and apparent I confess that I lay down my official responsibilities in this field with a definite sense of disappointment.'[4]

Following Kennedy's inauguration on January 20, 1961, Eisenhower retired to his beloved farm in Gettysburg. He was given an office in Gettysburg College and he took an active interest in the College's affairs. One of his main activities was the writing of his memoirs. With the assistance of a team of researchers, he published *Mandate for Change, 1953–56*, in 1963, and *Waging Peace, 1956–61* in 1965.

Eisenhower was not impressed by the performance in office of his Democratic successors, John F. Kennedy, 1961–63 and Lyndon Johnson, 1963–69. He regretted that Kennedy's economic policies resulted in budget deficits in 1961 and 1962 rather than the budget surpluses that Eisenhower had planned. To an even greater extent, he deplored the extreme liberal approach of Lyndon Johnson in his War on Poverty and Great Society. As for foreign policy, he disagreed with Kennedy's defence build-up, even after Kennedy could see that there was no missile gap – or, more accurately, that there was a large gap but that the shortfall was on the Soviet side rather than on the American side. With regard to Vietnam, the commitment of American troops by Kennedy and the massive escalation of the war by Johnson was a serious departure from Eisenhower's foreign policy of caution, restraint and avoidance of a land war in Asia. Nevertheless, Eisenhower had consistently regarded Vietnam as a cornerstone in the edifice of containment in Asia. He was consulted on Vietnam, as on other matters, by Kennedy and even more extensively by Johnson. He gave loyal support, discretely refraining from even a hint of public criticism. But in his declining years he was saddened by the course of events in the nation's public life. He supported Nixon for president in 1968 unreservedly, and he was delighted that before his death in March, 1969, Nixon was inaugurated as president in January, 1969, and his grandson, David, married Nixon's daughter, Julie.

From the mid-1960s his health deteriorated and he suffered several further heart attacks. In 1968 he was moved to Walter Reed Hospital in Baltimore, where he remained until his death. On March 28, 1969, he sensed that his end was approaching. With his son, John, and grandson, David, at his bedside, he asked to be pulled up straight in bed, so that he was sitting firmly upright. In his last words he said, 'I want to go. God, take me.' He then sank into a coma and died a few hours later.[5]

While Eisenhower had been unimpressed by the dynamic activism of the early to mid-1960s, this mood of the times played an important part in the contemporary portrayal of his presidency as ineffective, unimaginative and in serious need of replacement. To Kennedy's admirers, Eisenhower was a useful counterpoise of a tired old leader, lacking in vigour or ideas, in contrast to the exciting, dynamic, charismatic JFK. Liberals viewed Eisenhower with scorn. Arthur Schlesinger, Jr, dismissed him as 'an indifferent and passive president'.[6] The New Frontiersmen of the Kennedy administration, as Jim Heath puts it, 'exuded confidence in their ability to solve problems, right wrongs and make the world a better, safer place to live. Particularly after the drabness of the Eisenhower administration.'[7] Schlesinger wrote that America of the Eisenhower era had projected an image of 'an old nation of old men, weary, played out, fearful of ideas, change and the future', compared to the brilliance of John F. Kennedy, who 'lifted us beyond our capacities and gave the country back to its best self'.[8] This resulted in very unfavourable evaluations of Eisenhower's term in office. Norman Graebner wrote that 'Never has a popular leader who dominated so completely the national scene affected so negligibly the essential historical processes of his time.'[9] Commentators such as Walter Lippman, Marquis Childs and William Shannon were scathing in their assessment of Eisenhower's presidency. 'Eisenhower is a transitional figure,' Shannon wrote. 'He has not shaped the future nor tried to repeal the past. He has not politically organized nor intellectually defined a new consensus . . . The Eisenhower era is the time of the great postponement.'[10]

Shortly before his death in 1969 the first signs had begun to appear of Eisenhower revisionism. The new generation of the 1960s, full of self-proclaimed intellectual brilliance and contemptuous of confining restraints, found that social problems were not so susceptible to rapid solutions and that intervention in war did not necessarily produce swift success by means of clever new technology and the use of Green Berets. By the end of the 1960s, the 'best and the brightest', as David Halberstam described them, seemed to have led America into disaster and division, produced by their arrogance, conceit and imprudence.[11] In the changing circumstances the image that Eisenhower had conveyed as president, which New Frontier liberals had derided as old-fashioned and stale, began to be re-viewed as appealingly sensible and reassuring. In 1967, Murray Kempton published the first Eisenhower revisionist article, which attracted wide attention.[12]

In the 1970s the opening of Eisenhower's papers in his presidential library in Abilene produced a flood of books on Eisenhower that thoroughly revised the interpretations of his presidency that had been written in the late 1950s and early 1960s. These revisionist accounts totally debunked the caricature image of the dim-witted soldier who spent most of his time on the golf course and who was out of his depth in politics and was manipulated by powerful subordinates. No serious student of Eisenhower's presidency gives any credence to this interpretation of Eisenhower. The matter, however, is more complex. Eisenhower's skilful, deliberate cultivation of a 'hidden-hand' approach brought him considerable political benefits, but it deceived not only the general public but also the writers of the first accounts of his presidency, so that it needed the revisionists of the 1970s and 1980s to peel back some of the layers of deliberate deception, which Eisenhower had created, in order to gain a better appreciation of the much more complex figure underneath. The rather surprising nature of the discovery that Eisenhower was much more guileful and politically shrewd than expected, led, as post-revisionists validly argued, to an overemphasis on Eisenhower's political skills and methodology at the expense of a balanced evaluation of the substance of his policies.

Before presenting such an assessment, however, it is necessary to evaluate his methodology in some detail. His celebrated hidden-hand approach was a contributory factor to his consistent popularity, which was reflected in his high standing in the opinion polls, which averaged 64 per cent throughout his presidency. This added considerable weight to his authority. As Godfrey Hodgson has written, 'The President's effective power is very much a function of his standing in the polls.'[13] Hence, for example, only twice in his eight years in office was his veto overridden in Congress. His popularity, however, was derived from more fundamental matters than merely presenting a somewhat folksy, apolitical image. Eisenhower succeeded to an important extent in fulfilling the role of the president who embodies the aspirations of the American people. The presidency of the United States involves a great deal more than leadership of the government. As Clinton Rossiter put it, 'The framers of the Constitution took a momentous step when they fused the dignity of a king and the power of a prime minister in one elective office.'[14] As Erwin Hargrove has written, 'It is appropriate to study the presidency as intellectual history.'[15] Hence, just as important as any policies that were enacted is what the president symbolised to the nation, and the feelings and reactions that the president generated among the people. Eisenhower symbolised, above all, stability and reassurance. 'He was a stabilising force in a time of conflict,' as Herbert Parmet observes.[16] Clinton Rossiter suggests that Eisenhower fulfilled the role that had been inadvertently created when the framers of the Constitution 'gave us a father figure that should satisfy even the most demanding political Freudians'.[17] The need for stability was obvious, following the traumas of the Great Depression, the Second World War and the beginning of the Cold War. One of Eisenhower's main qualifications which enabled him to provide the required stability and reassurance was equally obvious, namely, his successful command of the armed forces in the Second World War. Yet, to an almost surprising degree, Eisenhower's style of presidential leadership lacked any semblance of military bearing. Dressed in civilian clothes, with a lack of hauteur and a punctilious concern for every detail of constitutional propriety, his approach was wholly civilian. Nevertheless, there was a fundamental awareness that he was a leader who had discharged enormous responsibilities in successful command during times of great trial in war, and this added immeasurably to his authority. Moreover, he conveyed the sense of duty of the old soldier reluctantly recalled to service rather than a self-serving, conniving politician. He was quite an effective communicator. His public image was enhanced by his very photogenic smile, while his personality defect of a very nasty temper was reserved only for private life and was never displayed in public. More substantially, he was a competent, if not particularly inspiring public speaker. His most significant form of communication was through news conferences. He held more news press conferences than any president before or since. Held almost every week throughout the presidency and televised from 1955 onwards, very few of his news conferences reveal anything of either the bumbling garbled syntax of his caricature image or the cunning deception of the hidden-hand approach. Overwhelmingly, the news conferences were straightforward, well-informed, relatively brief, reasonable answers to reporters' questions.

The methodology that Eisenhower employed with the greatest success was similar to his approach as a military commander, namely, the development of a consensual approach. As David Kennedy has written, Eisenhower's skill lay in his ability 'to fathom and manipulate the human equation . . . A careful student of war, Ike was a still more careful student of human psychology, especially of those elements that made up the mysterious compound of effective leadership.'[18] Eisenhower's appeal, Robert Dallek suggests, 'derived from a genuine personality and unaffected naturalness'.[19] He did not exploit his war hero status and he lacked the elements of the characteristics that would win the application of the term 'charismatic'. But he had a somewhat magnetic appeal, which enabled him to energise others, combined with considerable skill in defusing crises, enabling disparate groups and individuals to work together and in drawing out the best in people rather than creating clashes.

At a more mundane level, Eisenhower's methodology was effective in that it was tidy and well-organised. Contrary to the myth of his excessive delegation of power, he employed an effective staff system of administration, which created a pyramid of power, freeing him from involvement in small details but leaving the final decision on important matters to the president. Emmet J. Hughes wrote that Eisenhower was 'a weak and irresolute man' who 'delegated the powers of the presidency slackly and carelessly'.[20] A study of the full record of Eisenhower's administration demonstrates overwhelmingly that this is simply not true. Eisenhower had a carefully organised system, which employed delegation sensibly and effectively. He did not delegate in the manner of Ronald Reagan's somewhat lazy approach nor did he immerse himself in every minute detail in the style of Jimmy Carter. Neither did he tolerate the sloppy, disorderly administrative methods of Bill Clinton or Franklin Roosevelt. He maintained a well-organised administrative system, which enabled him to conduct affairs in a business-like fashion and which left the final decision on important matters to himself.

Of more substantial significance, however, than an evaluation of Eisenhower's methodology is an assessment of his policy achievements. As Erwin Hargrove has written, 'The debate about whether Ike was a skilful politician cannot enlighten us until we perceive the president's purpose.'[21] As Michael Mayer puts it, 'Once the old image of Eisenhower had been laid to rest the scholars began to debate the nature and wisdom of Eisenhower's policies.'[22]

Eisenhower's record of achievement, viewed in its most complimentary terms, can be summed up in the phrase, peace and prosperity. Both of those matters, however, require detailed analysis in order to gain a balanced evaluation of Eisenhower's achievements.

Stephen Ambrose summarises Eisenhower's foreign policy accomplishments in the phrase, 'He made a peace and he kept the peace.'[23] The debate continues on how Eisenhower was able to make peace early in his administration by ending the Korean War. Clearly there were conditions, such as war weariness on all sides and a new government in the Soviet Union, which made more possible the attainment of peace. Moreover, it is a debatable matter whether Eisenhower's tactics to end the war, stepping up bombing and making veiled threats about the possible use of atomic weapons, were instrumental in leading to the ceasefire. It is clearly the case, however, that when the opportunity arose to end hostilities in

Korea, for whatever reasons this opportunity arose, Eisenhower responded vigorously and skilfully to take the opportunity and to bring the fighting to an end. With his campaign promise of an end to the Korean War fulfilled, Eisenhower's leading priority was to keep the peace, which he succeeded in doing. As to how this was accomplished, Richard Damms, in a post-revisionist account, places emphasis on 'contingency and luck'.[24] Eisenhower most emphatically felt otherwise. As he said in an interview with Stephen Ambrose, 'We kept the peace. People ask how it happened – by God it didn't just happen, I'll tell you that.'[25] The evidence broadly supports Eisenhower's view and suggests that the grudging post-revisionist view is an inadequate explanation.

The major policy which Eisenhower pursued for the preservation of peace was the steady pursuit of containment. Once the furore over the 1952 campaign pledge of liberation had settled down, Eisenhower continued the policy, which had been established in the late 1940s, of a sustained build-up of Western strength, involving a clear, long-term commitment to international involvement, including close ties with NATO allies and heavy expenditure in Mutual Security programmes, in order to deter Soviet aggression and to enhance stability. In such crises as over Hungary and Berlin Eisenhower maintained a firm hand in defence of Western interests, while trying to avoid provocation or misunderstanding. Eisenhower built up formidable American military strength, but by placing greater reliance on the nuclear deterrent rather than on conventional weapons he ensured that the cost of defence did not overstrain the American economy. At the same time, with his eloquent speeches on the wasteful diversion of resources from peaceful to military purposes, he gave clear signals of his desire for a peaceful resolution of problems. Moreover, his embodiment of a decent, democratic American approach helped to allay anxieties at home and abroad. His quest for détente built up slowly and gradually and was on the verge of attaining fulfilment by 1960, when it was blown off course by the U-2 incident, which distorted his record by producing an atmosphere of crisis and tension at the end of his administration rather than of peaceful progress.

Eisenhower's critics, however, suggest that there were serious flaws in his foreign policy. He squandered opportunities for détente, it is argued, especially early in his administration. He maintained an ideologically rigid stance, which was confrontational and dangerous. His misreading of progressive, nationalistic movements as Kremlin-backed insurgencies created serious problems in both his administration and in leaving to his successor poisoned chalices in places such as Cuba and Vietnam. His projection of an image of decent, democratic values was overwhelmed by the image of the ugly American – domineering, hegemonistic, self-righteous and hypocritical, supporting undemocratic, repressive régimes whenever it suited American interests.

Eisenhower manifestly adhered consistently to an approach of virulent anti-Communism. His wartime cooperation with the Soviets and his willingness in 1945–47 to consider the possibilities of continuing Soviet–American cooperation did not leave an enduring mark upon him. From 1947 onwards his stance was unreserved condemnation of Communism as a system and of the ruthless and wicked means that Communists employed to seize and hold on to power. This led him undoubtedly to tend to view all conflicts, especially in the Third World, through the prism of a Cold War perspective. The left-wing government of Mossadegh in Iran was regarded as Communist, as was the régime in Guatemala of Arbenz. The overthrow of Mossadegh and his replacement by the Shah was regarded as holding back the advance of Communism in Iran, which the Soviets had been attempting since the end of the Second World War. The overthrow of Arbenz in Guatemala was felt to have reduced the prospects of Kremlin-backed Communism spreading throughout Latin America. Similar approaches were employed in such countries as the Congo and, above all, in Cuba, following Castro's accession to power. Eisenhower rigidly pursued a policy of undermining régimes and movements that were regarded as Communist, with virtually no consideration of a more flexible, tolerant, pluralistic approach, accepting different social and political systems rather than insisting on black and white differences between the free world and Communist tyranny. It is not the case that John Foster Dulles ran American foreign policy in the Eisenhower years. It is true, however, that Eisenhower, who made the ultimate decisions on foreign policy, agreed essentially with the morally rigid position that Dulles more visibly embodied and articulated, such as refusal to accept neutralism but insistence on a clear stance on one side or the other in the ideological conflict.

Eisenhower realised that poverty and deprivation were the fertile breeding ground of Communism and that the United States should play a leading role in assisting in social and economic development in more backward countries as a means to encourage them to choose a non-Communist direction. Eisenhower was liberal in his support for foreign aid. He was willing to give support to nationalistic movements, even if they were radical, provided that they were not Communist. In the Middle East, for example, the United States was willing to support Nasser in the early 1950s. Once a movement seemed to show any sign of turning towards Communism, such as Nasser in the late 1950s, or Castro in 1959–60, the Eisenhower administration turned strongly against it. Although Eisenhower did not support Britain in invading Nasser's Egypt, the United States moved swiftly after the Suez crisis to restore good relations with Britain and France, so that in the late 1950s the United States did not retain any benefit that had been acquired in the Arab world for the American stance in the Suez crisis, but instead was seen as a self-righteous, domineering power, obsessed by narrow-minded anti-Communism. It is a matter of debate whether events in Cuba and Vietnam after 1960 were set on a course by the Eisenhower administration from which his successors had little choice but to follow or whether Eisenhower could have handled the issues without American involvement in conflict. It is beyond dispute, however, that Eisenhower's legacy in these two countries was of a situation of dire peril. Nor is the evidence convincing that Eisenhower's personality significantly altered the image of America abroad in the 1950s. Eisenhower is open to the criticism that he did not attempt to utilise his advantage as an internationally-recognised war hero and liberator and the embodiment of America as a land of opportunity for even a boy from a humble rural background in Kansas. His tours in 1959 and 1960 were of benefit in this regard, but throughout his presidency anti-Americanism was strong even in friendly countries such as Britain.

Eisenhower's caution in his pursuit of détente is perhaps more defensible. In the uncertain world of 1953, with serious divisions and apprehensions with America, the opportunity for solid progress towards détente was perhaps not as great as it may superficially have seemed following Stalin's death in March, 1953. With the Hungarian Revolution and Berlin crisis, the prospects for détente in the later 1950s did not seem good. Yet gradually Eisenhower built up a foundation for détente following the interchange of visits in 1959, culminating in Khrushchev's visit to the United States. With arrangements in place for a four-power summit meeting in May, 1960, followed by a visit by Eisenhower to the Soviet Union in June, which it was hoped would initiate a system of regular top level Soviet–American meetings, along with a broadening of cultural exchanges and people-to-people contacts, the scene appeared to be set for the flowering of détente at the end of Eisenhower's presidency. All of this was, of course, blown apart by the U-2 incident. On the one hand, it might be argued that this resulted from Eisenhower's weakness, agreeing to the final flight of the U-2 against his better judgement and, more fundamentally, arising from Eisenhower's inclination to seek quick-fix solutions by technological means rather than by patient, diplomatic negotiations. On the other hand, Eisenhower was clearly unfortunate that Soviet capabilities to shoot down a U-2 were developed just before the

Paris summit. The impact of the U-2 on the end of the Eisenhower administration was profound, including its impact on the 1960 presidential election and on the evaluation of Eisenhower's presidency. Without the U-2 incident, Nixon would probably have won the 1960 election and been well placed to pursue in the early 1960s the policy of détente that he so effectively pursued a decade later in the 1970s. Such an ending and succession to the Eisenhower presidency would have been likely to have produced a very different evaluation of Eisenhower's presidency by commentators and historians in the early 1960s.

Eisenhower's primary interest as president was in foreign affairs, but by no means to the neglect of domestic affairs. Richard Nixon said that 'I've always thought this country could run itself domestically without a president. All you need is a competent Cabinet to run the country at home . . . The President makes foreign policy.'[26] Eisenhower did not share this view. Unlike presidents such as Nixon and George H. W. Bush, Eisenhower was almost as interested and absorbed in domestic issues as in international affairs. This was particularly the case with regard to the economy. Eisenhower was proud of his record with regard to the economy. Median family income grew 30 per cent in the 1950s from $3,083 to $5,657. Prices rose a mere 1.4 per cent per annum. Eisenhower proudly wrote in his memoirs that 'The 1953 dollar had lost only $5\frac{1}{2}$ cents of its value by 1961.'[27] Unemployment was relatively low, at an average of 4.6 per cent. There were recessions in 1953–54, 1957–58 and 1960–61, but measures of government intervention had helped to ensure that the economy did not plunge into deep depression but instead recovered fairly rapidly. There were serious problems in agriculture, but the difficulties arose from abundance rather than scarcity. Underlying economic and scientific developments in agricultural production, together with strong political opposition to his policies in the farm states, rendered Eisenhower's agricultural policies ineffective. 'The whole farm situation remains a national disgrace,' he wrote in disillusionment.[28] In fact, however, the issue of government subsidies and supports for agriculture proved to be extremely difficult in all Western countries as well as in administrations before and after Eisenhower.

The prosperity of the times was in many ways due to underlying economic conditions rather than the consequence of government policies. For example, world economic conditions were particularly favourable to America, with competitors in Europe and Japan slowly recovering from the devastation of the Second World War, from which America had emerged unscathed and stronger. Nevertheless, the policies of the Eisenhower administration, together with the confidence that was given by

Eisenhower's presence in the White House, played a role of considerable importance in producing an enviable record of steady economic stability and prosperity.

The affluence of the society provided the basis for the development of an atmosphere of good feelings. Yet, it was a time of deep anxiety and fear as well as of prosperity and contentment. Eisenhower played an important role in providing calming reassurance, so that, despite the underlying tensions, he presided over a period of national goodwill. Legitimate debate continues over his approach to McCarthyism, but by the mid-1950s the poisonous atmosphere of the Red Scare and of the scandals of the last days of the Truman administration had given way to a much more relaxed atmosphere. Popular culture and entertainment flourished, especially film, television and music. Disneyland, Doris Day, Coca-Cola, *I Love Lucy*, John Wayne, Pat Boone, Elvis Presley, McDonald's, James Stewart, Marilyn Monroe, Rodgers and Hammerstein, drive-in movie theatres and much else besides provided a glut of popular culture that, despite the sneers of some intellectuals, was not only the envy of the world but made an enormous impact on the rest of the world. To an even greater extent than with regard to the economy, this flowering of American popular culture was largely due to underlying conditions within society rather than in any way the consequence of government policy. Nevertheless, Eisenhower seemed in some way to embody this aspect of the America of his time and, again, his reassuring presence as president contributed to the confidence and stability, which helped to produce an atmosphere in which such diverse creativity thrived.

Critics suggest, however, that Eisenhower encouraged a bland, uncritical, self-satisfied and self-congratulatory outlook, which blinded Americans from the grave social, political, cultural and environmental issues of the time. Emmet John Hughes accused Eisenhower of 'letting the political conscience of the nation slumber'.[29] Theodore Roosevelt stated that the presidency 'is pre-eminently a place of moral leadership'.[30] Eisenhower, his critics charge, presided over an era of 'the bland leading the bland'. The extent of poverty was not so much ignored as not even noticed. The same blindness was demonstrated with regard to environmental issues, in an age of gaudy, gas-guzzling automobiles. Charles Alexander writes that, 'the American people went on something of an ecological binge'.[31] Instead of facing up to the deficiencies within America, it is argued, self-glorification in extolling the wonderful virtues and successes of America predominated to an extreme extent. Eisenhower's defenders argue that the generation of Americans who lived through the Great Depression and the Second World War were entitled to the enjoyment of the material prosperity of their time and were justifiably proud of a prosperous and successful society in which so many were able to fulfil the American dream. Nevertheless, there is undoubtedly at least an element of truth in the view that American society of the 1950s was somewhat excessively self-glorifying and that Eisenhower to an extent encouraged such an outlook. In February, 1960, he set up a President's Commission on National Goals, but this did not report until after the election in November, 1960, and made little impact.

The charge of abdication of moral responsibility is made most strongly against Eisenhower with regard to civil rights. In his defence it is argued that his administration passed the first pieces of civil rights legislation since Reconstruction. Moreover, Eisenhower had an important point and reasonable argument in his advocacy of a gradualist approach to such a sensitive social issue, with emphasis on local initiative rather than the imposition of all-encompassing Federal programmes to be introduced rapidly, abrasively and with a tone of moral self-righteousness and in contempt for the local customs of Southerners. Nevertheless, it is clear that the Civil Rights Acts of 1957 and of 1960 were essentially token gestures, which were largely ineffective. Eisenhower, from an all-white small town in Kansas, who served for decades in a segregated army and who had many Southern friends and associates, manifestly had the racial prejudices of his time and background and favoured a pace of change in race relations so gradual as to be almost imperceptible. As Thomas Borstelman puts it, Eisenhower 'remained in part blinded by . . . nostalgia for the stability of the white-ruled era now slipping away'.[32] He did not even respond to any great extent, as might have been expected, to the damage to the reputation of the United States internationally by the crises in race relations in the 1950s. Pach and Richardson conclude that 'Civil rights revealed more dramatically than any other issue the shortcomings of Eisenhower's philosophy of government restraint.'[33] Even Eisenhower's strongest admirers have tended to be very critical of his record on civil rights. Stephen Ambrose writes that 'He missed a historic opportunity to provide moral leadership.'[34] Roy Wilkins, Secretary of the NAACP (National Association for the Advancement of Colored People), quipped that 'If Eisenhower had fought World War II the way he fought for civil rights, we would all be speaking German today.'[35] Eisenhower's record on civil rights is undoubtedly one of the most serious blemishes on his record.

A serious deficiency of a different nature was, it might be suggested, Eisenhower's inability to bequeath a legacy of modern Republicanism or to groom a like-minded successor and to work effectively for his successor's electoral victory in 1960. Eisenhower had strong political convictions, which became very apparent throughout his presidency. These were fundamentally homespun philosophical attitudes from his small-town origins, but they had been developed with a degree of sophistication in his dealings within the political process during his military career, especially with regard to budgetary procedures. Eisenhower was at the same time aware of the political price paid by the Republican party in Herbert Hoover's time for its policies, which gave the impression of a lack of concern for social and economic issues during a time of depression. Yet Eisenhower was unable to mould the Republican party into his image and to make it the majority party in the country and the natural party of government. The degree of government intervention in the recessions in 1953–54, 1957–58 and 1960–61 was popularly regarded as too limited, which, together with his very strong stand in favour of a balanced budget in 1959–60, resulted in a failure to lay to rest the ghost of Herbert Hoover. The result was that the Republican party paid the price in defeat in the Congressional elections from 1954 to 1960. Indeed, the cumulative loss of all offices across the nation by the Republicans from 1952 to 1960 was a somewhat staggering 24 per cent.[36] At the same time, the right wing of the Republican party regarded Eisenhower as too liberal. Eisenhower failed to mend fences with the right wing. He indulged in bitter denunciations of the extreme right, while presiding over a continuing and growing split, which further weakened the party's electoral prospects. Richard V. Damms seems to be justified in his conclusion that 'Eisenhower proved to be a rather ineffective party leader.'[37] Eisenhower's ineffectiveness can be explained to some extent by the nature of his symbolic representation of the nation's values rather than acting as a grasping, partisan politician, and Eisenhower played this broader role effectively. Also, as the landslide victories in the re-election victories of Nixon in 1972 and Reagan in 1984 illustrated, even a landslide victory in the presidential election does not necessarily result in similar levels of support for the president's party in the Congressional elections. Nevertheless, compared, for example, to Franklin Roosevelt, who successfully combined symbolic embodiment of the nation's ideals and at the same time party advantage, Eisenhower's performance as party leader seems weak. Given his strong convictions and his desire to leave a lasting impact on policy, Eisenhower's performance was unimpressive in winning broad support within his party or in enabling his party to win elections.

Eisenhower was even more inept in grooming a like-minded successor. He had obvious, well-publicised reservations about Nixon's suitability as his successor. Yet, while he humiliated and weakened Nixon by some of his remarks, he did not take effective steps to promote another more suitable candidate. His support for Robert Anderson, who, whatever his merits in some respects, had no political base or clear political skills, was naïve. Hence, instead of passing on the torch in January, 1961, to a reasonably like-minded successor, with a party broadly in line with his political philosophy of modern Republicanism, Eisenhower handed over power to a Democratic president who held somewhat liberal views, with a Democratic majority in Congress, while the Republican party was characterised by increasingly widening divisions as it headed towards its disastrous split and massive defeat in 1964.

Nevertheless, setting Eisenhower's blemishes and failures against his successes, Eisenhower's accomplishments provide an impressive record of achievement. Revisionist historians re-evaluated Eisenhower largely on the basis of his surprisingly high level of political skill. Post-revisionists accepted that Eisenhower was no political novice, but they questioned his accomplishments with regard to substantial achievement. It might be argued, however, that some of Eisenhower's most serious weaknesses were not in the area of substantial policy but – perhaps surprisingly – in the field of political skill, especially an inability to project policy achievements in a manner that reaped political rewards and benefits. His policies on keeping down defence costs, for example, and viewing sceptically the claims of Soviet military superiority were thoroughly sound, yet he was unable to win the political contest on this issue, allowing himself to be portrayed as unsound on defence and permitting a missile gap, which was part of the reason for his fatal decision to agree to the final U-2 mission. On economic policy he was unable to capitalise politically on a record of solid economic growth and prosperity but instead allowed the debate to be dominated by critics who either charged that his policies were neo-Hooverite or that they retarded stronger economic growth which more 'imaginative', riskier policies could achieve or, as right-wingers charged, they were modified New Deal measures.

The revisionists punctured the myth of the caricature of Eisenhower as a disengaged political neophyte, yet they perhaps created a new myth of a brilliant, Machiavellian political manipulator, whose historical reputation soared on the basis of his subtle political skills rather than, as post-revisionists objected, on the basis of an evaluation of his policy attainments. Post-revisionists in their turn created, if not a myth, then at least a distorted assessment, which was so reserved as to be disparaging about Eisenhower's substantial accomplishments. The reality, it might be suggested, is that Eisenhower's policy achievements were, in spite of a number of blemishes, very impressive, creating peace, prosperity and national goodwill, while his political skills were impressive in a number of respects but weak in other respects, causing him to fail to gain full political advantage from some of his most important policy achievements.

The evaluation of a president's record in office, however, is inevitably determined not only by the events during his time in office but by events in subsequent years. This is clearly the case with regard to Eisenhower. In the years since his term of office in the 1950s a tidal wave of social and political change has swept across America, profoundly altering American politics and society. This sweep of social change, including the sexual revolution, the women's movement, oil shocks, changing attitudes to race relations, mass immigration from Third World countries, and other such developments, transformed America in the last decades of the twentieth century. In many ways these changes were no doubt for the better, but they caused insecurities and uncertainties, which created a nostalgia for an apparently simpler time, such as the 1950s with Eisenhower in the White House. Such matters are of debatable validity in an evaluation of Eisenhower, since they relate to issues over which neither Eisenhower nor his successors had very much control. Of greater validity are comparisons between Eisenhower's policies and his successors' on matters over which the president had a greater degree of control, such as involvement in a land war in Asia, corruption in government or budget deficits. Following decades in which Kennedy and Johnson plunged America into the quagmire of Vietnam, Nixon created a constitutional crisis over Watergate, Ford and Carter presided over economic stagnation, Reagan and the two Bushes engaged in wild deficit spending and Clinton disgraced the office of president by scandal, it seems reasonable to judge that Eisenhower was a more successful president than any of his successors.

In comparison to his predecessors, Eisenhower could not be held to rise to the status of the greatest presidents, such as Abraham Lincoln or Franklin Roosevelt. The fairest comparison is with earlier presidents who, like Eisenhower, wielded power as a general before holding office as president. Of these the one with whom Eisenhower would be closely ranked is George Washington. Eisenhower would not be placed above the founding father of the nation. But if George Washington is justifiably acclaimed as first in war, first in peace and first in the hearts of his countrymen, Eisenhower can justifiably be ranked as a good second.

Notes

Introduction

1 John R. Alden, *George Washington: A Biography* (Baton Rouge: Louisiana State University Press, 1984), p.304.

2 Marquis Childs, *Captive Hero: A Critical Study of the General and the President* (New York: Harcourt, Brace, 1958); Emmet J. Hughes, *The Ordeal of Power: A Political Memoir of the Eisenhower Years* (New York: Atheneum, 1963).

3 Herbert S. Parmet, *Eisenhower and the American Crusades* (New York: Macmillan, 1972); Charles C. Alexander, *Holding the Line: The Eisenhower Era, 1952–1961* (Bloomington: Indiana University Press, 1975); Blanche W. Cook, *The Declassified Eisenhower: A Startling Reappraisal of the Eisenhower Legacy* (Garden City, NY: Doubleday & Co., 1981); R. Alton Lee, *Dwight D. Eisenhower: Soldier and Statesman* (Chicago: Nelson-Hall, 1981); Fred I. Greenstein, *The Hidden Hand Presidency: Eisenhower as Leader* (New York: Basic Books, 1982); Stephen E. Ambrose, *Eisenhower* (2 vols; New York: Simon and Schuster, 1983–84); Robert F. Burk, *Dwight D. Eisenhower: Hero and Politician* (Boston: Twayne Publishers, 1986).

4 Chester J. Pach and Elmo Richardson, *The Presidency of Dwight D. Eisenhower* (rev edn; Lawrence: University Press of Kansas, 1991), p.xiii. Recent books in the post-revisionist mould are Richard V. Damms, *The Eisenhower Presidency, 1953–1961* (London: Pearson, 2002) and Tom Wicker, *Dwight D. Eisenhower* (New York: Henry Holt, 2002). Recent works which are more adulatory but somewhat uncritical are William B. Pickett, *Dwight D. Eisenhower and American Power* (Wheeling, Ill: Harlan Davidson, 1995) and Geoffrey Perret, *Eisenhower* (New York: Random House, 1999).

5 Robert J. Donovan, *Confidential Secretary: Ann Whitman's Twenty Years with Eisenhower and Rockefeller* (New York: E. P. Dutton, 1988).

6 A discussion of studies of the major topics and personalities of the Eisenhower period and of works on the American presidency is contained in the Bibliography.

Prologue

1 Tom Wicker, *Dwight D. Eisenhower* (New York: Henry Holt, 2002), p.4.

2 Douglas Kinnard, *Eisenhower: Soldier-Statesman of the Twentieth Century* (Washington, DC: Brassey's, 2002), p.4.

3 Robert Griffith, ed., *Ike's Letters to a Friend, 1941–1958* (Lawrence: University Press of Kansas, 1984).

4 R. Alton Lee, *Dwight D. Eisenhower: Soldier and Statesman* (Chicago: Nelson-Hall, 1981), p.34.

5 Dwight D. Eisenhower, *At Ease: Stories I Tell to Friends* (Garden City, NY: Doubleday, 1977), p.181.

6 Matthew F. Holland, *Eisenhower Between the Wars: The Making of a General and a Statesman* (Westport, Conn.: Praeger, 2001), p.222.

7 Mark A. Stoler, *Allies and Adversaries: The Joint Chiefs of Staff, the Grand Alliance and US Strategy in World War II* (Chapel Hill: University of North Carolina Press, 2000).

8 John S. D. Eisenhower, *Allies: Pearl Harbour to D-Day* (Garden City, NY: Doubleday & Co., 1982), p.xxiii.

9 *Ibid.*, p.103.

10 Dwight D. Eisenhower, *Crusade in Europe* (Garden City, NY: Doubleday & Co., 1948), p.4.

11 Winston S. Churchill, *Second World War*, Vol. V, *Closing the Ring* (London: Cassell, 1952), p.418.

12 John S. D. Eisenhower, *Allies*, p.xiii.

13 Winston S. Churchill, *Second World War*, Vol. VI, *Triumph and Tragedy* (London: Cassell, 1954), p.476.

14 Griffith, ed., *Ike's Letters to a Friend*, p.111.

15 Eisenhower, *Crusade in Europe*, p.444.

16 Merle Miller, *Plain Speaking: An Oral Biography of Harry S. Truman* (New York: C. P. Putnam's Sons, 1973), pp.339–340.

17 *Life*, November 9, 1942.

18 Susan Eisenhower, *Mrs Ike: Memoirs and Reflections of the Life of Mamie Eisenhower* (New York: Farrar, Strauss & Giroux, 1996), pp.193–194.

19 John S. D. Eisenhower, ed., *Letters to Mamie* (Garden City, NY: Doubleday & Co., 1978), pp.104–105.

20 Kay Summersby Morgan, *Past Forgetting: My Love Affair with Dwight D. Eisenhower* (New York: Simon and Schuster, 1976).

21 John Eisenhower, ed., *Letters to Mamie*, p.11.

22 Stephen E. Ambrose, *Eisenhower: Soldier and President* (New York: Simon and Schuster, 1990), p.210.

23 John Eisenhower, ed., *Letters to Mamie*, pp.11–12.

24 John R. Deane, *The Strange Alliance: The Story of Our Efforts at Wartime Cooperation with Russia* (New York: Viking Press, 1947), p.217.

25 Ambrose, *Eisenhower: Soldier and President*, p.218.

26 Peter Lyon, *Eisenhower: Portrait of the Hero* (Boston: Little, Brown, 1974), p.356.

27 *Ibid.*, p.365.

28 Ambrose, *Eisenhower: Soldier and President*, p.225.

29 *Ibid*, p.233.

30 John S. D. Eisenhower, *Strictly Personal* (Garden City, NY: Doubleday & Co., 1974), p.172.

31 Churchill to Eisenhower, July 27, 1948, *Columbia University*, Vol. 10 of Louis Galambos et al., eds, *The Papers of Dwight D. Eisenhower* (Baltimore: Johns Hopkins University Press, 1978), p.686.

32 Herbert S. Parmet, *Eisenhower and the American Crusades* (New York: Macmillan, 1972), p.59.

33 Dwight D. Eisenhower, *The White House Years*, Vol. I, *Mandate for Change, 1953–1956* (Garden City, NY: Doubleday & Co., 1963), p.10.

34 Travis B. Jacobs, *Eisenhower at Columbia* (New Brunswick, NJ: Transaction Publishers, 2001), p.327.

35 Ambrose, *Eisenhower: Soldier and President*, p.232.

36 Eisenhower, *At Ease*, pp.371–372.

37 H. W. Brands, *Cold Warriors: Eisenhower's Generation and American Foreign Policy* (New York: Columbia University Press, 1988), p.189.

38 Milton S. Eisenhower, *The President is Calling* (Garden City, NY: Doubleday & Co., 1974), p.241.

39 *New York Times*, January 8, 1952.

40 William B. Pickett, *Eisenhower Decides To Run* (Chicago: Ivan R. Dee, 2000), p.213.

41 Robert H. Ferrell, *Ill-Advised: Presidential Health and the Public Trust* (Columbia: University of Missouri Press, 1992), pp.53–150.

42 Geoffrey Perret, *Eisenhower* (New York: Random House, 1999), pp.405–408.

43 Richard M. Nixon, *RN: The Memoirs of Richard Nixon* (New York: Grosset & Dunlap, 1978), p.98.

44 Emmet John Hughes, *The Ordeal of Power: A Political Memoir of the Eisenhower Years* (New York: Atheneum, 1963), p.42.

45 Robert Griffith, *The Politics of Fear: Joseph R. McCarthy and the Senate* (2nd edn; Amherst: University of Massachusetts Press, 1987), pp.190–194.

46 Ambrose, *Eisenhower: Soldier and President*, p.284.

47 *New York Times*, October 25, 1952.

Chapter 1

1 Milton S. Eisenhower, *The President Is Calling* (Garden City, NY: Doubleday & Co., 1974), p.309.

2 Diary Entry, May 14, 1953, Robert H. Ferrell, ed., *The Eisenhower Diaries* (New York: W. W. Norton, 1981), p.238.

3 Fred I. Greenstein, *The Hidden-Hand Presidency: Eisenhower as Leader* (New York: Basic Books, 1982), pp.vii–viii.

4 Richard M. Nixon, *Six Crises* (Garden City, NY: Doubleday & Co., 1962), p.161.

5 Remarks at Dartmouth College Commencement Exercises, June 14, 1953, *Public Papers of the Presidents of the United States, 1953* (Washington, DC: US Government Printing Office, 1960), p.415. (Hereinafter cited as PP, followed by the relevant year.)

6 Robert Griffith, *The Politics of Fear: Joseph R. McCarthy and the Senate* (2nd edn; Amherst: University of Massachusetts Press, 1987), p.199.

7 James T. Patterson, *Grand Expectations: The United States, 1945–1974* (New York: Oxford University Press, 1996), p.266.

8 David Caute, *The Great Fear: The Anti-Communist Purge under Truman and Eisenhower* (New York: Simon and Schuster, 1978), pp.305–306.

9 Thomas C. Reeves, *The Life and Times of Joe McCarthy* (New York: Stein & Day, 1982), p.307.

10 Emmet John Hughes, *The Ordeal of Power: A Political Memoir of the Eisenhower Years* (New York: Atheneum, 1963), p.92.

11 Eisenhower to Harry A. Bullis, May 18, 1953, White House Central Files, 1953–1961, Official File, Box 368, 99-R, Dwight D. Eisenhower Library, Abilene, Kansas (hereinafter cited as WHCF, OF, DDEL).

12 Greenstein, *The Hidden-Hand Presidency*, pp.155–227.

13 Jeff Broadwater, *Eisenhower and the Anti-Communist Crusade* (Chapel Hill: University of North Carolina Press, 1992), pp.137–166.

14 Eisenhower to Milton Eisenhower, January 6, 1954, Ann Whitman File, Name Series, Box 12, Eisenhower, Milton, 1954 (3), DDEL (Ann Whitman File hereinafter cited as AWF).

15 Iwan W. Morgan, *Eisenhower versus the Spenders: The Eisenhower Administration, the Democrats and the Budget, 1953–1960* (London: Pinter Publications, 1990); John W. Sloan, *Eisenhower and the Management of Prosperity* (Lawrence: University Press of Kansas, 1990).

16 Sloan, *Eisenhower and the Management of Prosperity*, p.13.

17 Annual Budget Message to the Congress, January 21, 1954, PP, 1954, p.89.

18 Dwight D. Eisenhower, *Mandate for Change, 1953–1956* (Garden City, NY: Doubleday & Co., 1963), p.376.

19 Remarks at the Lincoln Day Box Supper, February 5, 1954, PP, 1954, p.242.

20 The President's News Conference, January 27, 1954, PP, 1954, p.211.

21 Annual Message Transmitting the Economic Report to the Congress, January 28, 1954, PP, 1954, p.216.

22 Annual Budget Message to the Congress, January 21, 1954, PP, 1954, p.89.

23 Annual Message to the Congress on the State of the Union, February 2, 1953, PP, 1953, p.20.

24 The President's News Conference, April 30, 1953, PP, 1953, p.249.

25 Patterson, *Grand Expectations*, p.289.

26 Annual Message to the Congress on the State of the Union, February 2, 1953, PP, 1953, p.21.

27 Eisenhower to Everett ('Swede') Hazlett, July 21, 1953, Robert Griffith, ed., *Ike's Letters to a Friend, 1941–1958* (Lawrence: University Press of Kansas, 1984), p.111.

28 'A Chance for Peace', address delivered before the American Society of Newspaper Editors, April 16, 1953, PP, 1953, p.182.

29 Special Message to the Congress on the Mutual Security Program, May 5, 1953, PP, 1953, p.257.

30 Annual Message to the Congress on the State of the Union, February 2, 1953, PP, 1953, p.17.

31 Eisenhower to General Alfred Guenther, May 4, 1953, AWF, Administration Series, Box 16, Guenther, General Alfred, 1952–53 (3), DDEL.

32 Saki Dockrill, *Eisenhower's New Look Security Policy, 1953–1961* (Basingstoke: Macmillan, 1996), p.25.

33 Special Message to the Congress Transmitting Re-organization Plan 6 concerning the Department of Defense, April 30, 1953, PP, 1953, p.227.

34 138th Meeting of the NSC, March 25, 1953, AWF, NSC Series, Box 4, DDEL.

35 Michael J. Hogan, *A Cross of Iron: Harry S. Truman and the Origins of the National Security State, 1945–54* (Cambridge: Cambridge University Press, 1998).

36 204th Meeting of NSC, June 24, 1954, AWF, NSC Series, Box 5, DDEL.

37 Minutes of Cabinet Meeting, May 22, 1953, AWF, Cabinet Series, Box 2, DDEL.

38 Annual Budget Message to the Congress, January 21, 1954, PP, 1954, p.86.

39 Annual Message Transmitting the Economic Report to the Congress, January 28, 1954, PP, 1954, p.215.

40 Sloan, *Eisenhower and the Management of Prosperity*, p.4.

41 Clinton Rossiter, *The American Presidency* (rev edn; Harcourt, Brace & World, 1959), pp.36–37.

42 Eisenhower to Gabriel Hauge, February 4, 1953, AWF, Administration Series, Box 18, Hauge, Gabriel, 1952–55 (7), DDEL.

43 Annual Message Transmitting the Economic Report to the Congress, January 28, 1954, PP, 1954, p.216.

44 Thomas Borstelmann, *The Cold War and the Color Line: American Race Relations in the Global Arena* (Cambridge, Mass.: Harvard University Press, 2001), p.93.

45 Address to the Congress on the State of the Union, February 2, 1953, PP, 1953, p.30.

46 Stanley I. Kutler, 'Eisenhower, the Judiciary and Desegregation', in Günter Bischof and Stephen E. Ambrose, eds, *Eisenhower: A Centenary Assessment* (Baton Rouge: Louisiana State University Press, 1995), p.100.

47 Robert F. Burk, *The Eisenhower Administration and Black Civil Rights* (Knoxville: University of Tennessee Press, 1984), p.142.

48 The President's News Conference, May 19, 1954, PP, 1954, p.491.

49 Chester Pach and Elmo Richardson, *The Presidency of Dwight D. Eisenhower* (rev edn; Lawrence: University Press of Kansas, 1991), p.157.

50 Hughes, *Ordeal of Power*, p.201.

51 Michael S. Mayer, 'Eisenhower and Racial Moderation', Chapter III in Mayer, ed., *The Eisenhower Presidency and the 1950s* (Boston: Houghton Mifflin Company, 1998), p.118.

52 Diary Entry, April 1, 1953, Ferrell, ed., *The Eisenhower Diaries*, p.234.

53 Diary Entry, January 18, 1954, Ferrell, ed., *The Eisenhower Diaries*, p.270.

54 Diary Entry, June 15, 1954, AWF, Ann Whitman Diary Series, Box 2, ACW Diary, June, 1954, DDEL.

55 James P. Pfiffner, *The Modern Presidency* (New York: St Martin's Press, 1994), p.135.

56 The President's News Conference, April 2, 1953, PP, p.158.

57 Washington to Foreign Office, February 23, 1954, FO 371/109009/AU 1001/1, Public Record Office, National Archives, Kew. (Hereinafter referred to as PRO, NA.)

58 Eisenhower to Swede Hazlett, December 8, 1954, Griffith, ed., *Ike's Letters to a Friend, 1941–1958*, p.138.

59 Diary Entry, April 1, 1953, Ferrell, ed., *The Eisenhower Diaries*, p.234.

60 Eisenhower to Clifford Roberts, December 7, 1954, AWF, DDE Diary Series, Box 8, DDE Diary, December, 1954 (2), DDEL.

Chapter 2

1 Fred I. Greenstein and Richard H. Immerman, 'Effective National Security Advisors: Recovering the Eisenhower Legacy', *Political Science Quarterly*, Vol. 115, No. 3 (Fall, 2000), pp.335–345.

2 John Foster Dulles, *War, Peace and Change* (New York: Harper Bros, 1939).

3 Dwight D. Eisenhower, *Mandate for Change, 1953–56* (Garden City, NY: Doubleday & Co., 1963), p.181.

4 Second Restricted Meeting of the Heads of Government, Mid Ocean Club, Bermuda, December 7, 1953, *Foreign Relations of the United States, 1952–54*, Vol. V: *Western European Security* (2 parts; Washington, DC: US Government Printing Office, 1983), Part 2, p.1811 (hereinafter cited as *FRUS*, followed by relevant volume and year).

5 William W. Stueck, *The Korean War: An International History* (Princeton: Princeton University Press, 1995), p.120.

6 *Ibid.*, p.121.

7 X (George F. Kennan), 'The Sources of Soviet Conduct', *Foreign Affairs*, Vol. 25, No. 4 (July, 1947), pp.566–582.

8 James Burnham, *Containment and Liberation* (New York: John Day, 1953), pp.42–43.

9 Richard H. Immermann, *John Foster Dulles: Piety, Pragmatism and Power in U.S. Foreign Policy* (Wilmington, Del.: Scholarly Resources, 1990), p.44.

10 John Foster Dulles, 'A Policy of Boldness', *Life*, May 19, 1952, p.151.

11 *New York Times*, October 5, 1952.

12 Gregory Mitrovich, *Undermining the Kremlin: America's Strategy to Subvert the Soviet Bloc, 1947–1956* (Ithaca, NY: Cornell University Press, 2000); Peter Gross, *Operation Rollback: America's Secret War behind the Iron Curtain* (Boston: Houghton Mifflin, 2000);

Scott Lucas, *Freedom's War: The U.S. Crusade Against the Soviet Union, 1945–1956*, (Manchester: Manchester University Press, 1998); Arch Paddington, *Broadcasting Freedom: The Cold War Triumphs of Radio Free Europe and Radio Liberty* (Lexington: University of Kentucky Press, 2000); Ronald R. Krebs, *Dueling Visions: U.S. Strategy Towards Eastern Europe under Eisenhower* (College Station, Texas: Texas A&M University Press, 2001).

13 Bennett Kovrig, *Of Walls and Bridges: The United States and Eastern Europe* (New York: Oxford University Press, 1991), p.35.

14 John W. Young, *Winston Churchill's Last Campaign: Britain and the Cold War, 1951–1955* (Oxford: Clarendon Press, 1996).

15 Churchill to Eisenhower, March 11, 1953, Peter G. Boyle, ed., *The Churchill–Eisenhower Correspondence, 1953–1955* (Chapel Hill: University of North Carolina Press, 1990), p.31.

16 Eisenhower to Churchill, March 11, 1953, *ibid.*, p.32.

17 Churchill to Eisenhower, March 9, 1954, *ibid.*, p.124.

18 Eisenhower to Churchill, March 19, 1954, *ibid.*, p.126.

19 Churchill to Eisenhower, August 6, 1954, *ibid.*, pp.166–167.

20 Eisenhower to Churchill, December 14, 1954, *ibid.*, p.182.

21 Eisenhower, *Mandate for Change*, p.253.

22 Eisenhower to Milton Eisenhower, December 11, 1953, Louis Galambos and Daun Van Ee, eds, *The Papers of Dwight David Eisenhower, The Presidency: The Middle Way* (Baltimore: Johns Hopkins University Press, 1996), Vol. XV, p.760.

23 Richard G. Hewlett and Jack M. Holl, *Atoms for Peace and War, 1953–1961: Eisenhower and the Atomic Energy Commission* (Berkeley: University of California Press, 1989), p.66.

24 Memorandum of a Special Meeting of the National Security Council, March 31, 1953, *FRUS*, 1952–54, Vol. II; *National Security Affairs*, Part I, p.278.

25 Diary Entry, April 1, 1953, Robert H. Ferrell, ed., *The Eisenhower Diaries* (New York: W. W. Norton, 1981), p.233.

26 Duane Tanabaum, *The Bricker Amendment Controversy: A Test of Eisenhower's Political Leadership* (Ithaca, NY: Cornell University Press, 1988).

27 Dwight D. Eisenhower, *Crusade in Europe*, (Garden City, NY: Doubleday & Co., 1948), p.443.

28 McGeorge Bundy, *Danger and Survival: Choices about the Bomb in the First Fifty Years* (New York: Random House, 1988), p.245.

29 148th Meeting of NSC, June 4, 1953, AWF, NSC Series, Box 4, DDEL.

30 Richard J. Aldrich, *Hidden Hand: Britain, America and Cold War Secret Intelligence* (London: John Murray, 2001); William E. Burrows, *By Any Means Necessary: America's Secret Air War in the Cold War* (New York: Farrar, Strauss and Giroux, 2001); Curtis Peebles, *Shadow Flights: America's Secret War Against the Soviet Union* (Novato, Calif.: Presidio Press, 2000).

31 Chris Pocock, *The U-2 Spyplane: Toward the Unknown: A New History of the Early Years* (Atglen, Pa.: Schiffer Publications, 2000); Norman Polmar and Mike Haenggi, eds, *Spyplane: The U-2 History Declassified* (Osceola, Wis.: MBI, 2000); Michael R. Beschloss, *Mayday: Eisenhower, Khrushchev and the U-2 Affair* (New York: Harper and Row, 1986).

32 Gayle B. Montgomery and James W. Johnston, *One Step From the White House: The Rise and Fall of Senator William F. Knowland* (Berkeley: University of California Press, 1998), pp.166–180.

33 Eisenhower to Alfred M. Gruenther, July 7, 1954, AWF, Administration Series, Box 16, Gruenther, General Alfred, 1954 (3), DDEL.

34 213th Meeting of NSC, September 9, 1954, AWF, NSC Series, Box 6, DDEL.

35 Second Restricted Meeting of the Heads of Government, Mid-Ocean Club, Bermuda, December 7, 1953, *FRUS, 1952–54*, Vol. V, Part 2, p.1809.

36 The President's News Conference, April 7, 1954, PP,1954, p.383.

37 John Prados, *President's Secret Wars: CIA and Pentagon Covert Operations from World War II through the Persian Gulf* (rev edn; Chicago: Ivan R. Dee, 1996), pp.115–116.

38 Excerpts from Remarks to a Group of Correspondents About to Return to the Scene of the Normandy Invasion, June 2, 1954, PP, 1954, p.535.

39 179th Meeting of NSC, January 8, 1954, Whitman File, NSC Series, Box 5, DDEL.

40 Robert H. Ferrell, ed., *The Diary of James C. Hagerty: Eisenhower in Mid-Course, 1954–1955* (Bloomington: University of Indiana Press, 1983), p.15.

41 Chester Pach and Elmo Richardson, *The Presidency of Dwight D. Eisenhower* (rev edn; Lawrence: University Press of Kansas, 1991), p.98.

42 Eisenhower, *Mandate for Change*, p.163.

43 British Memorandum, Persia: Political Review of the Recent Crisis, September 2, 1953, *FRUS, 1952–54*, Vol. X: *Iran, 1951–1954*, p.784.

44 160th Meeting of the NSC, August 27, 1953, AWF, NSC Series, Box 4, DDEL.

45 Milton Eisenhower, United States-Latin American Relations: Report to the President, November 23, 1953, AWF, Name Series, Box 13, Eisenhower, Milton, South American Report, 1953 (2), DDEL.

46 Eisenhower, *Mandate for Change*, p.83.

47 Stephen G. Rabe, *Eisenhower and Latin America, The Foreign Policy of Anticommunism* (Chapel Hill: University of North Carolina Press, 1988), pp.42–63; Piero Gleijeses, *Shattered Hope: The Guatemalan Revolution and the United States, 1944–1954* (Princeton, NJ: Princeton University Press, 1991).

48 135th Meeting of NSC, March 4, 1953, AWF, NSC Series, Box 4, DDEL.

Chapter 3

1 Diary Entry, January 10, 1955, Robert H. Ferrell, ed., *The Eisenhower Diaries* (New York: W. W. Norton, 1981), p.291.

2 Robert Dallek, *Lone Star Rising: Lyndon Johnson and His Times, 1908–1960* (New York: Oxford University Press, 1991), pp.467–591.

3 Annual Budget Message to the Congress, January 16, 1956, PP, 1956, p.78.

4 Letter to the Secretary of Defense on National Security Requirements, January 5, 1955, PP, 1955, p.3.

5 The President's News Conference, June 6, 1956, PP, 1956, p.554.

6 Letter to the Secretary of Defense on National Security Requirements, January 5, 1955, PP, 1955, p.5.

7 Annual Message Transmitting the Economic Report to the Congress, January 24, 1956, PP, 1956, p.180.

8 C. Wright Mills, *The Power Elite* (New York: Oxford University Press, 1956); C. Wright Mills, *White Collar: The American Middle Classes* (New York: Oxford University Press, 1951).

9 David Halberstam, *The Fifties* (New York: Fawcett Columbia, 1994), p.x.

10 Annual Message Presenting the Economic Report to the Congress, January 20, 1955, PP, 1955, p.200.

11 John P. Diggins, *The Proud Decades: America in War and in Peace, 1941–1960* (New York: W. W. Norton, 1989), p.178.

12 Paul Boyer, *Promises to Keep: The United States since World War I* (rev edn; Lexington, Mass.: D. C. Heath, 1999), p.175.

13 The President's News Conference, May 4, 1955, PP, 1955, p.465.

14 Dwight D. Eisenhower, *Waging Peace, 1956–1961* (Garden City, NY: Doubleday & Co., 1965), p.16.

15 Robert F. Burk, *The Eisenhower Administration and Black Civil Rights* (Knoxville: University of Tennessee Press, 1984), p.150.

16 The President's News Conference, March 14, 1956, PP, 1956, p.305.

17 The President's News Conference, September 5, 1956, PP, 1956, p.736.

18 The President's News Conference, March 14, 1956, PP, 1956, p.304.

19 The President's News Conference, August 31, 1956, PP, 1956, p.724.

20 The President's News Conference, March 14, 1956, PP, 1956, p.304.

21 The President's News Conference, September 5, 1956, PP, 1956, p.736.

22 The President's News Conference, March 14, 1956, PP, 1956, p.304.

23 Herbert S. Parmet, *Eisenhower and the American Crusades* (New York: Macmillan, 1972), p.576.

24 The President's News Conference, March 21, 1956, PP, 1956, p.335.

25 James T. Patterson, *Grand Expectations: The United States, 1945–1974* (New York: Oxford University Press, 1996), p.405.

26 Annual Message to the Congress on the State of the Union, January 5, 1956, PP, 1956, pp.25–26.

27 Diary Entry, December 7, 1954, Ferrell, ed., *The Eisenhower Diaries*, p.275.

28 Diary Entry, April 1, 1953, *ibid*, p.234.

29 Eisenhower to Swede Hazlett, December 24, 1953, Robert Grifith, ed., *Ike's Letters to a Friend* (Lawrence: University Press of Kansas, 1984), p.117.

30 Address at the Cow Palace, San Francisco, on Accepting the Nomination of the Republican National Convention, August 23, 1956, PP, 1956, p.704.

31 Clarence G. Lasby, *Eisenhower's Heart Attack* (Lawrence: University Press of Kansas, 1997).

32 Eisenhower to Swede Hazlett, June 4, 1955, Griffith, ed., *Ike's Letters to a Friend*, p.162.

33 Diary Entry, February 13, 1953, Ferrell, ed., *The Eisenhower Diaries*, p.230.

34 Eisenhower to Swede Hazlett, August 15, 1955, Griffith, ed., *Ike's Letters to a Friend*, p.148.

35 Eisenhower to Milton Eisenhower, December 11, 1953, Louis Galambos and Daun Van Ee, *The Papers of Dwight David Eisenhower, The Presidency: The Middle Way* (Baltimore: Johns Hopkins University Press, 1996), Vol. XV, p.760.

36 Eisenhower to Swede Hazlett, June 4, 1955, Griffith, ed., *Ike's Letters to a Friend*, p.145.

37 Eisenhower to Swede Hazlett, December 8, 1954, *ibid.*, pp.138–139.

38 Eisenhower to Swede Hazlett, December 24, 1953, *ibid.*, p.117.

39 *Ibid.*, p.118.

40 Eisenhower to Swede Hazlett, December 8, 1954, *ibid.*, p.138.

41 Eisenhower to Swede Hazlett, December 24, 1954, *ibid.*, pp.117–118.

42 Diary Entry, July 27, 1954, Robert H. Ferrell, ed., *The Diary of James C. Hagerty: Eisenhower in Mid-Course, 1954–1955* (Bloomington: Indiana University Press, 1983), p.100.

43 Eisenhower to Swede Hazlett, August 15, 1955, Griffith, ed., *Ike's Letters to a Friend*, p.149.

44 Diary Entry, December 13, 1955, Ferrell, ed., *The Diary of James C. Hagerty*, p.241.

45 Eisenhower to Swede Hazlett, August 3, 1956, Griffith, ed., *Ike's Letters to a Friend*, p.165.

46 Diary Entry, December 12, 1955, Ferrell, ed., *The Diary of James C. Hagerty*, p.240.

47 *Ibid.*, p.242.

48 Emmet John Hughes, *The Ordeal of Power: A Political Memoir of the Eisenhower Years* (New York: Atheneum, 1963), p. 173.

49 Richard M. Nixon, *RN: The Memoirs of Richard Nixon* (New York: Grosset & Dunlap, 1978), pp.167–168.

50 The President's News Conference, January 25, 1956, PP, 1956, p.195.

51 The President's News Conference, August 22, 1956, PP, 1956, p.698.

52 The President's News Conference, January 25, 1956, PP, 1956, p.196.

53 The President's News Conference, March 14, 1956, PP, 1956, pp.302–303.

54 Nixon, *RN: The Memoirs of Richard Nixon*, p.180.

55 Radio and Television Remarks Following the Election Victory, November 7, 1956, PP, 1956, p.1090.

56 Nixon, *RN: The Memoirs of Richard Nixon*, p.181.

Chapter 4

1 Eisenhower to Anthony Eden, April 8, 1955, AWF, International Series, Box 21, Eden 4/6/55–12/31/55 (6), DDEL.

2 Eisenhower to Anthony Eden, May 6, 1955, *ibid.*

3 Roger Makins to Harold Macmillan, March 17, 1955, FO 371/114364/AU1022/16, PRO, NA.

4 Curtis Peebles, *Shadow Flights: America's Secret War Against the Soviet Union* (Novato, Calif.: Presidio Press, 2000), pp.106–123.

5 *Ibid.*, p.140.

6 Richard J. Aldrich, *Hidden Hand: Britain, America and Cold War Secret Intelligence* (London: John Murray, 2001), pp.523–525.

7 Eden to Eisenhower, May 17, 1956, AWF, International Series, Box 21, Eden 1/16/56–6/26/56 (3), DDEL.

8 Peebles, *Shadow Flights*, p.143.

9 *Ibid.*, p.148.

10 The President's News Conference, June 6, 1956, PP, 1956, p.556.

11 Address at the Cow Palace, San Francisco, on Accepting the Nomination of the Republican Convention, August 23, 1956, PP, 1956, p.713.

12 Radio and Television Address Opening the President's Campaign for the Election, September 19, 1956, PP, 1956, p.785.

13 Address at the Annual Dinner of the American Society of Newspaper Editors, April 21, 1956, PP, 1956, p.419.

14 Letter to the Secretary of Defense on National Security Requirements, January 5, 1955, PP, 1955, pp.2–3.

15 The President's News Conference, April 4, 1956, PP, 1956, p.376.

16 The President's News Conference, June 6, 1956, PP, 1956, p.554.

17 The President's News Conference, February 23, 1955, PP, 1955, p.290.

18 The President's News Conference, April 4, 1956, PP, 1956, p.376.

19 Special Message to the Congress on the Foreign Economic Policy of the United States, January 10, 1955, PP, 1955, p.33.

20 *Ibid.*, p.32.

21 Aleksander Stylakin, 'The Hungarian Crisis of 1956: The Soviet Role in the Light of New Archival Documents', *Cold War History*, Vol. 2, No. 1 (October, 2001), pp.113–144.

22 Dwight D. Eisenhower, *Mandate for Change, 1953–1956* (Garden City, NY: Doubleday & Co., 1963), p.469.

23 The President's News Conference, March 16, 1955, PP, 1955, p.333.

24 Churchill to Eisenhower, February 15, 1955, Peter G. Boyle, ed., *The Churchill–Eisenhower Correspondence, 1953–1955* (Chapel Hill: University of North Carolina Press, 1990), p.193.

25 Eisenhower to Churchill, February 18, 1955, *ibid.*, p.195.

26 Chester Pach and Elmo Richardson, *The Presidency of Dwight D. Eisenhower* (rev edn; Lawrence: University Press of Kansas, 1991), p.98.

27 *Ibid.*, p.104.

28 Gordon H. Chang, *Friends and Enemies: The United States, China and the Soviet Union, 1948–1972* (Stanford, Calif.: Stanford University Press, 1990), pp.141–142.

29 Robert A. Divine, *Eisenhower and the Cold War* (New York: Oxford University Press, 1981), pp.65–66.

30 Stephen E. Ambrose, *Eisenhower: The President, 1952–1969* (New York: Simon and Schuster, 1984) p.245.

31 David L. Anderson, *Trapped by Success: The Eisenhower Administration and Vietnam, 1953–1961* (New York: Columbia University Press, 1991), p.ix.

32 George C. Herring, *America's Longest War: The United States and Vietnam, 1950–1975* (3rd edn; New York: McGraw-Hill, 1996), p.49.

33 Robert D. Schulzinger, *A Time for War: The United States and Vietnam, 1945–1975* (New York: Oxford University Press, 1997), p.71.

34 Address at the Annual Dinner of the American Society of Newspaper Editors, April 21, 1956, PP, 1956, p.423.

35 Robert Mann, *A Grand Delusion: America's Descent into Vietnam* (New York: Basic Books, 2001), p.196.

36 Eisenhower to Anthony Eden, July 31, 1956, AWF, International Series, Box 21, Eden, 7/18/56–11/7/56 (8), DDEL.

37 Eisenhower to Anthony Eden, September 3, 1956, AWF, International Series, Box 21, Eden, 7/18/56–11/7/56 (5), DDEL.

38 Keith Kyle, *Suez* (London: Weidenfeld and Nicolson, 1991), pp.291–401.

39 Eisenhower to Swede Hazlett, November 2, 1956, Robert Griffith, ed., *Ike's Letters to a Friend* (Lawrence: University Press of Kansas, 1984), p.175.

40 *Ibid.*, p.176.

41 Kyle, *Suez*, pp.425–533.

42 Emmet John Hughes, *The Ordeal of Power: A Political Memoir of the Eisenhower Years* (New York: Atheneum, 1963), p.220.

43 A. J. Goodpaster, Memorandum for the Record, November 7, 1956, AWF, DDE Diary Series, Box 19, Nov '56 Diary: Staff Memos, DDEL.

44 A. J. Goodpaster, Memorandum of a Conference with the President, November 20, 1956, AWF, DDE Diary Series, Box 19, Nov '56 Diary: Staff Memos, DDEL.

45 Cole Kingseed, *Eisenhower and the Suez Crisis of 1956* (Baton Rouge: Louisiana State University Press, 1995), p.148.

46 Washington to Foreign Office, March 6, 1956, FO371/120310/AU1011/1, PRO, NA.

47 Lodge to Eisenhower, December 21, 1956, AWF, Administration Series, Box 24, Lodge, Henry Cabot, 1956 (1), DDEL.

Chapter 5

1 Second Inaugural Address, January 21, 1957, PP, 1957, p.61.

2 Eisenhower to George Humphrey, July 22, 1958, AWF, Administration Series, Box 21, Humphrey, George M., 1957–58 (1), DDEL.

3 The President's News Conference, January 30, 1957, PP, 1957, p.100.

4 Eisenhower to Harold Macmillan, November 11, 1958, AWF, International Series, Box 24, Macmillan, October 1, 1958–March 20, 1959 (6), DDEL.

5 Eisenhower to Lewis Douglas, May 2, 1958, WHCF, OF, 144, Box 561, 1958, 114 (7), DDEL.

6 Special Message to the Congress on Federal Aid to Education, January 28, 1957, PP, 1957, p.90.

7 Annual Message to the Congress on the State of the Union, January 10, 1957, PP, 1957, p.25.

8 Supplementary Notes, Legislative Leaders Meeting, May 14, 1957, AWF, Legislative Meeting Series, Box 2, Legislative Leaders Meetings, May–June (3), DDEL.

9 The President's News Conference, January 23, 1957, PP, 1957, p.85.

10 Ibid., p.86.

11 Annual Message Transmitting the Economic Report to the Congress, January 23, 1957, PP, 1957, p.65.

12 Eisenhower to Arthur Burns, March 12, 1958, AWF, Administration Series, Box 9, Burns, Dr. Arthur F., 1958–59 (2), DDEL.

13 Dwight D. Eisenhower, Waging Peace 1956–1961 (Garden City, NY: Doubleday & Co., 1965), pp.205–206.

14 William L. O'Neill, American High: The Years of Confidence, 1945–1960 (New York: Free Press, 1986), p.272.

15 Eisenhower, Waging Peace, p.360.

16 Supplementary Notes, Legislative Leaders Meeting, February 4, 1958, AWF, Legislative Meetings Series, Box 3, DDEL.

17 David L. Snead, The Gaither Committee, Eisenhower and the Cold War (Columbus: Ohio State University Press, 1999), pp.91–129.

18 Eisenhower to Swede Hazlett, November 18, 1957, Robert Griffith, ed., Ike's Letters to a Friend, 1941–1958 (Lawrence: University Press of Kansas, 1984), p.190.

19 Stephen E. Ambrose, Eisenhower: The President, 1952–1969 (New York: Simon and Schuster, 1984), p.435.

20 Radio and Television Address to the American People on Science and National Security, November 7, 1957, PP, 1957, p.794.

21 A. J. Goodpaster, Memorandum of Conference with the President, June 23, 1958, AWF, DDE Diary Series, Box 33, June, 1958: Staff Notes, DDEL.

22 Radio and Television Address to the American People on Science and Security, November 7, 1957, PP, 1957, p.798.

23 Robert Dallek, *An Unfinished Life: John F. Kennedy* (Boston: Little, Brown, 2003), p.224.

24 Radio and Television Address to the American People on Science and Security, November 7, 1957, PP, 1957, p.798.

25 Radio and Television Address to the American People on Our Future Security, November 13, 1957, PP, 1957, p.815.

26 Memo of a Conference with the President, December 5, 1957, *FRUS, 1955–57*, Vol. XIX: *National Security Policy*, p.703.

27 Eisenhower to Frank Altschul, October 25, 1957, AWF, DDE Diary Series, Box 27, DDE Diary, October, 1957, DDEL.

28 Ambrose, *Eisenhower: The President*, p.435.

29 Robert A. Divine, *The Sputnik Challenge* (New York: Oxford University Press, 1993), p.vii.

30 *Ibid.*, p.viii.

31 Chester Pach and Elmo Richardson, *The Presidency of Dwight D. Eisenhower* (rev edn; Lawrence: University Press of Kansas, 1991), p.170.

32 Divine, *The Sputnik Challenge*, p.vii.

33 Sherman Adams, *First Hand Report: The Inside Story of the Eisenhower Administration* (New York: Harper and Row, 1961), p.355.

34 The President's News Conference, October 3, 1957, PP, 1957, p.708.

35 *Ibid.*, p.707.

36 *Ibid.*

37 Mary Dudziak, *Cold War Civil Rights* (Princeton: Princeton University Press, 2000), p.151.

38 Radio and Television Address to the American People on the Situation in Little Rock, September 24, 1957, PP, 1957, p.694.

39 Lodge to Eisenhower, September 25, 1957, AWF, Administration Series, Box 24, Lodge, Henry Cabot, 1957–58 (3), DDEL.

40 The President's News Conference, February 6, 1957, PP, 1957, p.128.

41 Robert Dallek, *Lone Star Rising: Lyndon Johnson and His Times* (New York: Oxford University Press, 1991), p.564.

42 Remarks at Meeting of Negro Leaders Sponsored by the National Newspaper Association, May 12, 1958, PP, 1958, p.393.

43 Adams, *First-Hand Report*, pp.315–317.

44 Eisenhower to Paul Hoffman, June 24, 1958, AWF, Administration Series, Box 19, Hoffman, Paul (1), DDEL.

45 Herbert S. Parmet, *Eisenhower and the American Crusades* (New York: Macmillan, 1972), p.495.

46 Remarks at the Republic National Committee Meeting in Chicago, August 27, 1958, PP, 1958, p.651.

47 Iwan W. Morgan, *Eisenhower versus The Spenders: The Eisenhower Administration, the Democrats and the Budget, 1953–1960* (London: Pinter Publications, 1990), p.123.

48 John W. Sloan, *Eisenhower and the Management of Prosperity* (Lawrence: University Press of Kansas, 1991), p.11.

49 Eisenhower to Harold Macmillan, November 11, 1958, AWF, International Series, Box 24, Macmillan, October 1, 1958–March 20, 1959 (6), DDEL.

50 *Ibid.*

Chapter 6

1 Letter to Nikita Khrushchev, Chairman, Council of Ministers, USSR, July 2, 1958, PP, 1958, p.509.

2 Curtis Peebles, *Shadow Flights: America's Secret War Against the Soviet Union* (Novato, Calif.: Presidio Press, 2000), pp.164–205.

3 *Ibid.*

4 *Ibid.*, pp.207–215.

5 Radio and Television Address to the American People on Science and National Security, November 7, 1957, PP, 1957, p.793.

6 Richard J. Aldrich, *Hidden Hand: Britain, America and Cold War Secret Intelligence* (London: John Murray, 2001), p.563.

7 Special Message to the Congress on the Mutual Security Program, February 19, 1958, PP, 1958, p.168.

8 The President's News Conference, February 26, 1958, PP, 1958, p.192.

9 Radio and Television Address to the American People on the Need for Mutual Security in Waging the Peace, May 21, 1957, PP, 1957, p.386.

10 Remarks and Address at the Dinner of the National Conference on the Foreign Aspects of National Security, February 25, 1958, PP, 1958, p.178.

11 Remarks and Address at the Dinner of the National Conference on the Foreign Aspects of National Security, February 25, 1958, PP, 1958, p.17.

12 Robert A. Divine, *Blowing on the Wind: The Nuclear Test Ban Debate, 1954–1960* (New York: Oxford University Press, 1978), pp.113–261; Caroline Pruden, *Conditional Partners: Eisenhower, the United Nations and the Search for a Permanent Peace* (Baton Rouge: Louisiana State University Press, 1998), pp.144–172.

13 Letter to Nikita Khrushchev, Chairman, Council of Ministers, USSR, April 8, 1958, PP, 1958, p.290.

14 Harold Macmillan, *Riding the Storm, 1956–1959* (London: Macmillan, 1971), p.562.

15 Dwight D. Eisenhower, *Waging Peace, 1956–1961* (Garden City, NY: Doubleday & Co., 1965), p.304.

16 David L. Anderson, *Trapped by Success: The Eisenhower Administration and Vietnam, 1953–1961* (New York: Columbia University Press, 1991), p.200.

17 H. W. Brands, *Into the Labyrinth: The United States and the Middle East, 1945–1993* (New York: McGraw-Hill, 1994), pp.69–72.

18 Staff Notes, Memorandum of a Conference with the President, July 15, 1958, AWF, DDE Diary Series, Box 35, July, 1958, Staff Memos (2), DDEL.

19 Eisenhower, *Waging Peace*, p.290.

20 A. J. Goodpaster, Memorandum of Conference with the President, July 23, 1958, AWF, DDE Diary Series, Box 35, July, 1958, Staff Memos (1), DDEL.

21 Lodge to Eisenhower, March 11, 1957, AWF, Administration Series, Box 24, Lodge, Henry Cabot, 1957–58 (3), DDEL.

22 Second Inaugural Address, January 21, 1957, PP, 1957, p.63.

23 Eisenhower to George Humphrey, March 27, 1957, AWF, Administration Series, Bos 21, Humphrey, George M., 1957–58 (3), DDEL.

24 Burton I. Kaufman, *Trade and Aid: Eisenhower's Foreign Economic Policy, 1953–1961* (Baltimore: Johns Hopkins University Press, 1982), p.99.

25 Eisenhower to George Humphrey, March 27, 1957, AWF, Administration Series, Box 21, Humphrey, George M., 1957–58 (3), DDEL.

Chapter 7

1 Arthur J. Schlesinger, Jr, *A Thousand Days: John F. Kennedy in the White House* (New York: André Deutsch, 1965), p.15.

2 Annual Review of 1959, January 1, 1960, FO371/148576/AU1011/1, PRO, NA.

3 Annual Budget Message to the Congress, Fiscal Year 1961, January 18, 1960, PP, 1960–61, p.40.

4 Annual Message to the Congress on the State of the Union, January 7, 1960, PP, 1960–61, p.13.

5 Address in Los Angeles to the Nationwide 'Dinner with Ike' Rallies, January 27, 1960, PP, 1960–61, p.141.

6 Statement by the President on the Annual Budget Message, January 19, 1959, PP, 1959, p.113.

7 Remarks of the President on Future Budgets, Cabinet Meeting, November 27, 1959, WHO, OSS, Cabinet Series, Box 5, C-52 (4), DDEL.

8 Robert M. Collins, *More: The Politics of Economic Growth in Postwar America* (New York: Oxford University Press, 2000), pp.42–51.

9 The President's News Conference, January 13, 1960, PP, 1960–61, p.26.

10 The President's News Conference, February 17, 1960, PP, 1960–61, p.198–99.

11 Address at the Republican National Convention in Chicago, July 26, 1960, PP, 1960–61, p.594.

12 The President's News Conference, February 25, 1959, PP, 1959, p.218.

13 *Ibid.*

14 The President's News Conference, July 8, 1959, PP, 1959, p.516.

15 The President's News Conference, April 27, 1960, PP, 1960–61, pp.362–363.

16 Peter J. Roman, *Eisenhower and the Missile Gap* (Ithaca, NY: Cornell University Press, 1995), p.147.

17 A. J. Goodpaster, Memorandum of Conference with the President, March 11, 1960, AWF, DDE Diary Series, Box 48, Staff Notes, March, 1960 (3), DDEL.

18 A. J. Goodpaster, Memorandum of Conference with the President, February 9, 1959, AWF, DDE Diary Series, Box 39, Staff Notes, February, 1959 (2), DDEL.

19 The President's News Conference, February 4, 1959, PP, 1959, p.161.

20 Notes on Legislative Leadership Meeting, March 10, 1959, AWF, Legislative Meetings Series, Box 3, Legislative Meetings, 1959 (3), March–April, DDEL.

21 George B. Kistiakowsky, *A Scientist at the White House* (Cambridge, Mass.: Harvard University Press, 1976), p.293.

22 Dwight D. Eisenhower, *Waging Peace, 1956–61* (Garden City, NY: Doubleday & Co., 1965), p.418.

23 A. J. Goodpaster, Memorandum of Conference with the President, February 10, 1959, White House Office, Office of the Staff Secretary, Subject Series, Alphabetical Subseries, Box 15, Intelligence Matters (8), DDEL (hereinafter cited as WHO, OSS).

24 Roman, *Eisenhower and the Missile Gap*, p.129.

25 A. J. Goodpaster, Memorandum of Conference with the President, February 10, 1959, WHO, OSS, Subject Series, Alphabetical Subseries, Box 15, Intelligence Matters (8), DDEL.

26 The President's News Conference, January 28, 1959, PP, 1959, p.21.

27 Annual Message to the Congress on the State of the Union, January 9, 1959, PP, 1959, p.8.

28 The President's News Conference, February 4, 1959, PP, 1959, p.160.

29 Annual Message to the Congress on the State of the Union, January 7, 1954, PP, 1954, pp.22–23.

30 Michael Harrington, *The Other America: Poverty in the United States* (New York: Macmillan, 1962).

31 The President's News Conference, September 7, 1960, PP, 1960–61, p.682.

32 Eisenhower to Ralph McGill, February 26, 1959, AWF, Name Series, Box 23, DDEL.

33 Robert F. Burk, *The Eisenhower Administration and Black Civil Rights* (Knoxville: University of Tennessee Press, 1984), p.259.

34 Peter J. Ling, *Martin Luther King* (London: Routledge, 2002), pp.70–75.

35 Remarks and Discussion at the National Press Club, January 14, 1949, PP, 1959, p.23.

36 David W. Reinhard, *The Republican Right since 1945* (Lexington: University of Kentucky Press, 1983), p.158.

37 Remarks at the Republican National Committee Breakfast, Chicago, Illinois, July 27, 1960, PP, 1960–61, p.604.

38 The President's News Conference, January 28, 1959, PP, 1959, p.135.

39 Reinhard, *The Republic Right since 1945*, p.158.

40 The President's News Conference, February 17, 1960, PP, 1960–61, p.196.

41 The President's News Conference, February 3, 1960, PP, 1960–61, p.144.

42 Reinhard, *The Republican Right since 1945*, p.155.

43 The President's News Conference, August 26, 1960, PP, 1960–61, p.658.

44 *Ibid.*, pp.653, 657.

45 Charles C. Alexander, *Holding the Line: The Eisenhower Era, 1952–1961* (Bloomington: University of Indiana Press, 1975), p.278.

46 Richard M. Nixon, *RN: The Memoirs of Richard Nixon* (New York: Grosset & Dunlap, 1978), p.222.

47 Stephen E. Ambrose, *Eisenhower: The President, 1952–1969* (New York: Simon and Schuster, 1984), p.594.

48 The President's News Conference, February 10, 1959, PP, 1959, p.177.

49 The President's News Conference, January 21, 1959, PP, 1959, p.130.

50 The President's News Conference, February 10, 1959, PP, 1959, p.177.

51 Legislative Leaders Meeting, February 24, 1959, WHO, OSS, Legislative Meetings Series, Box 5, L-55 (1), DDEL.

52 The President's News Conference, May 5, 1959, PP, 1959, p.363.

53 The President's News Conference, January 18, 1961, PP, 1960–61, pp.104–105.

54 Sherman Adams, *First-hand Report: The Story of the Eisenhower Administration* (New York: Harper and Brothers, 1961), p.227.

55 Michael Beschloss, *Mayday: Eisenhower, Khrushchev and the U-2 Affair* (New York: Harper & Row, 1986), p.3.

56 Stephen E. Ambrose, *Nixon, Vol. I: The Education of a Politician, 1913–1962* (New York: Simon and Schuster, 1987), p.548.

57 Diary Entry, November 20, 1960, AWF, DDE Diary Series, Box 54, Diary, November, 1960, DDEL.

58 Ambrose, *Nixon*, Vol. I, p.548.

59 Robert Dallek, *An Unfinished Life: John F. Kennedy, 1917–1963* (Boston: Little, Brown, 2003), p.302.

Chapter 8

1 Annual Message to the Congress on the State of the Union, January 9, 1959, PP, 1959, p.15.

2 Radio and Television Address to the American People: Security in the Free World, March 16, 1959, PP, 1959, p.273.

3 The President's News Conference, March 11, 1959, PP, 1959, p.248.

4 John S. D. Eisenhower, Memorandum of Conference with the President, March 6, 1959, AWF, DDE Diary Series, Box 39, Staff Notes, March 1–15, 1959, DDEL.

5 William L. O'Neill, *American High: The Years of Confidence, 1945–1960* (New York: Free Press, 1986), p.281.

6 Chester Pach and Elmo Richardson, *The Presidency of Dwight D. Eisenhower* (rev edn; Lawrence: University Press of Kansas, 1991), p.200.

7 The President's News Conference, February 25, 1959, PP, 1959, p.209.

8 Radio and Television Address to the American People: Security and the Free World, March 16, 1959, PP, 1959, p.273.

9 *Ibid.*, p.278.

10 Remarks and Discussion at the National Press Club, January 14, 1959, PP, 1959, p.27.

11 Despatch from the Embassy in the Soviet Union to the Department of State, January 26, 1959, *FRUS, 1958–60*, Vol. X: *Eastern Europe Region*, Part I, p.276.

12 Strobe Talbott, ed., *Khrushchev Remembers* (New York: André Deutsch, 1971), p.361.

13 Annual Message to the Congress on the State of the Union, January 7, 1960, PP, 1960–61, p.3.

14 Memorandum of Conversation, March 20, 1959, AWF, International Series, Box 24, Macmillan Visit, March 20–22, 1959 (1), DDEL.

15 The President's News Conference, June 17, 1959, PP, 1959, p.465.

16 Harold Macmillan, *Pointing the Way, 1959–1961* (London: Macmillan, 1972), p.191.

17 Eisenhower to Harold Macmillan, March 18, 1960, AWF, International Series, Box 25(b), Macmillan, Harold, January 1–August 4, 1960 (7), DDEL.

18 John S. D. Eisenhower, Memorandum for Record, February 12, 1959, WHO, OSS, Subject Series, Alphabetical Subseries, Box 15, Intelligence Matters (8), DDEL.

19 *Ibid.*

20 *Ibid.*

21 A. J. Goodpaster, Memorandum of Conference with the President, April 7, 1959, WHO, OSS, Subject Series, Alphabetical Subseries, Box 15, Intelligence Matters (10), DDEL.

22 Memorandum of Conference with the President, July 8, 1959, WHO, OSS, Subject Series, Alphabetical Subseries, Box 15, Intelligence Matters (12), DDEL.

23 Richard J. Bissell, *Reflections of a Cold Warrior: From Yalta to the Bay of Pigs* (New Haven: Yale University Press, 1996), pp.124–125.

24 Michael R. Beschloss, *Mayday: Eisenhower, Khrushchev and the U-2 Affair* (New York: Harper & Row, 1986), p.296.

25 Adam Ulam, *The Rivals: America and Russia since the Second World War* (New York: Viking, 1971), pp.311–312.

26 George B. Kistiakowski, *Scientist at the White House* (Cambridge, Mass.: Harvard University Press, 1976), p.375.

27 Bissell, *Reflections of a Cold Warrior*, p.127.

28 Curtis Peebles, *Shadow Flights: America's Secret War Against the Soviet Union* (Novato, Calif.: Presidio Press, 2000), p.276.

29 Stephen G. Rabe, *Eisenhower and Latin America: The Foreign Policy of Anticommunism* (Chapel Hill: University of North Carolina Press, 1988), p.126.

30 *Ibid.*, p.131.

31 Macmillan to Eisenhower, July 25, 1960, AWF, International Series, Box 25(b), Macmillan, Harold, January 1–August 4, 1960 (3), DDEL.

32 Annual Address to Congress on the State of the Union, January 7, 1960, PP, 1960–61, p.5.

33 Mark T. Gilderhus, *The Second Century: US–Latin American Relations since 1889* (Washington, DC: Scholarly Resources, 2000), p.171.

34 Washington to Foreign Office, January 1, 1960, FO 371/148576/AU/1011/1, PRO, NA.

35 Robert Mann, *A Grand Delusion: America's Descent into Vietnam* (New York: Basic Books, 2001), p.217.

36 Address at the Gettysburg College Convocation: The Importance of Understanding, April 4, 1959, PP, 1959, p.313.

37 A. J. Goodpaster, Memorandum of Conference with the President, December 31, 1960, AWF, DDE Diary Series, Box 55, Staff Notes, December, 1960, DDEL.

38 A. J. Goodpaster, Memorandum of Conference with the President, January 3, 1961, AWF, DDE Diary Series, Box 55, Staff Notes, January, 1961, DDEL.

39 Richard M. Nixon, *Six Crises* (Garden City, NY: Doubleday & Co., 1962), p.335.

Conclusion

1 Farewell Radio and Television Address to the American People, January 17, 1961, PP, 1960–61, p.1038.

2 *Ibid.*, p.1037.

3 *Ibid.*, pp.1039–1040.

4 *Ibid.*, p.1039.

5 John S. D. Eisenhower, *Strictly Personal* (Garden City, NY: Doubleday & Co., 1974), p.337.

6 Arthur M. Schlesinger, Jr, *A Thousand Days: John F. Kennedy in the White House* (New York: André Deutsch, 1965), p.34.

7 Jim F. Heath, *Decade of Disillusionment: The Kennedy–Johnson Years* (Bloomington: Indiana University Press, 1975), p.60.

8 Schlesinger, *A Thousand Days*, p.871.

9 Shirley Anne Warshaw, ed., *Re-examining the Eisenhower Presidency* (Westport, Conn.: Greenwood Press, 1983), p.210.

10 William V. Shannon, 'Eisenhower as President,' *Commentary*, November 26, 1958, p.390.

11 David Halberstam, *The Best and the Brightest* (New York: Random House, 1972).

12 Murray Kempton, 'The Underestimation of Dwight Eisenhower', *Esquire*, September, 1968, pp.108–109, 156.

13 Godfrey Hodgson, *All Things to All Men: The False Promise of the Modern American Presidency* (London: Weidenfeld and Nicolson, 1980), p.260.

14 Clinton Rossiter, *The American Presidency* (rev edn; Baltimore: Johns Hopkins University Press, 1987), p.5.

15 Edwin C. Hargrove, *The President as Leader* (Lawrence: University Press of Kansas, 1998), p.579.

16 Herbert S. Parmet, *Eisenhower and the American Crusades* (New York: Macmillan, 1972), p.577.

17 Rossiter, *American Presidency*, p.5.

18 David M. Kennedy, *Freedom from Fear: The American People in Depression and War, 1929–1945* (New York: Oxford University Press, 1999), pp.689–690.

19 Robert Dallek, *Hail to the Chief: The Making and Unmaking of American Presidents* (New York: Hyperion, 1996), p.145.

20 Emmet John Hughes, *The Ordeal of Power: A Political Memoir of the Eisenhower Years* (New York: Atheneum, 1963), p.329.

21 Hargrove, *The President as Leader*, p.252.

22 Michael S. Mayer, ed., *The Eisenhower Presidency and the 1950s* (Boston: Houghton Mifflin, 1998), p.xvi.

23 Stephen E. Ambrose, *Eisenhower: Soldier and President* (New York: Simon and Schuster, 1990), p.576.

24 Richard V. Damms, *The Eisenhower Presidency, 1955–1961* (London: Pearson, 2002), p.111.

25 Stephen E. Ambrose, *Eisenhower: The President, 1952–1969* (New York: Simon and Schuster, 1984), p.626.

26 Theodore H. White, *The Making of the President, 1960* (New York: Pocket Books, 1961), p.171.

27 Dwight D. Eisenhower, *Waging Peace, 1956–1961* (Garden City, NY: Doubleday & Co., 1965), p.464.

28 Dwight D. Eisenhower, *Mandate for Change, 1953–56* (Garden City, NY: Doubleday & Co., 1963), p.563.

29 Hughes, *Ordeal of Power*, p.6.

30 James M. Burns, *The Three Roosevelts* (New York: Atlantic Monthly Press, 2001), p.245.

31 Charles C. Alexander, *Holding the Line: The Eisenhower Era, 1952–1961* (Bloomington: Indiana University Press, 1975), p.106.

32 Thomas Borstelman, *The Cold War and the Color Line: American Race Relations in the Global Arena* (Cambridge, Harvard University Press, 2001), p.134.

33 Chester Pach and Elmo Richardson, *The Presidency of Dwight D. Eisenhower* (rev edn; Lawrence: University Press of Kansas, 1991), p.137.

34 Ambrose, *Eisenhower: The President*, p.192.

35 Harvard Sitkoff, *The Struggle for Black Equality, 1954–1992* (rev edn; New York: Hill and Wang, 1993), p.36.

36 David W. Reinhard, *The Republican Right since 1945* (Lexington: University of Kentucky Press, 1985), p.158.

37 Damms, *The Eisenhower Presidency, 1953–1961*, p.108.

Haven: Yale University Press, 1996), Herbert Brownell, *Advising Ike: The Memoirs of Attorney-General Herbert Brownell* (Lawrence: University Press of Kansas, 1993), Robert Cutler, *No Time for Rest* (Boston: Little, Brown, 1996), Allen Dulles, *The Craft of Intelligence* (New York: Harper and Row, 1963), John S. D. Eisenhower, *Strictly Personal* (Garden City, NY: Doubleday & Co., 1974), Milton S. Eisenhower, *The President is Calling* (Garden City, NY: Doubleday & Co., 1974), Barry Goldwater, *The Conscience of a Conservative* (Shepardsville, Ky: Victor Publishing, 1960), Robert H. Ferrell, ed., *The Diary of James C. Hagerty: Eisenhower in Mid-Course, 1954–55* (Bloomington: Indiana University Press, 1983), Emmet John Hughes, *The Ordeal of Power: A Political Memoir of the Eisenhower Years* (New York: Atheneum, 1963), George F. Kennan, *Memoirs, 1950–1963* (Boston: Little, Brown, 1972), James R. Killian, *Sputnik, Scientists and Eisenhower* (Cambridge, Mass.: MIT Press, 1977), George B. Kistiakowsky, *A Scientist at the White House* (Cambridge, Mass.: Harvard University Press, 1976), Arthur Larson, *Eisenhower: The President Nobody Knew* (New York: Charles Scribner's Sons, 1968), Henry Cabot Lodge, *The Storm Has Many Eyes: A Personal Narrative* (New York: W. W. Norton, 1973), Merle Miller, *Plain Speaking: An Oral History of Harry S. Truman* (New York: C. P. Putnam's Sons, 1973), Kay Summersby Morgan, *Past Forgetting: My Love Affair with Dwight D. Eisenhower* (New York: Simon and Schuster, 1976), E. Frederick Morrow, *Black Man in the White House* (New York: Coward McCann, 1963), Robert Murphy, *Diplomat Among Warriors* (Garden City, NY: Doubleday & Co., 1964), Richard M. Nixon, *RN: The Memoirs of Richard Nixon* (New York: Grossat and Dunlop, 1978), Richard M. Nixon, *Six Crises* (Garden City, NY: Doubleday & Co., 1962), Francis Gary Powers, *Operation Overflight* (New York: Holt, Reinhart and Winston, 1970), James Reston, *Deadline: A Memoir* (New York: Random House, 1992), Nelson A. Rockefeller, *A Republican Approach to the Great Issues* (Garden City, NY: Doubleday & Co., 1960), Kermit Roosevelt, *Countercoup: The Struggle for the Control of Iran* (New York: McGraw-Hill, 1978), Raymond J. Saulnier, *Constructive Years: The U.S. Economy under Eisenhower* (Lanham, Md.: University Press of America, 1991), Lewis L. Strauss, *Men and Decisions* (Garden City, NY: Doubleday & Co., 1962), Robert Taft, *A Foreign Policy for Americans* (Garden City, NY: Doubleday & Co., 1951), Maxwell Taylor, *An Uncertain Trumpet* (New York: Harpers and Sons, 1960), Earl Warren, *The Memoirs of Earl Warren* (Garden City, NY: Doubleday & Co., 1977), Kenneth W. Thompson, ed., *The Eisenhower Presidency: Eleven Intimate Perspectives of Dwight D. Eisenhower* (Lanham, Md.: University Press of America, 1984). Useful accounts by non-Americans are Anthony Eden, *The Memoirs of the Right Hon. Anthony Eden* (3 vols; London: Cassell, 1960–65), Harold Macmillan, *Memoirs* (6 vols; London, Macmillan, 1966–1973), Harold Macmillan, *War Diaries: Politics and War in the Mediterranean, January, 1943–May, 1945* (London: Macmillan, 1984), Peter Catterell, ed., *The Macmillan Diaries: The Cabinet Years, 1950–57* (London: Macmillan, 2003), Strobe Talbott, ed., *Khrushchev Remembers* (New York: André Deutsch, 1971).

Interesting contemporary journalistic accounts are provided by Marquis Childs, *Captive Hero: A Critical Study of the General and the President* (New York: Harcourt, Brace, 1958), Robert Donovan, *Eisenhower: The Inside Story* (New York: Harper Bros., 1956), Merlo J. Pusey, *Eisenhower the President* (New York: Macmillan, 1956), Richard Rovere, *The Eisenhower Years* (New York: Farrar, Strauss and Cudahy, 1956), Merriman Smith, *The President's Odyssey* (New York: Harper Bros., 1961), I. F. Stone, *The Haunted Fifties* (New York: Random House, 1963).

The most important biographies of Eisenhower are Stephen E. Ambrose, *Eisenhower* (2 vols; New York: Simon and Schuster, 1984), Stephen E. Ambrose, *Eisenhower: Soldier and President* (New York: Simon and Schuster, 1990), Michael R. Beschloss, *Eisenhower: A Centennial Life* (New York: Edward Burlingame Books, 1990), Piers Brendon, *Ike: His Life and Times* (New York: Harper and Row, 1986), Robert F. Burk, *Dwight D. Eisenhower: Hero and Politician* (Boston: Twayne Publishers, 1986), Douglas Kinnard, *Eisenhower: Soldier-Statesman of the Twentieth Century* (Washington, DC: Brassey's, 2002), R. Alton Lee, *Dwight D. Eisenhower: Soldier and Statesman* (Chicago: Nelson-Hall, 1981), Peter Lyon, *Eisenhower: Portrait of the Hero* (Boston: Little, Brown, 1974), Geoffrey Perret, *Eisenhower* (New York: Random House, 1999), Tom Wicker, *Dwight D. Eisenhower* (New York: Henry Holt and Company, 2002).

Studies of Eisenhower's presidency include Charles C. Alexander, *Holding the Line: The Eisenhower Era, 1952–1961* (Bloomington: Indiana University Press, 1975), Blanche W. Cook, *The Declassified Eisenhower* (Garden City, NY: Doubleday & Co., 1981), Richard V. Damms, *The Eisenhower Presidency, 1953–1961* (London: Pearson, 2002), Fred I. Greenstein, *The Hidden-Hand Presidency: The President as Leader* (New York: Basic Books, 1982), William B. Ewald, Jr, *Eisenhower the President: Crucial Days, 1951–1960* (Englewood Cliffs, NJ: Prentice-Hall, 1981), Chester Pach and Elmo Richardson, *The Presidency of Dwight D. Eisenhower* (rev edn; Lawrence: University Press of Kansas, 1990), Herbert S. Parmet, *Eisenhower and the American Crusades* (New York: Macmillan, 1972), William B. Pickett, *Dwight D. Eisenhower and American Power* (Wheeling, Ill.: Harlan Davidson, 1995).

Useful edited collections on Eisenhower include Günter Bischof and Stephen E. Ambrose, eds, *Eisenhower: A Centenary Assessment* (Baton Rouge: Louisiana State University Press, 1995), Dale Carter, ed., *Cracking the Ike Age: Aspects of Fifties America* (Aarhus, Denmark: Aarhus University Press, 1992), Joann P. Krieg, ed., *Dwight D. Eisenhower: Soldier, President, Statesman* (New York: Greenwood Press, 1987), Michael S. Mayer, ed., *The Eisenhower Presidency and the 1950s* (Boston: Houghton Mifflin, 1998), Richard Melanson and David Mayers, eds, *Re-evaluating Eisenhower: American Foreign Policy in the 1950s* (Urbana: University of Illinois Press, 1989), Shirley Anne Warshaw, ed., *Re-examining the Eisenhower Presidency* (Westport: Greenwood Press, 1993).

Among accounts of aspects of Eisenhower's pre-presidential career the most significant include Carlo d'Este, *Eisenhower: A Soldier's Life* (New York: Henry Holt, 2002), Matthew F. Holland, *Eisenhower Between Wars: The Making of a General and a Statesman* (Westport, Ct.: Praeger, 2001), John S. D. Eisenhower, *Allies: Pearl Harbor to D-Day* (Garden City, NY: Doubleday, 1982), Mark A. Stoler, *Allies and Adversaries: The Joint Chiefs of Staff, the Grand Alliance and US Strategy in World War II* (Chapel Hill: University of North Carolina Press, 2000), Rick Atkinson, *An Army at Dawn: The War in North Africa, 1942–43* (New York: Henry Holt, 2002), David Eisenhower, *Eisenhower at War, 1943–1945* (New York: Random House, 1986), Stephen E. Ambrose, *The Supreme Commander* (Garden City, NY: Doubleday & Co., 1970), Travis B. Jacobs, *Eisenhower at Columbia* (New Brunswick, NJ: Transactions Publishers, 2001), Steve Neal, *Harry and Ike: The Partnership That Remade the Postwar World* (New York: Scribner's 2000), William B. Pickett, *Eisenhower Decides to Run: Presidential Politics and Cold War Strategy* (Chicago: Ivan R. Dee, 2000).

There are many useful studies of contemporary figures. Among the more important are Sheri L. Dew, *Ezra Taft Benson* (Salt Lake City: Deseret Book Co., 1987), Roy Jenkins, *Churchill* (London: Macmillan, 2001), Richard N. Smith, *Thomas E. Dewey and His Times* (New York: Simon and Schuster, 1982), Byron C. Hulsey, *Everett Dirksen and His Presidents* (Lawrence: University Press of Kansas, 2000), Peter Grose, *Gentleman Spy: The Life of Allen Dulles* (Boston: Houghton Mifflin, 1994), Richard H. Immerman, *John Foster Dulles: Piety, Pragmatism and Power in U.S. Foreign Policy* (Wilmington, Del.: Scholarly Resources, 1999), David Dutton, *Anthony Eden: A Life and Reputation* (London: Arnold, 1997), Susan Eisenhower, *Mrs. Ike: Memoirs and Reflections on the Life of Mamie Eisenhower* (New York: Farrar, Strauss and Giroux, 1996), Robert A. Goldberg, *Barry Goldwater* (New Haven: Yale University Press, 1995), Rudy Abramson, *Spanning the Century: The Life of W. Averell Harriman* (New York: William

Morrow, 1992), Robert Dallek, *Lone Star Rising: Lyndon Johnson and His Times, 1908–1960* (New York: Oxford University Press, 1991), Hugh Brogan, *Kennedy* (London: Longman, 1996), Robert Dallek, *An Unfinished Life: John F. Kennedy* (Boston: Little, Brown, 2003), Peter J. Ling, *Martin Luther King* (London: Routledge, 2002), Gayle B. Montgomery and James V. Johnson, *One Step from the White House: The Rise and Fall of Senator William F. Knowland* (Berkeley: University of California Press, 1998), William Taubman, *Khrushchev: The Man and His Era* (New York: W. W. Norton, 2003), Thomas C. Reeves, *The Life and Times of Joe McCarthy* (New York: Stein and Day, 1982), Alistair Horne, *Macmillan* (2 vols; London: Macmillan, 1988–89), Stephen E. Ambrose, *Nixon* (3 vols; New York: Simon and Schuster, 1987–91), Iwan Morgan, *Nixon* (London: Arnold, 2000), John B. Martin, *Adlai Stevenson of Illinois* (Garden City, NY: Doubleday, 1976), Linda McFarlane, *Cold War Strategist: Stuart Symington and the Search for National Security* (Westport, Ct.: Praeger, 2001), James T. Patterson, *Mr. Republican: A Biography of Robert A. Taft* (Boston: Houghton Mifflin, 1972), Robert J. Donovan, *Confidential Secretary: Ann Whitman's Twenty Years with Eisenhower and Rockefeller* (New York: E. P. Dutton, 1988).

There is a very extensive historical literature on most of the important topics of the Eisenhower years. Of the most significant works, the most useful studies of the Red Scare and McCarthyism are Jeff Broadwater, *Eisenhower and the Anti-Communist Crusade* (Chapel Hill: University of North Carolina Press, 1992), Ellen Schrecker, *The Age of McCarthyism: A Brief History with Documents* (2nd edn; New York: Palgrave, 2002), Richard Fried, *Nightmare in Red: The McCarthy Era in Perspective* (New York: Oxford University Press, 1990), Robert Griffith, *The Politics of Fear: Joseph R. McCarthy and the Senate* (2nd edn; Amherst: University of Massachusetts Press, 1987), David Caute, *The Great Fear: The Anti-Communist Purge under Truman and Eisenhower* (New York: Simon and Schuster, 1978). On the Bricker Amendment, see Duane Tanabaum, *The Bricker Amendment Controversy: A Test of Eisenhower's Political Leadership* (Ithaca, NY: Cornell University Press, 1988). On the economy, the most important studies are Iwan W. Morgan, *Eisenhower versus the Spenders: The Eisenhower Administration, the Democrats and the Budget, 1953–1960* (London: Pinter Publishers, 1990), John W. Sloan, *Eisenhower and the Management of Prosperity* (Lawrence: University Press of Kansas, 1991), Robert M. Collins, *More: The Politics of Economic Growth in Postwar America* (New York: Oxford University Press, 2000), Mark H. Rose, *Interstate: Express Highway Politics, 1941–1956* (Lawrence: University Press of Kansas, 1979), Ken A. Ingersent and A. J. Rayner, *Agricultural Policy in Western Europe and the*

United States (Northampton: Edward Elgar Publishing, 1999), Burton I. Kaufman, *Trade and Aid: Eisenhower's Foreign Economic Policy* (Baltimore: Johns Hopkins University Press, 1982). On civil rights, the most important works are Robert F. Burk, *The Eisenhower Administration and Black Civil Rights* (Knoxville: University of Tennessee Press, 1984), Harvard Sitkoff, *The Struggle for Black Equality, 1954–1992* (rev edn; New York: Hill and Wang, 1993), Taylor Branch, *Parting the Waters: America in the King Years, 1954–63* (New York: Simon and Schuster, 1988), James T. Patterson, *Brown v Board of Education: A Civil Rights Milestone and Its Troubled Legacy* (New York: Oxford University Press, 2001), John A. Kirk, *Redefining the Color Line: Activism in Little Rock, Arkanses, 1940–1970* (Gainesville: University of Florida Press, 2002), Mary L. Dudziak, *Cold War Civil Rights: Race and the Image of American Democracy* (Princeton: Princeton University Press, 2000), Thomas Borstelmann, *The Cold War and the Color Line: American Race Relations in the Global Era* (Cambridge, Mass.: Harvard University Press, 2001). On party politics, useful works include Gary W. Reichard, *The Re-affirmation of Republicanism: Eisenhower and the Eighty-Third Congress* (Knoxville: University of Tennessee Press, 1975), David W. Reinhard, *The Republican Right since 1945* (Lexington: University of Kentucky Press, 1985), Theodore H. White, *The Making of the President, 1960* (New York: Pocket Books, 1961). On defence policy and defence spending, the most important books are Saki Dockrill, *Eisenhower's New Look Security Policy, 1953–1961* (Basingstoke: Macmillan, 1996), Michael J. Hogan, *A Cross of Iron: Harry S. Truman and the National Security State, 1945–54* (Cambridge: Cambridge University Press, 1998), Gerard H. Clarfield, *Security with Solvency: Dwight D. Eisenhower and the Shaping of the American Military Establishment* (Westport, Ct: Praeger, 1999), Robert A. Divine, *The Sputnik Challenge* (New York: Oxford University Press, 1993), David L. Snead, *The Gaither Committee, Eisenhower and the Cold War* (Columbus: Ohio State University Press, 1999), Peter J. Roman, *Eisenhower and the Missile Gap* (Ithaca, NY: Cornell University Press, 1985). On relations with the Soviet Union, among the most important works are Robert A. Divine, *Eisenhower and the Cold War* (New York: Oxford University Press, 1981), H. W. Brands, *Cold Warriors: Eisenhower's Generation and American Foreign Policy* (New York: Columbia University Press, 1988), McGeorge Bundy, *Danger and Survival: Choices About the Bomb in the First Fifty Years* (New York: Random House, 1988), Robert R. Bowie and Richard H. Immerman, *Waging Peace: How Eisenhower Shaped an Enduring Strategy* (New York: Oxford University Press, 1998), Campbell Craig, *Destroying the Village: Eisenhower and Thermonuclear War* (New York: Columbia University Press, 1998), Raymond L. Garthoff,

Assessing the Adversary: Estimates by the Eisenhower Administration of Soviet Intentions and Capabilities (Washington, DC: Brookings Institution, 1991), Andreas Wenger, *Living with Peril: Eisenhower, Kennedy and Nuclear Weapons* (New York: Rowman and Littlefield, 1997), Kenneth A. Osgood, 'Form before Substance: Eisenhower's Commitment to Psychological Warfare and Negotiations with the Enemy,' *Diplomatic History*, Vol. 24, No. 4 (September, 2000), pp.405–433, Fred I. Greenstein and Richard H. Immerman, 'Effective National Security Advisers: Recovering the Eisenhower Legacy', *Political Science Quarterly*, Vol. 115, No. 3 (Fall, 2000), pp.335–345. On a test ban and disarmament, see Robert A. Divine, *Blowing on the Wind: The Nuclear Test Ban Debate, 1954–60* (New York: Oxford University Press, 1978), Richard G. Hewlett and Jack M. Holl, *Atoms for Peace and War, 1953–1961: Eisenhower and the Atomic Energy Commission* (Berkeley: University of California Press, 1989), Lawrence S. Witner, *Resisting the Bomb: A History of the World Nuclear Disarmament Movement* (Stanford, Calif: Stanford University Press, 1997), Martha Smith-Norris, 'The Eisenhower Administration and the Nuclear Test Ban Talks, 1958–1960: Another Challenge to "Revisionism",' *Diplomatic History*, Vol. 27, No. 4 (September, 2003), pp.503–541. On liberation and relations with Eastern Europe, the most significant works are Ronald R. Krebs, *Dueling Visions: US Strategy Towards Eastern Europe under Eisenhower* (College Staton: Texas A&M University Press, 2001), Peter Grose, *Operation Rollback: America's Secret War behind the Iron Curtain* (Boston: Houghton Mifflin, 2000), Gregory Mitrovich, *Undermining the Kremlin: America's Strategy to Subvert the Soviet Bloc, 1947–1956* (Ithaca, NY: Cornell University Press, 2000), Scott Lucas, *Freedom's War: The U.S. Crusade Against the Soviet Union, 1945–1956* (Manchester: Manchester University Press, 1999), Bennett Kovrig, *Of Walls and Bridges: The United States and Eastern Europe* (New York: Oxford University Press, 1991), Arch Paddington, *Broadcasting Freedom: The Cold War Triumphs of Radio Free Europe and Radio Liberty* (Lexington: University of Kentucky Press, 2000), Aleksander Stykalin, 'The Hungarian Crisis of 1956: The Soviet Role in the Light of New Archival Documents', *Cold War History*, Vol. 2, No. 1 (October, 2001), pp.113–144. On relations with Western Europe, see Pascaline Winand, *Eisenhower, Kennedy and the United States of Europe* (Basingstoke: Macmillan, 1993). On Anglo-American relations, see John Charmley, *Churchill's Grand Alliance: The Anglo-American Special Relationship, 1940–1957* (London: Hodder and Stoughton, 1995), G. Wyn Rees, *Anglo-American Approaches to Alliance Security, 1955–1960* (Basingstoke: Macmillan, 1996). On relations with the United Nations, see Caroline Prudens, *Conditional Partners: Eisenhower, the United Nations and the*

Search for a Permanent Peace (Baton Rouge: Louisiana State University Press, 1998). On relations with the Third World, the most useful works are H. W. Brands, *The Specter of Neutralism: The United States and the Emergence of the Third World, 1947–1960* (New York: Columbia University Press, 1989), Peter L. Hahn and Mary Ann Heiss, eds, *Empire and Revolution: The United States and the Third World since 1945* (Columbus: Ohio State University Press, 2001), Robert J. McMahon, 'Eisenhower and Third World Nationalism: A Critique of the Revisionists', *Political Science Quarterly*, Vol. 101, No. 3 (Fall, 1986), pp.453–473. On policy towards Latin America, the most important books are Stephen G. Rabe, *Eisenhower and Latin America: The Foreign Policy of Anticommunism* (Chapel Hill: University of North Carolina Press, 1988), Mark T. Gilderhus, *The Second Century: US-Latin American Relations since 1989* (Wilmington, Del.: Scholarly Resources, 2000), Richard H. Immerman, *The CIA in Guatemala: The Foreign Policy of Intervention* (Austin: University of Texas Press, 1982), Piero Gleijeses, *Shattered Hope: The Guatemalan Revolution and the United States, 1944–1954* (Princeton, NJ: Princeton University Press, 1991), Richard E. Welch, *Response to Revolution: The United States and the Cuban Revolution* (Chapel Hill: University of North Carolina Press, 1985), Thomas G. Paterson, *Contesting Castro: The United States and the Triumph of the Cuban Revolution* (New York: Oxford University Press, 1994), Trumbull Higgens, *The Perfect Failure: Kennedy, Eisenhower and the CIA at the Bay of Pigs* (New York: W. W. Norton, 1987). On policy towards China, the most significant studies are Gordon H. Chang, *Friends and Enemies: The United States, China and the Soviet Union, 1948–1972* (Stanford, Calif.: Stanford University Press, 1990), Quiang Zhai, *The Lion, the Dragon and the Eagle: Chinese–British–American Relations, 1949–1958* (Kent, Ohio: Kent State University Press, 1994), Shu Guang Zhang, *Deterrence and Strategic Culture: Chinese-American Confrontations, 1949–1958* (Ithaca, NY: Cornell University Press, 1993), Thomas J. Christenson, *Useful Adversaries: Grand Strategy, Domestic Mobilization and Sino-American Conflict, 1947–1958* (Princeton, NJ: Princeton University Press, 1996). On the Korean War, particularly the negotiations to bring an end to the war, see William W. Stueck, *The Korean War: An International History* (Princeton, NJ: Princeton University Press, 1995), William W. Stueck, *Rethinking the Korean War: A New Diplomatic and Strategic History* (Princeton, NJ: Princeton University Press, 2002), Rosemary Foot, *A Substitute for Victory: The Politics of Peacemaking at the Korean Armistice Talks* (Ithaca, NY: Cornell University Press, 1990). On Vietnam, amongst the vast number of works on the subject the most useful are David L. Anderson, *Trapped by Success: The Eisenhower*

Administration and Vietnam, 1953–1961 (New York: Columbia University Press, 1991), Robert Mann, *A Grand Delusion: America's Descent into Vietnam* (New York: Basic Books, 2001), Robert D. Schulzinger, *A Time for War: The United States and Vietnam, 1941–1975* (New York: Oxford University Press, 1997), George C. Herring, *America's Longest War: The United States and Vietnam, 1950–1975* (3rd edn; New York: McGraw-Hill, 1996), Melanie Billings-Yun, *Decision Against War: Eisenhower and Dien Bien Phu, 1954* (New York: Columbia University Press, 1988), Fred I. Greenstein, *How Presidents Test Reality: Decisions on Vietnam, 1954 and 1965* (New York: Russell Sage Foundation, 1989). On policy towards the Middle East, the most important works are H. W. Brands, *Into the Labyrinth: The United States and the Middle East, 1945–1993* (New York: McGraw-Hill, 1993), Douglas Little, *American Orientalism: The United States and the Middle East since 1945* (Chapel Hill: University of North Carolina Press, 2003), Peter L. Hahn, *The United States, Great Britain and Egypt, 1945–1956: Strategy and Diplomacy in the Early Cold War* (Chapel Hill: University of North Carolina Press, 1991), Keith Kyle, *Suez* (London: Weidenfeld and Nicolson, 1991), W. Scott Lucas, *Divided We Stand: Britain, the United States and the Suez Crisis* (London: Hodder and Stoughton, 1991), Cole Kingseed, *Eisenhower and the Suez Crisis of 1956* (Baton Rouge: Louisiana State University Press, 1995), Nigel J. Ashton, *Eisenhower, Macmillan and the Problem of Nasser: Anglo-American Relations and Arab Nationalism, 1955–1959* (London: Macmillan, 1996), Salim Yaqub, *Containing Arab Nationalism: The United States, the Arab Middle East and the Eisenhower Doctrine* (Chapel Hill: University of North Carolina Press, 2003), Irene L. Gendzier, *Notes from the Minefield: United States Intervention in Lebanon and the Middle East, 1945–1958* (New York: Columbia University Press, 1996), Mary Ann Heiss, *Empire and Nationhood: The United States, Great Britain and Iranian Oil* (New York: Columbia University Press, 1997), Mark I. Gasiorowski, *US Foreign Policy and the Shah: Building a Client State in Iran* (Ithaca, NY: Cornell University Press, 1991), Nathan I. Citino, *From Arab Nationalism to OPEC: Eisenhower, King Sa'ud and the Making of US-Saudi Relations* (Bloomington: Indiana University Press, 2002), Abraham Ben-Zui, *Decade of Transition: Eisenhower, Kennedy and the Origins of the American-Israeli Alliance* (New York: Columbia University Press, 1998). On intelligence, the most important works include Richard J. Aldrich, *Hidden Hand: Britain, America and Cold War Secret Intelligence* (London: John Murray, 2001), Rhodri Jeffreys-Jones, *The CIA and American Democracy* (2nd edn; New Haven, Conn: Yale University Press, 1998), John Prados, *President's Secret Wars* (rev edn; Chicago: Ivan R. Dee, 1996), Stephen E. Ambrose, *Ike's Spies: Eisenhower and the Intelligence Establishment* (Garden City, NY: Doubleday & Co., 1981), Curtis Peebles, *Shadow Flights: America's Secret War Against the Soviet Union* (Novato, Calif.: Presidio Press, 2000), William E. Burrows, *By Any Means Necessary: America's Secret Air War in the Cold War* (New York: Farrar, Strauss and Giroux, 2001), Chris Pocock, *The U-2 Spyplane: Towards the Unknown: A New History of the Early Years* (Atglen, Pa.: Schiffer Publishing, 2000), Norman Polmar and Mike Haenggi, eds, *Spyplane: The U-2 Declassified* (Osceola, Wis.: Motorbooks International, 2001), Michael R. Beschloss, *Mayday: Eisenhower, Khrushchev and the U-2 Affair* (New York: Harper and Row, 1986).

On Eisenhower's administrative methods, see Alfred D. Sander, *Eisenhower's Executive Office* (Westport, Ct.: Greenwood Press, 1999). On relations with the media, useful works are Craig Allen, *Eisenhower and the Mass Media: Peace, Prosperity and Prime-time TV* (Chapel Hill: University of North Carolina Press, 1992), Martin J. Medhurst, *Dwight D. Eisenhower: Strategic Communicator* (Westport, Conn.: Greenwood Press, 1993), Martin J. Medhurst, ed., *Eisenhower's War of Words: Rhetoric and Leadership* (East Lansing: Michigan State University Press, 1994). On Eisenhower's health, see Robert H. Ferrell, *Ill-Advised: Presidential Health and the Public Trust* (Columbia: University of Missouri Press, 1992), Clarence G. Lasby, *Eisenhower's Heart Attack* (Lawrence: University Press of Kansas, 1997).

Useful general histories of the Eisenhower period include Paul Bowyer, *Promises to Keep: The United States since World War II* (rev edn; Lexington, Mass.: D. D. Heath, 1999), Gary A. Donaldson, *Abundance and Anxiety: America, 1945–1960* (Westport, Ct.: Praeger, 1997), David Halberstam, *The Fifties* (New York: Fawcett Columbia, 1994), James T. Patterson, *Grand Expectations: The United States, 1945–1974* (New York: Oxford University Press, 1996), William L. O'Neill, *American High: The Years of Confidence, 1945–1960* (New York: Free Press, 1986), John P. Diggins, *The Proud Decades: America in Peace and War, 1941–1960* (New York: W. W. Norton, 1989). Cultural and intellectual trends are covered in Richard H. Pells, *The Liberal Mind in a Conservative Age: American Intellectuals in the 1940s and 1950s* (2nd edn; Middleton, Conn.: Wesleyan University Press, 1989), William Whyte, *The Organization Man* (New York: Simon and Schuster, 1956), C. Wright Mills, *White Collar: The American Middle Classes* (New York: Oxford University Press, 1951), C. Wright Mills, *The Power Elite* (New York: Oxford University Press, 1956), Stephen Whitfield, *The Culture of the Cold War* (2nd edn; Baltimore: Johns Hopkins University Press, 1996).

In the growing literature on the American presidency, useful studies include Philip Abbott, *Strong Presidents: A Theory of Leadership* (Knoxville:

University of Tennessee Press, 1998), Robert Dallek, *Hail to the Chief: The Making and Unmaking of American Presidents* (New York: Hyperion, 1996), Robert E. Diclerico, *The American President* (5th edn; Upper Saddle River, NJ: Prentice-Hall, 2000), Ethan M. Fishman, *The Prudential Presidency: An Aristotelian Approach to Presidential Leadership* (Westport, Ct.: Praeger, 2001), Carol Golderman, *All the President's Words: The Bully Pulpit and the Creation of the Virtual Presidency* (New York: Walker and Co., 1997), Michael A. Genovese, *The Power of the American Presidency* (New York: Oxford University Press, 2001), Lewis C. Gould, *The Modern American Presidency* (Lawrence: University Press of Kansas, 2002), Erwin C. Hargrove, *The President as Leader* (Lawrence: University Press of Kansas, 1998), Godfrey Hodgson, *All Things to All Men: The False Promise of the Modern American Presidency* (London: Weidenfeld and Nicolson, 1980), John Kentleton, *President and Nation: The Making of Modern America* (London: Palgrave Macmillan, 2002), William W. Lammers and Michael A. Genovese, *The Presidency and Domestic Policy: Comparing Leadership Styles, FDR to Clinton* (Washington, DC: C Q Press, 2000), Marc Landy and Sidney M. Milkens, *Presidential Greatness* (Lawrence: University Press of Kansas, 2000), William E. Leuchtenburg, *In The Shadow of FDR: From Harry Truman to Bill Clinton* (rev edn; Ithaca, NY: Cornell University Press, 1993), Louis W. Liebovich, *The Press and the Presidency* (2nd edn; Westport, Ct.: Praeger, 2001), Richard E. Neustadt, *Presidential Power and Modern Presidents: The Politics of Leadership from Roosevelt to Reagan* (New York: The Free Press, 1990), James P. Pfiffner, *The Modern Presidency* (New York: St Martin's Press, 1994), Clinton Rossiter, *The American Presidency* (rev edn; Baltimore: Johns Hopkins University Press, 1987), Craig A. Smith and Kathy B. Smith, *The White House Speaks: Presidential Leadership and Persuasion* (Westport, Ct.: Praeger, 1994), Richard W. Waterman, *The Image-is-Everything Presidency: Dilemmas in American Leadership* (Boulder, Col.: Westview Press, 1999), Philip Abbott, 'Eisenhower, King Utopus and the Fifties Decade in America', *Presidential Studies Quarterly*, Vol. 33, No. 1 (March, 2002), pp.7–29.

Useful historiographical articles include Alan Brinkley, 'A President for Certain Seasons', *Wilson Quarterly*, Vol. XIV, No. 2 (Spring, 1990), pp.110–119, Richard H. Immerman, 'Confessions of an Eisenhower Revisionist: An Agonising Reappraisal', *Diplomatic History*, Vol. 14, No. 3 (Summer, 1990), pp.319–342, Stephen G. Rabe, 'Eisenhower Revisionism: A Decade of Scholarship', *Diplomatic History*, Vol. 17, No. 1 (Winter, 1993), pp.97–115, Peter G. Boyle, 'Update: Eisenhower', *The Historian*, No. 43 (Autumn, 1994), pp.9–11.

Index